Furiously
Happy

Also by Jenny Lawson

Let's Pretend This Never Happened

Furiously Happy

{ A Funny Book About Horrible Things }

Jenny Lawson

FLATIRON
BOOKS
NEW YORK

This book is dedicated to
my daughter,
the giggling witness to the strange
and wonderful world her family
has created out of insanity
(both real and hyperbolic).

God help us when she's old enough
to write her own memoir.

---

www.flatironbooks.com

All photos courtesy of the author unless otherwise indicated.

Endpaper illustrations by Sarah Mensinga

Library of Congress Cataloging-in-Publication Data

Lawson, Jenny, 1979–
    Furiously happy : a funny book about horrible things / Jenny Lawson.
        pages cm
    ISBN 978-1-250-07700-4 (hardcover)
    ISBN 978-1-250-07701-1 (e-book)
  1. Lawson, Jenny, 1979–   2. Journalists—United States—Biography.
3. Humorists, American—21st century—Biography.   4. Mental illness—Humor.
I. Title.
    PN4874.L285A3 2015
    070.92—dc23

                                     2015022196

Our books may be purchased in bulk for promotional, educational, or business use. Please contact your local bookseller or the Macmillan Corporate and Premium Sales Department at (800) 221-7945, extension 5442, or by e-mail at MacmillanSpecialMarkets@macmillan.com.

First Edition: September 2015

10 9 8 7 6 5 4 3 2 1

It was the best of books, it was the worst of hairbrushes. Read it. Don't tease your hair with it. —CHARLES DICKENS

Jesus gave me this book when he was done with it, saying, "You have got to read this shit, Kevin. It's fucking fantastic." Jesus is terrible with names.
—ERNEST HEMINGWAY

There are few people whom I really love, and still fewer of whom I think well, but only one whose face I want to peel off and wear around my parlor. Lock thy door, Mrs. Lawson. —JANE AUSTEN

I can say without exaggeration: This is the finest coaster I have ever owned.
—DOROTHY PARKER

It's life that matters, nothing but life—the process of discovering, the everlasting and perpetual process, not the discovery itself, at all. That, and this book. This book is nice too. —FYODOR DOSTOYEVSKY

Who let you in here? —STEPHEN KING

I seem to have lost my coat. —WILLIAM SHAKESPEARE

You don't even know these people in your blurbs. Most of them are dead and Stephen King is probably going to press charges. We're really going to need to increase your visits. —MY CURRENT SHRINK

Contents

FURIOUSLY HAPPY

A funny book about horrible things
by Jenny Lawson

This is where I was going to put a simple Mary Oliver quote but instead I decided to replace it with the idea I had for the cover of this book because I'm pretty sure it'll never get accepted and I don't want it to go to waste. The great thing about this cover is that when you're holding the book up to read it, it will look like the bottom of your face has been replaced with an ecstatic raccoon smile. That way you look friendly and also terrifying to anyone passing by, which is nice because then people won't bother you while you're reading. In fact, you can rip out the previous page and glue photocopies of it on the covers of all of your other books because it's like a subtle "Do Not Disturb" sign. People may think you're a slow reader after a few years of this, but it's worth it for the uninterrupted peace, and the added joy of being half a raccoon. If you disagree then this is probably the wrong book for you.

You've been warned.

A Series of Unfortunate Disclaimers

No, no. I insist you stop right now.

Still here? *Awesome.* Now you're not allowed to blame me for anything in this book because I told you to stop reading and you just kept going. You're like Bluebeard's wife when she found all those heads in the closet. (Spoiler alert.) But personally I think that's a good thing. Ignoring the severed human heads in the closet doesn't make for a good relationship. It makes for an unsanitary closet and possible accessory charges. You have to confront those decapitated heads because you can't grow without acknowledging that we are all made up from the weirdness that we try to hide from the rest of the world. *Everyone* has human heads in their closet. Sometimes the heads are secrets, or unsaid confessions, or quiet fears. This book is one of those severed heads. You are holding my severed head in your hands. This is a bad analogy but in my defense, I did tell you to stop. I don't want to blame the victim, but at this point we're in this together.

⊢⊣

Everything in this book is mostly true but some details have been changed to protect the guilty. I know it's usually about "protecting the innocent" but why would they need protection? *They're innocent.* And they're also not nearly as fun to write about as the guilty, who always have more fascinating stories and who make you feel better about yourself by comparison.

⊢⊣

This is a funny book about living with mental illness. It sounds like a terrible combination, but personally, I'm mentally ill and some of the most hysterical people I know are as well. So if you don't like the book then maybe you're just not crazy enough to enjoy it. Either way, you win.

Note from the Author

Dear reader,

Right now you're holding this book in your hands and wondering if it's worth reading. It's probably not, but there's a $25 bill hidden in the binding so you should just buy it quickly before the clerk notices.[1]

You are welcome.

Furiously Happy is the name of this book. It's also a little something that saved my life.

My grandmother used to say, "Into everyone's life a little rain must fall—rain, assholes, and assorted bullshit." I'm paraphrasing. But she was right. We all get our share of tragedy or insanity or drama, but what we do with that horror is what makes all the difference.

---

1. My editor insists that I clarify that there isn't *actually* a $25 bill hidden in this book, which is sort of ridiculous to have to explain, because there's no such thing as a $25 bill. If you bought this book thinking you were going to find a $25 bill inside then I think you really just paid for a worthwhile lesson, and that lesson is, *don't sell your cow for magic beans*. There was another book that explained this same concept many years ago, but I think my cribbed example is much more exciting. It's like the *Fifty Shades of Grey* version of "Jack and the Beanstalk." But with fewer anal beads, or beanstalks.

I learned this firsthand a few years ago when I fell into a severe bout of depression so terrific that I couldn't see a way out of it. The depression wasn't anything new. I've struggled with many forms of mental illness since I was a kid, but clinical depression is a semiregular visitor and anxiety disorder is my long-term abusive boyfriend. Sometimes the depression is mild enough that I mistake it for the flu or mono, but this instance was one of the extreme cases. One where I didn't necessarily want my life to end, I just wanted it to stop being such a bastard. I reminded myself that depression lies, because it does. I told myself that things would get better. I did all of the normal things that sometimes help but I still felt hopeless and suddenly I found myself really angry. Angry that life can throw such curveballs at you. Angry at the seeming unfairness of how tragedy is handed out. Angry because I had no other emotions left to give.

So I took to my blog and wrote a post that would change the way that I would look at life from then on:

October 2010:

All things considered, the last six months have been a goddamn Victorian tragedy. Today my husband, Victor, handed me a letter informing me that another friend had unexpectedly died. You might think that this would push me over the edge into an irreversible downward spiral of Xanax and Regina Spektor songs, but no. It's not. I'm fucking *done* with sadness, and I don't know what's up the ass of the universe lately but *I've HAD IT. I AM GOING TO BE FURIOUSLY HAPPY, OUT OF SHEER SPITE.*

Can you hear that? That's me *smiling*, y'all. I'm smiling so loud you can fucking *hear it.* I'm going to destroy the goddamn universe with my irrational joy and I will spew forth pictures of clumsy kittens and baby puppies adopted by raccoons and MOTHERFUCK-ING NEWBORN LLAMAS DIPPED IN GLITTER AND THE BLOOD OF SEXY VAMPIRES AND IT'S GOING TO BE AWESOME. In fact, I'm starting a whole movement right now. **The FURIOUSLY HAPPY movement.** And it's going to be awesome because first of all, **we're all going to be VEHEMENTLY happy,** and secondly because it will freak the shit out of everyone that hates you because those assholes don't want to see you even vaguely amused, much less furiously happy, and it will make their world turn a little sideways and will probably scare the shit out of them. Which will make you even more happy. *Legitimately.* Then the world tips in our favor. Us: 1. Assholes: 8,000,000. That score doesn't look as satisfying as it should because they have a bit of a head start. Except you know what? *Fuck that.* We're starting from scratch.

Us: 1. Assholes: 0.

⊢⊣

Within a few hours #FURIOUSLYHAPPY was trending worldwide on Twitter as people loudly fought to take back their lives from the monster of depression. And that was just the beginning.

Over the next few years I pushed myself to say yes to anything ridiculous. I jumped into fountains that were not meant to be jumped into. I took impromptu road trips to hunt down UFOs. I chased tornados. I wore a wolf (who had died of kidney failure) to the local *Twilight* premiere while shouting "TEAM JACOB" at angry vampire fans. I rented sloths by the hour. My new mantra was "Decorum is highly overrated and probably causes cancer." In short, I went a little insane, in slow but certain spurts. And it was the best possible thing that could have happened to me.

This didn't mean that I wasn't still depressed or anxious or mentally ill. I still spent my share of weeks in bed when I simply couldn't get up. I still hid under my office desk whenever the anxiety got too heavy to battle standing up. The difference was that I had a storeroom in the back of my mind filled with moments of tightrope walking, snorkeling in long-forgotten caves, and running barefoot through cemeteries with a red ball gown trailing behind me. And I could remind myself that as soon as I had the strength to get up out of bed I would again turn my hand to being furiously happy. Not just to *save* my life, but to *make* my life.

There's something about depression that allows you (or sometimes forces you) to explore depths of emotion that most "normal" people could never conceive of. Imagine having a disease so overwhelming that your mind causes you to want to murder yourself. Imagine having a malignant disorder that no one understands. Imagine having a dangerous affliction that even *you* can't control or suppress. Imagine all the people living life in peace. Imagine the estate of John Lennon not suing me for using that last line. Then imagine that same (often fatal) disease being one of the most misunderstood disorders . . . one that so few want to talk about and one that so many of us can never completely escape from.

I've often thought that people with severe depression have developed such a well for experiencing extreme emotion that they might be able to experience extreme joy in a way that "normal" people also might never understand, and that's what FURIOUSLY HAPPY is all about. It's about taking those moments when things are fine and making them *amazing*, because those moments are what make us who we are, and they're the same moments we take into battle with us when our brains declare war on our very existence. It's the difference between "surviving life" and "living life." It's the difference between "taking a shower" and "teaching your monkey butler how to shampoo your hair." It's the difference between being "sane" and being "furiously happy."

Some people might think that this "furiously happy" movement is just an excuse to be stupid and irresponsible and invite a herd of kangaroos over to your house without telling your husband first because you suspect he would say no since he's never particularly liked kangaroos. And that would be ridiculous because *no one would invite **a herd** of kangaroos into their house.* Two is the limit. I speak from personal experience. My husband, Victor, says that "none" is the new limit. I say he should have been clearer about that before I rented all those kangaroos.

The FURIOUSLY HAPPY movement sparked the Silver Ribbon concept, an idea that grew from a blog post and resonated with thousands of people, in spite of the fact that none of us ever actually *made* any silver ribbons because we were all too depressed to do crafts. Here's the original post:

> When cancer sufferers fight, recover, and go into remission we laud their bravery. We wear ribbons to celebrate their fight. We call them survivors. Because they are.

> When depression sufferers fight, recover, and go into remission we seldom even know, simply because so many suffer in the dark... ashamed to admit something they see as a personal weakness... afraid that people will worry, and more afraid that they won't. We find ourselves unable to do anything but cling to the couch and force ourselves to breathe.

> When you come out of the grips of a depression there is an incredible relief, but not one you feel allowed to celebrate. Instead, the feeling of victory is replaced with anxiety that it will happen

again, and with shame and vulnerability when you see how your illness affected your family, your work, everything left untouched while you struggled to survive. We come back to life thinner, paler, weaker... but as survivors. Survivors who don't get pats on the back from coworkers who congratulate them on making it. Survivors who wake to more work than before because their friends and family are exhausted from helping them fight a battle they may not even understand.

I hope to one day see a sea of people all wearing silver ribbons as a sign that they understand the secret battle, and as a celebration of the victories made each day as we individually pull ourselves up out of our foxholes to see our scars heal, and to remember what the sun looks like.

I hope one day to be better, and I'm pretty sure I will be. I hope one day I live in a world where the personal fight for mental stability is viewed with pride and public cheers instead of shame. I hope it for you too.

But until then, it starts slowly.

I haven't hurt myself in three days. I sing strange battle songs to myself in the darkness to scare away the demons. I am a fighter when I need to be.

And for that I am proud.

I celebrate every one of you reading this. I celebrate the fact that you've fought your battle and continue to win. I celebrate the fact that you may not understand the battle, but you pick up the baton dropped by someone you love until they can carry it again. I survived and I remind myself that each time we go through this, we get a little stronger. We learn new tricks on the battlefield. We learn them in terrible ways, but we use them. We don't struggle in vain.

We win.
We are alive.

>———<

And we are.

I want this book to help people fighting with mental illness, and also those who have friends and family who are affected by it. I want to show people that there can be advantages to being "a bit touched," as my grandmother put it. I want my daughter to understand what's wrong with me and what's right with me. I want to give hope. I want to teach the world to sing in perfect harmony, but without selling any Coca-Cola products.

This book is less a sequel to my last one and more a collection of bizarre essays and conversations and confused thoughts stuck together by spilled boxed wine and the frustrated tears of baffled editors who have no choice but to accept my belief that it's perfectly acceptable to make up something if you need a word that doesn't already exist, and that punctuation is really more of a suggestion than a law. It's called "concoctulary,"[2] y'all. I hope you will find it to be the perfect follow-up

---

2. "Concoctulary" is a word that I just made up for words that you have to invent because they didn't yet exist. It's a portmanteau of "concocted" and "vocabulary." I was going to call it an "imaginary" (as a portmanteau of "imagined" and "dictionary") but turns out that the word "imaginary" was already concoctularied, which is actually fine because "concoctulary" sounds sort of unintentionally dirty and is also great fun to say. Try it for yourself. *Con-COC-chew-lary. It sings.*

to my last book . . . strange, funny, honest, and more than a little bit peculiar.

But in the best possible way.

Like all of us.

—Jenny Lawson[3]

---

3. *My* mental illness is not *your* mental illness. Even if we have the exact same diagnosis we will likely experience it in profoundly different ways. This book is my unique perspective on my personal path so far. It is *not* a textbook. If it were it would probably cost a lot more money and have significantly less profanity or stories about strangers sending you unexpected vaginas in the mail. As it is with all stories, fast cars, wild bears, mental illness, and even life, only one truth remains: your mileage may vary.

Furiously Happy. Dangerously Sad.

"You're not crazy. STOP CALLING YOURSELF CRAZY," my mom says for the eleventy billionth time. "You're just *sensitive*. And . . . a little . . . *odd*."

"And fucked up enough to require an assload of meds," I add.

"That's not crazy," my mom says as she turns back to scrubbing the dishes. "You're *not* crazy and you need to stop saying you are. It makes you sound like a lunatic."

I laugh because this is a familiar argument. This is the same one we've had a million times before, and the same one we'll have a million times again, so I let it lie. Besides, she's technically right. I'm not *technically* crazy, but "crazy" is a much simpler way of labeling what I really am.

According to the many shrinks I've seen in the last two decades I am a high-functioning depressive with severe anxiety disorder, moderate clinical depression, and mild self-harm issues that stem from an impulse-control disorder. I have avoidant personality disorder (which is like social anxiety disorder on speed) and occasional depersonalization disorder (which makes me feel utterly detached from reality, but in less of a "this LSD is awesome" kind of a way and more of a "I wonder what my face is doing right now" and "It sure would be nice to feel emotions again" sort of thing). I have rheumatoid arthritis and auto-immune issues. And, sprinkled in like paprika over a mentally unbalanced deviled egg, are things like mild OCD and trichotillomania—the urge to pull one's hair out—which is always nice to end on, because whenever people hear the word "mania" they automatically back off and give you more room on crowded airplanes. Probably because you're not supposed to talk about having manias when you're on a crowded airplane. This is one of the reasons why my husband, Victor, hates to fly with me. The other reason is I often fly with taxidermied creatures as anxiety service animals. Basically we don't travel a lot together because he doesn't understand awesomeness.

"You're not *a maniac*," my mom says in an aggravated voice. "You just like to pull your hair. You even did it when you were little. It's just soothing to you. Like . . . like petting a kitten."

"I like to pull my hair *out*," I clarify. "It's sort of different. That's why they call it a 'mania' and not 'kitten-petting disorder.' Which would honestly suck to have because then you'd end up with a bunch of semi-bald kittens who would hate you. *My God*, I hope I never get *overly enthusiastic kitten-fur-pulling disorder*."

My mother sighs deeply, but this is exactly why I love having these conversations with her. *Because she gives me perspective.* It's also why *she* hates having these conversations with me. *Because I give her details.*

"You are perfectly normal," my mom says, shaking her head as if even her body won't let her get away with this sort of lie.

I laugh as I tug involuntarily at my hair. "I have *never* been normal and I think we both know that."

My mom pauses for a moment, trying to think up another line of defense, but it's pretty hopeless.

⊢━⊣

I've always been naturally anxious, to ridiculous degrees. My earliest school memory is of a field trip to a hospital, when a doctor pulled out some blood samples and I immediately passed out right into a wall of (thankfully empty) bedpans. According to other kids present, a teacher said, "Ignore her. She just wants attention." Then my head started bleeding and the doctor cracked open an ammonia capsule under my nose, which is a lot like being punched in the face by an invisible fist of stink.

Honestly I didn't know *why* I'd passed out. My baseline of anxiety remained the same but my subconscious was apparently so terrified that it had decided that the safest place for me to be was fast asleep on a floor, surrounded by bedpans. Which sort of shows why my body is an idiot, because forced narcolepsy is pretty much the worst defense ever. It's like a human version of playing possum, which is only helpful if bears are trying to eat you, because apparently if you lie down in front of bears they're all, "What a badass. I attack her and she takes a catnap? I probably shouldn't fuck with her."

This would be the start of a long and ridiculous period of my life, which shrinks label "white coat syndrome." My family referred to it as *"What-the-hell-is-wrong-with-Jenny* syndrome." I think my family was more accurate in their assessment because passing out when you see doctors' coats is just damn ridiculous and more than slightly embarrassing, especially later when you have to say, "Sorry that I passed out on you. *Apparently I'm afraid of coats.*" To make things even worse, when I pass out I tend to flail about on the floor and apparently I moan gutturally. "Like a Frankenstein," according to my mom, who has witnessed this on several occasions.

Other people might battle a subconscious fear of adversity, failure, or being stoned to death, but *my* hidden phobia makes me faint at the sight of *outerwear*. I've passed out once at the optometrist's, twice at the dentist's office, and two horrifying times at the gynecologist's. The nice thing about passing out at the gynecologist's, though, is that if you're already in the stirrups you don't have far to fall—unless of course you're like me, and you flail about wildly while you're moaning and unconscious. It's pretty much the worst way to pass out with someone in your vagina. It's like having a really unattractive orgasm that you're not even awake for. I always remind my gynecologist that I might rather loudly pass out during a Pap smear and then she usually grimly informs me that *she didn't need me to remind her at all.* "Probably," my sister says, "because most people don't make as much of a theatrical show about fainting."

The *really* bad part about passing out at the gynecologist's is that you occasionally regain consciousness with an unexpected speculum inside your vagina, which is essentially the third-worst way to wake up. (The second-worst way to wake up is at the gynecologist's *without* a speculum inside of you because the gynecologist took it out when you passed out and now you have to start all over again, which is why I always tell gynecologists that if I pass out when they're in my vagina they should just take that opportunity to get everything out of the way while I'm out.

The first-worst way to wake up is to find bears eating you because your body thought its safest defense was to sleep in front of bears. That "playing possum" bullshit almost never works. Not that I know, because I'd never pass out in front of bears, because that would be ridiculous. In fact I've actually been known to run at bears to get a good picture of them. Instead, I pass out in front of *coats*, which—according to my brain—are the things that you *really* need to be concerned around.)

One time I loudly lost consciousness at my veterinarian's office when he called my name. Apparently my subconscious freaked out when I saw blood on the vet's coat and then I abruptly passed out right on my cat. (That's not a euphemism.) I woke up shirtless in the lobby with a bunch of strangers and dogs looking down at me. Evidently when I started moaning the vet called an ambulance and when the EMTs arrived they claimed they couldn't find my heartbeat so they ripped open my shirt. Personally I think they just wanted a cheap thrill. I think the dogs looking down on me agreed, as they seemed slightly embarrassed for me after watching the whole spectacle unfold. But you really can't blame the dogs because, first of all, who can look away from a train wreck like that, and secondly, dogs have no concept of modesty.

"Waking up shirtless with a bunch of concerned dogs staring at your bra because you're afraid of coats is about the seventh-worst way to wake up," I mutter aloud to my mother.

"Hmm," my mom replies noncommittally, raising a single eyebrow. "Well, okay, maybe you're not *normal* normal," she says grudgingly, "but who wants to be normal? *You're fine.* You are perfectly fine. *Better* than normal even, because you're so aware of what's wrong with you that you can recognize it and . . . sort of . . . *fix it.*"

I nod. She has a point, although the rest of the world might disagree with our definition of "fixing it."

When I was little I "fixed it" by hiding from the world in my empty toy box whenever my undiagnosed anxiety got too unbearable. In high school I fixed it by isolating myself from other people. In college I fixed it with eating disorders, controlling what I ate to compensate for the lack of control I felt with my emotions. Now, as an adult, I control it with medication and with shrink visits and with behavioral therapy. I control it by being painfully honest about just how crazy I am. I control it by allowing myself to hide in bathrooms and under tables during important events. And sometimes I control it by letting it control me, because I have no other choice.

Sometimes I'm unable to get out of bed for a week at a time. Anxiety attacks are still an uncomfortable and terrifying part of my life. But after my furiously happy epiphany, I've learned the importance of pushing through, knowing that one day soon I'll be happy again. (If this sentence seems confusing it's probably because you skipped over the author's note at the beginning like everyone else in the world does. Go back and read it because it's important and also because you might find money in there.)

This is why I sneak into other people's bathrooms in haunted hotels and once accepted a job as a political czar who reports directly to the stray cat that sleeps at city hall. I have staged live zombie apocalypse drills in crowded ballrooms and I've landed on aircraft carriers at sea. I once crowdfunded enough money to buy a taxidermied Pegasus. *I am furiously happy.* It's not a cure for mental illness . . . it's a weapon, designed to counter it. It's a way to take back some of the joy that's robbed from you when you're crazy.

"*Aaaaah!* You're *not* crazy," my mom says again, waving a wet plate at me. "Stop saying you're crazy. People will think you're a lunatic."

And it's true. They will. I Google the word "lunatic" on my phone and read her one of the definitions.

Lunatic: *(noun) Wildly or giddily foolish.*

My mom pauses, stares at me, and finally sighs in resignation, recognizing way too much of me in that definition. "Huh," she says, shrugging thoughtfully as she turns back to the sink. "So maybe 'crazy' isn't so bad after all."

I agree.

Sometimes crazy is just right.

I've Found a Kindred Soul and He Has a Very Healthy Coat

A few weeks ago I was at the pharmacy picking up my meds and I was staring into the drive-through window and thinking about how awesome it is that we live in a world where you can pick up drugs in a drive-through, and that's when I noticed something strange next to the pharmacist's register:

Yes. Those are dog biscuits.

And I thought, "Well, that's . . . *odd*. But maybe someone returned them because they were stale or something?" And then I thought it was even odder that someone could realize that dog biscuits had gone stale because dogs aren't usually very good at *not* eating cookies even if they're fairly shitty. I mean, dogs eat used diapers if you let them, so I'm pretty sure none of them are saying no to cookies. But then the pharmacist came back and while he was ringing me up *he reached over and picked up a handful of broken dog biscuits . . .*

AND.

ATE.

THEM.

And then I thought, "Wait. *Am I high right now?* Is *he* high? Am I being tested? Should I say something?" But I didn't, because I'm pretty sure you're not supposed to accuse the man giving you drugs of eating dog food. And then I signed for the drugs and drove away and I thought to myself, "Is it possible that he accidentally ate the dog biscuits? Or maybe someone is always stealing his food at work so he decided to put his tasty human cookies (made *for* humans, not *from* humans) in a Milk-Bone box to keep them safe? Or maybe he just likes to entertain himself by seeing if people will tell him that he's eating dog food. Those would be good people, probably."

I'm not one of those people.

But then I spent all day thinking, *"WHY THE DOG BISCUITS?"* and so I went back today to ask, but the dog biscuits were gone and the dog-biscuit-eating guy was also gone and I thought, "Can I ask this pharmacist if the other pharmacist who eats dog food is around, because I need to know the story?" And the answer is "No. No, I can't." But I really want to know because I suspect that I would be great friends with this guy because anyone who would hide crackers in a dog-food box seems like someone I'd like to hang out with. Although, someone who just eats dog food for fun seems slightly more questionable.

Except now I'm wondering if maybe Milk-Bones are really delicious and he's just a genius who's discovered really cheap cookies. Cookies that you don't have to call your judgmental vet about when your dog gets in the pantry and eats all of them. You still have to call the vet though when your cat has eaten a toy consisting of a tinkle bell and a feather and a poof ball all tied together with twine. That actually happened once and it was really the worst because the vet told me that I'd have to ply the cat with laxatives to make the toy pass easily through and that I'd need to inspect the poop to make sure the toy passed because otherwise they'd have to do open-cat surgery. And then it finally *did* start to pass, but just the first part with the tinkle bell, and the cat was freaked out because he was running away from the tinkle bell hanging out of his butthole and when I called the vet he said to definitely NOT pull on the twine because it could pull out his intestines, which would be the grossest piñata ever, and so I just ran after the cat with some scissors to cut off the tinkle bell (which, impressively, was still tinkling after seeing things no tinkle bell should ever see). Probably the cat was running away because of the tinkle bell *and* because I was chasing it with scissors screaming, "LET ME HELP YOU."

If I was good friends with that dog-food-eating pharmacist I would've called him to tell him all about the tinkle bell issue because he'd probably appreciate it, but I never found him again because I was worried that if I ever asked to see the dog-food-eating pharmacist the other pharmacists would stop giving me drugs.

This feels a bit discriminatory, but I can't explain exactly why.

My Phone Is More Fun to Hang Out with Than Me

When I wake up in the morning I often find messages left to me on my phone. Then I read the messages and I suspect that I'm being stalked by a madwoman. And I am. That madwoman is me. The calls are coming from inside the house.

Some of these notes are written while I'm waiting for my sleeping pills to kick in, but most are written at two a.m., when I'm convinced that I've come up with something brilliant that I'll forget if I don't jot it down immediately. Then in the morning I congratulate myself because I have forgotten what it was and am a little disappointed that the messages are less world-shattering and more just plain confusing. These missives from my brain are baffling, but I never delete them because it's nice to have a pen pal I don't have to write back to, and also because I can look at the strange notes and think, "Finally someone gets me."

These are a few of those notes:

"I'm not going to say I told you so" is pretty much the same thing as saying "I told you so." Except worse because you're saying "I told you so" and congratulating yourself for your restraint in not saying what you totally just said.

>—<

Are asparaguses just artichokes that haven't grown properly? Like they started smoking and got really skinny, like supermodels?

>—<

I bet marmalade was invented by the laziest person in the world.

>—<

Eating a peach is like eating a newborn baby's head. In that it's all soft and fuzzy. Not that peaches taste like babies. I don't eat babies. Or peaches, actually. Because they remind me of eating babies. Vicious circle, really.

>—<

Today at lunch the waiter told me that the soup of the day was "Beef and Human." And I was like, "What the shit?" He said he'd had some and it was "good but really heavy on the human." Victor was like, "That sounds great. I'll have a bowl of that," and I felt like I'd fallen into a *Twilight Zone* movie. But it turns out the waiter was saying "Beef and Cumin," which honestly sounds almost as gross.

》———《

Is it illegal to use shower curtains as regular curtains and vice versa? If not, what if you went shopping for a shower curtain but bought a valance? That seems like it should be a misdemeanor at least.

》———《

The phrase "Rest in peace" seems incredibly self-serving. It basically means, "Stay in your grave. Don't haunt me." The opposite would be "Fitfully toss" or "Go jogging."

》———《

I don't get the anti-slut-shaming movement. They're like, "Don't shame the sluts," and I'm like, "*You're the one calling them sluts.*" It's like having a "Lay off the fatties" campaign.

》———《

If the plural of "octopus" is "octopi" then why isn't the plural of "rabbit" "rabbi"? Is it just because "octopuses" is too much fun to say?

》———《

One of Victor's friends had a pet called "Terry the Truth Cat." When she was little and her father thought she was lying he would pick up the cat and say, "You kids tell me the truth or Terry gets it." I guess it was supposed to help with honesty but it seems pretty fucked up. Plus, I don't think I could threaten a cat. Maybe we could get Terry the Truth Turtle and threaten him with a fake gun. We'd be trying to get our daughter, Hailey, to tell the truth and he'd just hide his head in his shell like, "I'm not part of this. I'm not with you guys." But I don't like guns so maybe we could hold it over a pot of boiling water. But what if we accidentally steamed it? That would suck. Fuck it. I'd rather just let Hailey learn to lie really well.

>———<

"We wish you a merry Christmas" is the most demanding song ever. It starts off all nice and a second later you have an angry mob at your door scream-singing, "Now bring us some figgy pudding and bring it RIGHT HERE. WE WON'T GO UNTIL WE GET SOME SO BRING IT RIGHT HERE." Also, they're rhyming "here" with "here." That's just sloppy. I'm not rewarding unrequested, lazy singers with their aggressive pudding demands. There should be a remix of that song that homeowners can sing that's all "I didn't even ask for your shitty song, you filthy beggars. I've called the cops. *Who is this even working on? Has anyone you've tried this on actually given you pudding? Fig-flavored pudding? Is that even a thing?*" It doesn't rhyme but it's not like they're trying either. And then the carolers would be like, "SO BRING US SOME GIN AND TONIC AND LET'S HAVE A BEER," and then I'd be like, "Well, I guess that's more reasonable. Fine. You can come in for one drink." Technically that would be a good way to get free booze. Like trick-or-treat but for singy alcoholics. *Oh my God, I finally understand caroling.*

———

I almost never use B.C. and A.D. to describe time periods. I use BKCWC. Before Kirk Cameron Went Crazy. That's how I judge time.

———

Why is it "**in**capable" and "**un**able" instead of "**un**capable" and "**in**able?" You can have an inability but you can't be inable. I'm uncapable of understanding how these decisions were made.

———

If I were a dominatrix I would force my submissive to do my washing up and clean the fridge and brush the cats and whenever he tried to say the safety word ("banana") to make me stop because it wasn't what he wanted I would chuckle softly and say, "No, Gary. That's *definitely* not the safety word," and I would tighten the leash and hand him a mop and I'd say, "*So your wife won't do this for you?* That's so sad. Now finish the floors and go pick up my dry-cleaning." It would be ten years later and I'd still have someone to pick me up at the airport and do all the shit I didn't want to do and then on his deathbed I'd say, "Hey, Gary? I was just kidding. The secret word really *was* 'banana,'" and then we'd laugh and laugh.

———

Whenever Victor and I are fighting, I like to pull out my phone and take a selfie of us together because that way when he tells me to calm down I can prove that I'm less mad than he is because "How could you think I've lost my temper? Look at me in this picture. I look adorable. *You* look like the one with a temper problem." It's also nice because when I'm taking the picture he either has to smile or he has to choose to look shitty. Either way, I win. Plus, I have a terrible picture of him I can threaten to tweet out if he doesn't agree that I'm probably right about everything.

>———<

I wonder if when birds are new they ever try to land on clouds? And if so is it like when you think you've gone down the last stair but there's still another one and you step off and make that weird "oof" noise and everyone looks at you? That would suck. But at least birds are hidden when they fuck up and fall through clouds.

>———<

I find it very confusing that people refer to good days as "the salad days." No one wants salad. Is it because rich people always serve salad even though it usually gets thrown away? Does it mean that if you're rich enough to serve food just to be thrown away then you've "made it"? Because that makes sense.

>———<

Bruce Springsteen said you can't start a fire without a spark, but you can start it with a magnifying glass. It ruins the rhyme scheme but at the cost of science. And arson. But maybe it's still a spark even if it starts with a magnifying glass? Maybe the first flame is always a spark? But that's like saying you can't start a fire without a fire. That's just sloppy songwriting. Bruce Springsteen is obviously not the boss of scientific accuracy.

⊢——⊣

Do they call a crib a "crèche" because it sounds like "crotch" and babies come from crotches? If so, that seems very lazy, but it's nice that they put an accent in it because it adds a desperately needed touch of elegance.

⊢——⊣

Kids don't use paper book covers anymore. Why is that? They're missing out on the best part of school, which is doodling genitals and curse words and hiding them in flowery vines. There used to be advertisements on ours. Mostly for the cotton gin and the funeral home, which was weird because we were children and had no money or inclination for either. I never understood paying for burial when you could just let pigs eat your body. I mean, we were *surrounded* by pig farms and those pigs need to eat, so two birds/one stone. We'd just turn the covers backward (after we'd drawn an inappropriately erect man in a coffin) and use the fresh blank covers to practice future tattoo designs.

We also had leather notebooks at our school, which I'm told is not something everyone had. They were leather, zippered notebooks with your name hand-tooled on them by the local saddle maker. You used it to carry your homework and everyone had one but they were really expensive. I finally got one as a combo birthday/Christmas present when I was in eighth grade and was so excited. Basically, I got school supplies as a present and I was fuck-ing ecstatic. These were simpler times. The salad days. Possibly.

My point is, kids get super excited about the stupidest things and then the stupidest things become incredibly popular. That's why I now try to avoid popular things like school supplies, and instead I just lean toward unpopular things like being eaten by pigs. Conceptually, I mean. I've been around a lot of pigs and none of them have ever tried to eat me. The pig farmer next door told me that's because pigs are picky and won't eat people who are still alive. This seems odd because I think wanting to eat a corpse is sort of the *opposite* of being a picky eater, but I'll defer to the experts on this one.

>—<

Whenever Hailey tells me kids at school were mean to her I want to go find those kids and tell them that I'm them from the future and that they've failed *miserably*. And then I'd be like, *"And look how fat you got."*

>—<

Yesterday I was at the gas station and I saw a woman whose kid is in Hailey's Girl Scout troop, but I was in my pajamas so I was hiding in the back until she left. There was a collection of cards and I perused them to look normal but the one I'd picked up was a can of beans with googly eyes and I thought that was weird, but turns out it's one of those cards that sings and moves when you open it. So I'm standing there, holding a googly-eyed can of beans as it shakes and loudly farts the birthday song to me in a gas station. It was like I was competing for an award for being the most conspicuously uncool person ever. I waved weakly at the woman and said, "That wasn't me," but she wasn't buying it. I should have slapped the card to the ground and yelled, "Witchcraft!" but you always think about these things too late.

———

My blood test came back as low in magnesium and selenium, but instead of prescribing a vitamin my doctor prescribed "two brazil nuts a day." I always thought that in the future food was supposed to be in pill form. Now I'm taking pills in food form. We're going backward here. Also, it sort of sucks that the one nut I'm prescribed is the worst nut. The one everyone throws away. I need to start a fund-raiser where everyone in the world just sends me the two nuts always left at the bottom of the can.

I told Victor that I'd gotten my test results and "they've pre-scribed me nuts." Victor says I'm confusing "prescribed" with "di-agnosed."

———

Benedict Cumberbatch is like Alan Rickman Benjamin Buttoning.

———

I don't understand why people keep pushing that "Don't be some random person. BE UNIQUE" message. You're *already* incredibly unique. *Everyone* is incredibly unique. That's why the police use fingerprints to identify people. So you're *incredibly* unique ... *but in the exact same way that everyone else is.* (Which, admittedly, doesn't really sing and is never going to make it on a motivational T-shirt.) So none of us are unique in being unique because being unique is pretty much the *least* unique thing you can be, because it comes naturally to everyone. So perhaps instead of "BE UNIQUE" we should be saying, "Be as visibly fucked up as you want to be because being unique is already taken." *By **everyone**, ironically enough.*

Or maybe we should change the message to "Don't just be some random person. Be the MOST random person."

>——<

The amount of money I would pay for people to stop fucking up grammar is only *slightly* lower than the amount I'd give to ensure I never have grammatical errors in the statements I make calling others out on their grammatical errors.

>——<

If you put a bunch of chameleons on top of a bunch of chameleons on top of a bowl of Skittles what would happen? Is that science? Because if so, I finally get why people want to do science.

>——<

I should start the Museum of Missing Stuff. It'd be filled with empty glass cases of stuff that's not there. Also, a giant room of stray socks and keys. And my sense of rationalism. And Victor's sense of whimsy. And his patience. That place would be crammed. We might have to expand.

>——<

People who think it's so hard to find a needle in a haystack are probably not quilters. *Needles find you.* Just walk on the haystack for a second. You'll find the needle. They're worse than floor-Legos. And if that doesn't work just burn some fucking hay. They should change "like finding a needle in a haystack" to "like finding a pen that works in that drawer filled with pens that don't work."

>——<

People wonder how Victor and I have stayed married for so long even though he's Republican and I'm super liberal. I think it all comes down to communication and compromise. Like last week when Victor said, "If you renew your PETA membership I will run over a squirrel." He's bluffing though. Unless he was in someone else's car.

>——<

I'm allergic to latex and it makes me break out in a rash so most condoms are out for me because the last thing any of us wants is a vagina rash. The alternative is the ones made of sheepskin, but it always creeps me out because does that mean Victor and I are having sex with a sheep? A *dead* sheep, actually. So it's bestiality *and* necrophilia. And a three-way, I think. I actually mentioned that to Victor and he immediately booked a vasectomy, which is sweet because it's nice that he cares about me. He claimed it was less his caring and more "I'd rather have my nuts cut off than have to listen to you talk about having three-ways with dead sheep." But now I have all these leftover condoms. They make great water balloons though and I bet they'd be really good for championship bubblegum-blowing competitions. Really chewy sheep bubblegum. That might be cheating. I don't know the rules about bubblegum contests.

⊢——⊣

My grandmother used to say, "Those are not the kind of underwear you want to get hit by a bus in," but I don't think the underwear has been invented that would make me *want* to get hit by a bus. Plus, when you're hit by a bus I think your underwear is probably the last thing on your mind. In fact, when you die your bowels release and you shit yourself, so even if you were wearing clean underwear they would not be clean by the time your grandmother got there. That's why I think they should make underwear with defensive sayings on them like *"I swear these were totally clean this morning."* It's the equivalent of those old-fashioned day-of-the-week underwear without having to remember what day it is. I can barely manage to get dressed in the morning, much less pass a pop quiz given by my underwear on what day it is. And besides, why am I taking advice on underwear from my grandmother when "granny panties" are the most universally reviled underthings in existence? When we were kids our great-aunt Olly used to give my sister and me a roll of dimes and a pack of granny panties every Christmas. They were so enormous that we'd pull them up to our necks and pretend they were strapless leotards while we mimicked the dancers on *Fame*. Just in the privacy of our own house though. That would be mortifying in public. And actually if someone saw me wearing granny panties that went up to my armpits while trying to do the robot I'd probably throw myself in front of a bus. Full circle.

"The victim was wearing a strapless leotard when she shit herself. A roll of dimes was found on the body. Her grandmother has been contacted to inform her how badly she failed."

I Have a Sleep Disorder and It's Probably Going to Kill Me or Someone Else

If you were to ask me, "How did you sleep?" I'd usually say, "Pretty well, all things considered." But today it's a bit more complicated because this morning I lost both of my arms.

On the bright side, it gave me something to write about, although it was of course impossible to write about at the time because I didn't have any working arms.

(Editor's note: Start over. Sound less ludicrous.)

Fine.

This morning I got up at six a.m. to get Hailey off to school but then I went back to bed for a bit because I'd been up until three a.m. having a dead raccoon rodeo in the kitchen.

(Editor's note: You know what? Never mind.)

The dead raccoon's name was Rory. I fell in love with him the instant I saw him because he looked exactly like Rambo, the rescued, orphaned raccoon who lived in my bathtub when I was little. Rory hadn't been lucky enough to be adopted by a small child who'd dress him up in small shorts sets and let him turn her sink into his own tiny waterfall.

Instead, Rory had fallen in with a bad crowd and ended up as road-kill, but my friend Jeremy (a burgeoning taxidermist) saw great poten-tial (and very few tire marks) on the cadaver and decided that Rory's tiny spirit should live on in the most disturbingly joyous way possible.

(*Courtesy of Jeremy Johnson*)

Rory the Dead Raccoon stood up on his hind legs, his arms stretched out in glee. He looked like he was the most excited member of your surprise party, or like a Time Lord in the process of regenerating.

His bafflingly enormous smile caused people to giggle (usually ner-vously and somewhat involuntarily) whenever I presented him. Or sometimes they'd scream and back away. I guess it depends on if you're expecting an unnaturally cheerful dead raccoon to pop out at you.

Victor didn't *entirely* understand my love for Rory, but he couldn't disagree that Rory was probably the best raccoon corpse that anyone had ever loved. Rory's tiny arms perpetually reached out as if to say, "OHMYGOD, *YOU ARE MY FAVORITE. PERSON. EVER. PLEASE LET ME CHEW YOUR FACE OFF WITH MY LOVE.*" Whenever I'd accomplished a particularly impossible goal (like remembering to refill my ADD meds even though I have ADD and was out of ADD meds) Rory was always there, eternally offering supportive high fives because *he* understood the value of celebrating the small victories. Victor might have refused to congratulate me on the fact that I hadn't fallen down a well that week, but that dead raccoon always had my back and very few people can say that.

"Very few people would *want* to say that," Victor corrected.

"It's just nice to have unconditional encouragement and praise," I explained to him. "*Some* people get all stingy with their high fives, but Rory never leaves me hanging." In fact, it was physically impossible for Rory to leave me hanging and I momentarily considered having Victor one day taxidermied in the same happy, congratulatory pose, but then I realized that no one would recognize him and he'd probably just look sarcastic, like he was only offering me high fives when I slipped on things that weren't there, or when the electricity was cut off because I forgot to pay it again.

Victor thinks taxidermy is a waste of money, claiming that "there are only so many things you can do with a dead raccoon." But I have proven him wrong time and time again. Victor pointed out that what he'd *actually* said was "There are only so many things you *should* do with a dead raccoon," and honestly that does sound more like something he'd say, but I still disagree.

When Victor was making Skype calls for work, I'd silently crawl up behind him and have Rory slowly and menacingly rise up over Victor's shoulder until the person on the call froze because they noticed a mentally unbalanced raccoon was leaning in like a furry, eavesdropping serial killer. Then Victor would realize Rory was behind him and he'd sigh that sigh he does so well and remind himself to lock his office door. If anything, though, Victor should have thanked me, because the perfect test to see if your friends and coworkers really have your back is if they're willing to say, "Hey, there's a raccoon creeping on you." It's like the "Is-my-fly-down?" test, but times one thousand, because almost *anyone* can relate enough to clear their throat and raise an eyebrow at your junk until you realize you forgot to zip, but it takes a really concerned badass to interrupt a conference call and say, "WATCH OUT FOR THAT MOTHERFUCKING RACCOON, DUDE." To their credit, most of Victor's callers would mention something and I'd point out that they'd passed the test and then Rory would be like, "JAZZ HANDS!" Then Victor would lock us both out and I'd stick Rory's paw under his office door and say in a small raccoony voice, "I'm trying to help you. Let me help you."

When the mailman dropped off packages I'd open the door a few inches and have Rory peek outside. *"Well, helllllooo!"* Rory would say in a snooty British accent. *"I hope you don't need a signature because I seem to have misplaced my opposable thumbs."* Eventually the mailman just stopped ringing the bell and would leave the packages on the porch, which was nice because it cut down on awkward small talk.

Sometimes I'd hide him under the covers (Rory, not the mailman) so that when Victor turned down the bed there was Rory on his pillow, as if to say, "SURPRISE, MOTHERFUCKER! THERE'S A DEAD RACCOON IN YOUR BED AND HE WANTS SOME SNUGGLIN'." Then Victor would glare at me and make me switch pillows with him.

Victor can't understand Rory's frenzied kind of love, but I think he's starting to accept that this is my love language. Other women might show their adoration with baked goods or hand-knitted slippers, but mine is channeled through animal corpses. Victor tries to interpret it as best he can but he is a guy who keeps his emotions close to his vest when it comes to dead animals in bed, so honestly it's hard to know what that man is really thinking. He's an enigma, that one.

Last night I realized that Rory was perfectly suited to ride on the cats (as if they were small furry horses and he was a rodeo star) but apparently the cats didn't realize how awesome it would be and so they were *incredibly* uncooperative. I tried to create a photomontage of Rory the Rodeo Raccoon but they weren't having it. (I suspect if my cats had Instagram they'd be all over this, but they don't so they couldn't be bothered.) I'd perch Rory on their backs and they'd stand still for a second but by the time I'd backed up and gotten them in focus they'd turn around like, "What are you doing? Why is there a raccoon on my back? *Why do they even let you be in charge of things?*" and then they'd just flop over on their sides like a bunch of ingrates who didn't understand art. Rory would gently tumble onto the floor, which I suspect sent the cats mixed messages because he was still waving his hands in the air like he just didn't care, as if he were celebrating the cats being assholes, and I was like, "*You're killin' me, Smalls*," but then he just celebrated the fact that I was frustrated. *Honestly, it is impossible to stay mad at that raccoon.*

Sometime around two a.m., Ferris Mewler finally gave up and stayed upright, annoyed but resigned, as he carried an ecstatic Rory on his back and I was like, "YES! *FERRIS MEWLER, YOU ARE AMERICA'S NEXT TOP MODEL!*" But then Victor opened the bedroom door and yelled, "*WHAT IN THE HELL IS GOING ON OUT HERE? IT'S TWO O'CLOCK IN THE DAMN MORNING,*" and Ferris panicked at all the unexpected yelling and tore off down the hall but Rory was still stuck to his back as Ferris streaked through the living room. And then Victor was like, "HOLY SHIT. *WHAT IN THE HELL WAS THAT?*" because I guess his eyes hadn't adjusted to the light (or maybe to the sight of an ecstatic raccoon frolicking bareback on a house cat). I

considered acting just as shocked as he was and claiming it was probably a small chupacabra that had snuck in. But then I thought that
would just raise more questions so instead I lowered the camera and
said, "What was *what?*" as innocently as possible. I prayed he'd just go
away questioning his sanity, and he did, but probably less because I'd
fooled him and more because he'd married someone who took secret
pictures of cats wearing dead raccoons in the wee hours of the morning. It wasn't my fault though. I've had chronic insomnia for as long as
I can remember. These are the things that eventually happen when
you're alone at two a.m. often enough.

*(Editor: Remember three pages ago when you said you lost your arms?
How have we not gotten to that yet? Did you forget that's what this story
was about?)*

*(Me: I was just getting there. You can't just start off a story about missing
arms without the proper context. Apparently.)*

I finally went to sleep at three a.m., woke up a few hours later to take
Hailey to school, and then crawled back in bed for a quick nap. It was
lovely, but at nine thirty the alarm I'd set on my phone went off. I tried
to reach over to turn it off, and that's when I realized that my left arm
was missing.

And I thought, "Well, *that's* odd."

But then I looked over at my arm and was like, "Wait, no, there it is."

It was flung awkwardly over my head and was completely numb
because Hunter S. Thomcat was lying on it and had cut off the circulation. I threw my shoulder toward the phone and Hunter grudgingly
rolled over, but my arm just fell forward, zombielike. My hand *almost*
grazed the phone but I couldn't get my fingers to work enough to hit
the snooze button. I glared furiously at my fingers like I was trying to

telekinetically move an inanimate object, except that the inanimate object was my own hand. The alarm got louder and so I tried to prop myself up with my other arm but I ended up just flopping around like a fish out of water because my other arm was pinned behind me AND WAS ALSO ASLEEP. This has never happened to me before and it seemed such an astronomically weird coincidence that I started to worry that I was accidentally in some sort of partial coma that only affects arms. Or maybe I'd been selectively paralyzed, but that seemed unlikely since most people who've been paralyzed say "I CAN'T FEEL MY LEGS" rather than "My arms stopped working."

Hunter walked around to stare at me like "Why aren't you turning off that noise? *What is wrong with you?*" which was very unhelpful. I managed to Frankenstein myself up into a sitting position and kept tossing my helpless arms near the snooze button, but it wouldn't work and it got louder and louder and I could hear Victor angrily stomping toward the bedroom, yelling, "Oh my God, *ARE YOU **STILL** IN BED?*" I didn't want to tell him that not only was I still in bed but also my arms weren't even awake yet, and so I panicked and quickly rolled off the edge of the bed to hide behind it. Obviously I wasn't thinking straight because I forgot that I didn't have arms to help catch me and so I landed facedown with a dull thud and that's when I realized how helpful it is to have working arms. You never think to appreciate your arms until you need them to stop the floor from punching you in the face.

Hunter S. Thomcat looked over the edge of the bed at me quizzically, as if to say, "What in the hell are you doing? Is there food down there?" and he dropped to the floor beside me to check it out. Victor burst in, yelling, "WHY IS YOUR ALARM BLARING? *SOME* OF US ARE ON CONFERENCE CALLS, YOU KNOW," and I heard him huff and switch off the alarm.

I looked at Hunter like, "Shhh. Say nothing and we'll be fine," and he stared back at me like, "What do you mean 'we'?"

Victor paused and I saw his feet moving toward the bathroom, where he looked for me, and then he came back in and was like, "*WHERE ARE YOU?*" but I stayed quiet and waited for him to leave so I could sneak out to my desk and pretend I'd been up for hours. My plan would have worked perfectly if Hunter hadn't decided to jump onto my hip so he could peer over the side of the bed and look at Victor like, "Why are you people doing this? Is this a game?"

Then Victor walked around the bed and sighed, and I said, "NO ONE'S IN HERE," but it sounded muffled because of the floor. He accused me of hiding from him rather than working and I said, "*No, actually,* I'm down here trying to save you from the sight of your disabled and temporarily paralyzed wife BECAUSE I'M TRYING TO PROTECT YOU." Then Victor gave me what I guess was a look of pity, or maybe love. I don't know because I was still facing the floor but I'm giving him the benefit of the doubt because *that's* what marriage is all about.

I suddenly realized that all of this might make a pretty good chapter and I wanted to write it down but I still didn't have arms to write with. So instead I said, "I've actually been down here working on my book but I don't have a way to type. Can you just turn on the voice-recognition part of my phone and lay it by my face so I can dictate notes because my arms don't work right now?" and Victor said, "*Your arms don't work right now?*" and I said, "Yes. Apparently I slept wrong and lost circulation and they're both still asleep."

"Holy crap," he said. "You're so lazy that even your limbs are still sleeping while I'm talking to you."

"*Quite the contrary,*" I explained as I struggled to roll over onto my back. "I'm so hardworking that I'm awake even when my body is still partially unconscious and I'm like, '*Fuck you, arms. I'll still be productive without you.*' THAT'S HOW DEDICATED I AM."

I was starting to get some of the feeling back in my left arm and I lifted it to try to brush Hunter away from my nose but instead I just smacked myself in the face.

Victor stared at me with concerned resignation. "You just hit yourself."

"It's possible my arms might be rebelling. Just put the phone next to my face and leave me. I have important work to do here."

He shook his head with disappointment, but he still did it and I started dictating. But the transcription app kept autocorrecting my story to something less ridiculous because even my phone was against me at that point. Then Hunter saw the words on the phone moving and he kept pouncing on it and resetting the cursor. I laid my head down on the rug in defeat as the pain of pins and needles flooded my arms, and wondered how often this sort of shit happened to Hemingway.

Victor claims these kinds of things don't go on in normal households, but I'm pretty sure this entire incident could be blamed on the fact that I have several real-life sleep disorders. This is not too surprising considering that I collect neurological disorders like other people collect comic books. Basically I've become so talented at having disorders that *I can literally have one in my sleep.* Victor doesn't think this is really something to brag about, but that's probably because he doesn't have *any* disorders and he's jealous.

Jesus. *It's not a competition, Victor.*

(But if it were a competition I'd be winning. *Handily.*)

Victor had been pushing me into doing a sleep study for years, but I'd felt it was a waste of time and money. I already knew I had a problem so I didn't really want proof that I was fucked up even when I was unconscious.

Besides, I wasn't the only one with sleep problems, as Victor had been talking in his sleep since he was a kid. When he was eight he was traveling with his dad and sat up in a darkened hotel room at two a.m., opened his eyes, and raised his arm to point toward the dark hall, saying, "Who's that man standing in the corner?" Then he lay back down and went straight back to sleep while his father quietly shit himself. Metaphorically. Probably.

A few weeks ago Victor woke himself up yelling, "LADY. YOU HAVE THE WRONG NUMBER. OUR CAT ISN'T EVEN IN THE HOSPITAL. *HE DOESN'T WANT PAJAMAS.*" Poor Victor. Even in sleep he's plagued by assholes.

It might be hereditary because my dad also has major sleep issues. I never really noticed it when I was a kid because you always assume that your family is normal until you realize that no one else's father stops people in the middle of their conversation to tell them he needs a quick nap and then lies down on their living room floor for twenty minutes to snore so loudly it sounds as if he's the Big Bad Wolf, but in reverse. No matter where we were or who we were with, my dad would often stop, lie down, and immediately go to sleep until he'd wake himself up choking on a snore. Once, Victor took my dad deep-sea fishing during a storm and the boat was rocking like mad and there was water and blood on the bottom of the boat and everyone was seasick and Daddy said, "Well, if no one else is going to take a nap, I will," and he lay down in the fish blood and slept soundly (but not soundlessly) for forty minutes. To Victor (and everyone else on the boat) this seemed insane, but to me it seemed normal, and I thought Victor was overreacting and should just count himself lucky that my dad had kept his pants on.

I inherited insomnia from my mom and the snoring/daytime sleepiness from my dad. I also came up with my own brand of exhaustion and choking-related awesomeness and Victor eventually said he couldn't take it anymore and made me get help.

My doctor thought I was most likely snoring and exhausted because of the insomnia and prescribed a hypnotic sedative. It probably works really well for normal people, but the first time I took it I waited for it to make me sleepy and it never did. Several hours later Victor found me in a closet where I claimed I could see through postcards and that I'd found the fifth dimension. Victor assumed I'd had some sort of a breakdown, which is insulting because it's entirely possible that I *did* find the fifth dimension and he wasn't giving me the benefit of the doubt. Instead he just put me to bed and called the doctor, who explained that she'd forgotten to tell me that I have to go to bed immediately after I take the pill or my body will stay awake while my brain goes to sleep. She told Victor that the same thing had happened to her father (who was found wandering the front yard—wearing only socks—asking the trees why they hated him) and her mom ended up taking him to the ER because she assumed he must have had a stroke. That whole story freaked me out so I threw away the sedatives (and all hope of visiting the fifth dimension) and instead told Victor I'd go for a sleep study if he promised to stop videotaping me snoring and playing it next to me to wake me up so I could *"feel his pain."*

I made an appointment with a sleep doctor, who explained that during the sleep study people would be watching me sleep and monitoring my brain waves to see how I reacted during the four stages of sleep. I'd explain those stages if I could spell all the complicated words but they basically range from "Wide awake" to "Just barely not dead."

My sleep cycle is a bit more elaborate.

The seven stages of sleep (according to my body)

STAGE 1: You take the maximum dose of sleeping pills, but they don't work at all and then you glare at their smug bottles at three a.m., whispering, *"You lying bastards."*

STAGE 2: You fall asleep for eight minutes and you have that dream where you've missed a semester of classes and don't know where you're supposed to be and when you wake up you realize that even in sleep you're fucking your life up.

STAGE 3: You close your eyes for just a minute but never lose consciousness and then you open your eyes and realize it's been *hours* since you closed your eyes and you feel like you've lost time and were probably abducted by aliens.

STAGE 4: This is the sleep that you miss because you're too busy looking up "Symptoms of Alien Abduction" on your phone.

STAGE 5: This is the deep REM sleep that recharges you completely and doesn't actually exist but is made up by other people to taunt you.

STAGE 6: You hover in a state of half sleep when you're trying to stay under but someone is touching your nose and you think it's a dream but now someone is touching your mouth and you open your eyes and your cat's face is an inch from yours and he's like, "BOOP. I got your nose."

STAGE 7: You finally fall into the deep sleep you desperately need. Sadly, this sleep only comes after you're supposed to be awake, and you feel guilty about getting it because you should have been up hours ago but you've been up all night *and now your arms are missing.*

I suspected that the only stage of sleep I'd have during the sleep study would be the sleep you don't get because strangers are watching you.

It was disconcerting right from the beginning because I went after sundown and the entrance to the clinic was literally in a dark back alley. I knocked on the locked door (which startled a homeless man who had been ironically—or possibly sarcastically—sleeping heavily) and I was fairly certain that this was the sort of place that would probably sell abortions by the dozen, but then the nurse opened the door and it was very bright and pleasant and not very abortiony at all.

They put me in a bedroom and the nurse asked if I wanted to change into pajamas. I self-consciously explained that the sweats I was wearing *were* my pajamas and then I felt like I was improperly dressed for sleep. Aside from that, though, it was just like being home, except for the video camera, the constant observation, the oxygen tubes up my nose, the monitors taped to my fingers, and the electrodes glued to my scalp to track my brain waves. The electrode wires were the most uncomfortable because they ran all over my head like I was a Medusa with a bunch of anorexic snake hair. The silver lining was that the weight of the wires pulled my face back like a mini-facelift and so I looked

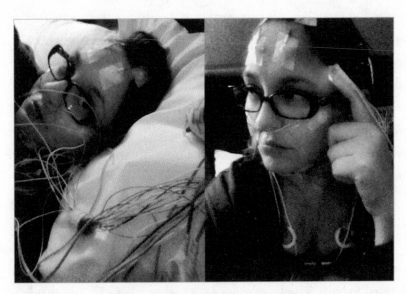

Because nothing says "sweet dreams" like electrodes
and wires from ankle to scalp.

surprisingly sexy if you ignored all of the anorexic snakes on my head. The nurse continually readjusted the forehead electrodes because she said they weren't picking up a signal and I'm pretty sure that's an insult.

My nurse warned me that one of the patients was a sleepwalker but that if he walked into my room they'd come get him, and that was comforting in a way that wasn't really comforting at all. After several hours of staring at the ceiling I drifted off and awoke to the sound of the woman next door screaming maniacally and I assumed she'd been stabbed to death by the sleepwalker. I shot bolt upright but the snakes in my hair were attached to the wall behind me so they jerked me back down onto the bed and I thought to myself, "Well, this is a really fucked-up way to die."

The nurse rushed in to assure me that everything was fine and that the screaming woman just suffered from night terrors. I nodded agreeably as I watched the sleepwalker knock over a chair outside my door. I briefly considered escaping but I was lightly shackled to the bed by wires and monitors, plus the nurses and orderlies were watching me, and for a minute I realized this was probably a lot like being in a mental institution, except even crazier because we'd all come here voluntarily, like some sort of terrible slumber party for weirdos. I was certain I wouldn't sleep again. But I must have, because at four a.m. a different nurse shook me awake and brusquely said, "You can go now. We got what we needed." She refused to tell me exactly what it was they'd gotten and I started to suspect it was my kidneys.

I was groggy but they made me leave out the back door while it was still dark. It was like I'd had a one-night stand with a sleep clinic.

A week later my doctor had my results and informed me that I have pretty much all of the sleep disorders except for the only one that I wanted to have, which is the apnea one where they give you that headgear that shoots oxygen up your nose. I wanted it because I'm pretty sure that's a smaller version of that oxygen chamber that Michael Jackson slept in to stop him from aging, and things seemed to work out pretty well for him.

Sadly, I didn't have sleep apnea but I had a number of other issues. A few things that are wrong with me when I'm not even conscious:

PERIODIC LIMB MOVEMENTS DURING SLEEP: It's like restless leg syndrome but it only happens after you're unconscious. I'm fine with it, though, because I think that means that my legs are jogging without me, which is honestly the only way you could ever get me to jog. When I was little we had a dog that I think had the same issue because he was always running while asleep on his side and we would look at his twitchy legs and say, "Aw! He's chasing rabbits in his sleep!" It's pretty much the most adorable sleep disorder ever. (Except, according to Victor, my version is not so much "running adorably" as it is some sort of ongoing exorcism, what with all the "terrifying jerking and writhing about.")

SNORING: They didn't see me choking during the sleep study but I often wake up choking and snoring loudly, although maybe that's because Victor's choking me for snoring loudly. I did snore a lot though, so my doctor prescribed these clips that go inside your nostrils to make it easier to breathe, except that you have clips in your nostrils now so it actually makes it *harder* to breathe. I tried it exactly once, which was enough time to realize that the *real* snoring cure here was slow suffocation, which admittedly is a very quiet death. I also had an allergic reaction to the plugs and both nostrils swelled up. This seemed like a more economical and organic way of smothering to death, but I still prefer snoring to asphyxiation. Call me crazy.

SEIZURES: "It looks like you might have an uncommon seizure disorder but there's no real cure for it." I asked the doctor what the point was in even telling me about it then. "Just keep an eye on it," he replied. I'm not sure how I would keep an eye on a disorder that only happens when I'm unconscious. I couldn't even tell if he was being sarcastic or not.

ALPHA INTRUSION: When you're asleep you're supposed to have delta brain waves, but apparently my brain is constantly getting interrupted with alpha waves, so I'm flooded with awakelike brain activity while my body is asleep, which means even when I'm asleep I'm still awake. I suspect my brain is working in collusion with my legs and my whole body is forcing me to do algebra and work out while I'm asleep. It's no wonder I'm so damn tired. And now that I think about it, alpha intrusion is all about part of you being asleep and the rest of you being awake . . . JUST LIKE MY ARMS THIS MORNING. *BAM.* It's like my brain just did a mic drop there.

When I told Victor the results he didn't take them very seriously until I pointed out that most people with alpha intrusion die. Then he looked concerned and I felt bad so I admitted that they actually don't die from alpha intrusion. Just, you know, most people die. Eventually. I can't imagine the intrusion helps though.

Victor sighed and assured me that "no one ever died from not enough sleep" but I'm pretty sure they have, and he paused and corrected himself. "Maybe it's 'No one ever died from *too* much sleep,'" and I was like, "I think you just described a coma. THIS ISN'T HELPING."

"*Fine,*" he said. "Everyone has to die of something but you're probably not going to die of sleep."

And he's wrong because *best-case scenario* I die in my sleep. I'll go to bed and then I'll never wake up. Worst-case scenario? I'm eaten by clowns.[1]

A footnote on Rory: There are actually two Rorys: Rory and his stunt double, Rory Too. The first time I saw Rory was on the Internet and I fell in love and told his maker, Jeremy, that I had to have him. I explained how Rory perfectly displayed that furiously happy smile and Jeremy agreed. Sadly, in between my falling in love with his photo and actually paying for him, Rory was involved in a tragic roller-coaster accident in Las Vegas. This sounds like something I just made up, but I assure you it's true. Rory's temporary guardians had taken him on a debaucherous Vegas weekend and he'd broken a few limbs. He'd also left all of his fingers and toes behind, proving the old adage "What happens [to break off] in Vegas stays in Vegas." Jeremy was furious and broke the news to me gently and he vowed to make me another Rory (better, stronger, and with wires inside so he was posable and could more effectively ride on the cats) with a raccoon corpse he had in his freezer.

"How does the first Rory's face look?" I asked.

"Still pleased as damn punch," he admitted. "But the rest of him is a hot mess."

I considered it for a moment and decided that a broken and tattered but still *ecstatically happy* Rory was pretty much exactly what being furiously happy was all about. After all, the most interesting of us have been broken and mended and broken again.

"I'll take him," I said. "Hell, I'll take them both."

And that's how I came to own two furiously happy raccoons. And I

---

1. But even then I'd probably lose consciousness before I died. In fact, pretty much *everyone's* final stage of death is the not-waking-up part. Although the whole never-having-insomnia-again thing sounds a bit nice, and it probably says something about me that I'm a bit envious of people taking the big dirt nap. Not that I'm ready for it now. It's just nice to know eventually I'll get some sleep.

love the flexible perfection of Rory Too (who is slightly larger, but you can't be picky when you're only dealing with roadkill raccoons) but Rory I is the one who makes me laugh every time I look at him. Jeremy had mended his broken arm and leg, and my father spent an afternoon sculpting new fingers and toes for him. Rory still looks a bit "off" but in a good sort of way and I'm currently looking for infant-sized adamantium Wolverine claws for him.

But even without the claws he's lovely . . . broken and flawed and so strange that even people who like taxidermy still think, "What the shit is going on here?" even as he's bringing joy and laughter into their lives. That raccoon is my goddamn role model. He is the worst and best Patronus ever, and I want to be *just* like him when I grow up.

Yes. Yes, they are.

How Many Carbs Are in a Foot?

I think I'm the last person left on earth who hasn't eaten kale or quinoa. People keep raving about their being the next big thing, but I'm still all frightened-rabbit from the time Victor made me the *last* big thing and I was like, "This rice has gone bad and I didn't even think rice could go bad." Then Victor explained that it was risotto and I was like, "The stuff Gordon Ramsay is always yelling about? This is *very* disappointing. It's as if risotto doesn't know if it's mashed potatoes or rice so it just decided to be both. *But badly.*"

Victor argued that it was really more like grits, but grits you can smother with cheese and butter, and that's pretty much cheating. I'd eat a human foot if it was smothered in enough cheese and butter. Then Victor called my bluff, saying, "You would *not* eat a human foot. *You won't even finish the damn risotto.*" I'm not sure if that was a dare, but it didn't matter because he's right. I'm *way* too lactose intolerant. Everyone else at the dinner party would be tucking into their cheesy-butter foot, and I'd have to eat *my* foot parboiled and plain. That's *my* struggle. And it's very real.[1,2]

---

1. Victor just read this and he says it sounds like I would eat my *own* foot, and that's just ridiculous. I'm not even sure why I have to clarify this but just to be clear, I wouldn't eat *my own foot*. That would be barbaric. Victor says that eating someone else's foot isn't exactly kosher but obviously I wouldn't do it unless the foot was ethically harvested. Like how some indigenous tribes eat their dead as a sign of respect. You couldn't turn that down without being insulting.

"Oh, your cheesy foot looks delicious but I *just* ate someone's gramma an hour ago and *I. am. stuffed.*"

No one is going to believe that.

But frankly I do sort of wonder how people taste. Cannibals say that we taste like pork, and bacon is my spirit animal, so we're probably delicious. I feel sorry for tribes that used to be cannibals but then stopped when the Christians came and inevitably ruined everything, because it would suck to be nostalgic for the comfort food of your childhood but then never have it again because now it's suddenly *not* cool to eat your dead uncle. That's a shitty craving to have. Not that I would know. I've never eaten a person before. Hell, *I've never even eaten kale.*

2. It just occurred to me that my footnote was *literally* a note about a foot. That's awesome. High five, me. I guess there's always a silver lining, even when it involves human feet you're too allergic to eat.

Pretend You're Good at It

It wasn't enough blood to be worrisome. Not even enough to demand a stitch. But it wouldn't stop dripping unceasingly from my swollen foot.

I was in New York in January, to record the audiobook version of my soon-to-be-released first book and to attend a prelaunch lunch held to publicize my book. This is fairly normal in book publishing but I was new to it and I was terrified on both accounts. The invitations to the luncheon were nicer than my wedding invites and everyone came. People from *The New York Times*, CBS, *O* magazine, and others I didn't even know. My agent and publisher did their best to keep me unaware of the importance of this luncheon, as they both knew that my anxiety disorder could be crippling and I'd already warned them (only half joking) that I might spend the lunch hiding under the table and they would have to just find a way to explain that writers are notoriously eccentric. And they are. But I knew I was more than that.

Mentally ill.

It's a phrase that once scared me, but now I wear it like an old jacket, comfortable but ugly. It keeps me warm when people look at me as if

I've lost my mind. I haven't. I'm mentally ill. There is a difference. At least to me there is. I am very aware of the fact that I'm not right. I know hiding under tables and in bathrooms isn't normal. I know that I've carved out a life that lets me hide when I need to because I wouldn't survive any other way. I know that when my anxiety attacks hit, my body isn't actually going to kill me, in spite of how it feels. I know that when I get suicidal thoughts stuck in my head I have to tell someone else who can help because depression is a cunning manipulator. I know that depression lies to you. I know that the few weeks a year when my face feels like a stranger's mask and nothing but physical pain can bring me back to my body there is a limit to how much I can hurt myself and still be safe in my own bed. I *know* that I am crazy. And *that* has made all the difference.

The luncheon went well. I mingled somewhat unsuccessfully with important people but I managed to intrigue them enough that they wanted to interview me for important pieces that might help the book I'd been writing for the last ten years. The book was a sort of dark comedy, and the cover featured a small, taxidermied mouse dressed as Hamlet and holding the skull of another dead mouse in his hands, as if it were a tiny Yorick. I'd asked my publisher to put my dead mouse, Hamlet von Schnitzel, on the cover of the book as a joke, but we could come up with nothing better for such a strange little book and that's why I was constantly apologizing to the sales team for making them have to sell a book with one and a quarter dead rodents on the cover.

After the first set of drinks was ordered, my editor, Amy, had a small but perfect speech, which would have been nicer than any speeches given at my wedding if I'd actually had friends when I was married who knew me enough to give speeches. Then she called me up to say a few words and I shakily welcomed everyone and thanked them for coming on this strange journey with me. And then I panicked a little because I couldn't think of how else to end the speech and that's when I found myself pulling one (and a quarter) dead mice out of my purse in the middle of a fancy New York restaurant. The waitstaff looked a little stunned and I think I might have hidden my face behind the tiny rodent and said something in a squeaky mouse voice about the importance of being true to yourself. Most of the people in the room knew nothing about me and even less about Hamlet von Schnitzel, but my vaguely panicked agent smiled encouragingly and so everyone else smiled along with her.

The whole luncheon was fuzzy but I think it was successful. My favorite part was when everyone was leaving and one of the waitresses snuck in to tell me that she was a huge fan and couldn't wait to read my book. I suspected my editor had paid her to say that but I saw her nervous, wild-eyed look barely masked by a skin of propriety and I realized she was part of my tribe. I hugged her tight and thanked her. She probably never realized how much I needed her right then . . . a keystone to keep me steady in a sea of normal semi-strangers.

I went straight from the luncheon to the small studio where I was recording my audiobook. I'd had to convince them to let me narrate my own book because most audiobooks are read by professional, velvet-toned actors, whereas my voice sounds like if Minnie Mouse were sick and spent too much time in Texas. I was terrified, certain that the pounding of my heart would be heard on the tape. They could literally pick up every rumble of my stomach. How could they fail to hear the terror in my voice?

The answer is, *they couldn't,* and so they'd stop me every few seconds and ask me to try the line again. Eventually they told me to take a break and clear my head and I left so that they could probably call Betty White to see if she could take over and that's when I realized how much I wanted to read my story in my own voice. I hid in the bathroom and sent out a frantic text to my friend Neil Gaiman (a brilliant author and narrator) telling him that I was panicked and was just about to lose the chance to tell my own story because my voice betrayed just how weak and insignificant I knew I was. He sent back a single line that has never left me:

"Pretend you're good at it."

It seemed too simple, but it was all I had so I scrawled the words on my arm and repeated it as a mantra. I walked back into the studio pretending to be someone who was amazing at reading her own story. I finished an entire paragraph without interruption. Then I looked up and the producer stared at me and said, "I don't know what you just did, but keep doing it." And I said, "I just did a *lot* of cocaine," and she looked a bit aghast and so I said, "No, I'm just kidding. I just got some really good advice from a friend."

The next day of recording was just as nerve-wracking as the day before, but I looked at the words on my arm again (*"PRETEND YOU'RE GOOD AT IT"*) and took a deep breath and pretended up the confidence I needed. Then I said, "You know what this audiobook needs? MORE COWBELL." And I sang the theme from *Annie* because I'd always wanted to sing on a New York stage and I figured that this was as close as I'd ever come. Then I suggested that they hire James Earl Jones to read the rest of the book. Or a Darth Vader impersonator if he wasn't available. They laughed. I laughed. I felt better. And I pretended I was good at it. And somehow? I was.

I write this mantra on myself *every single time* I have to get onstage or do a book reading. *"Pretend you're good at it."* I'd like to think that one day I'll be able to leave off the "pretend," but for now pretending works just fine. It gave me the confidence to finish the audiobook that day, and to be able to laugh and enjoy the experience instead of cowering in the bathroom.

But later that night in my hotel room I was hard-pressed to find something to laugh about. It was two a.m. and I was in the midst of a medium-sized panic attack. The kind where it seems like there are wild hamsters in your heart and you can feel the dread pressing down on you but you don't *quite* feel like you're dying yet. I took some anti-anxiety meds and tried to snap myself out of it by pacing, but the bitter cold had made my feet and hands swell from my rheumatoid arthritis and one foot was so swollen that the back of my heel split, seeping blood into my slipper. I sat with my foot in the bath, watching the water turn red as I waited for the bleeding to stop. I took deep, measured breaths and I tried to convince myself that being trapped in a tiny hotel room half of a country away from my home was fine . . . it was an adventure. One I was taking with a dead mouse and a foot they might have to amputate. And just when the panic attack got strong enough that I thought I might scream, I looked outside and saw the most amazing thing.

I saw snow.

To most people, snow is not a big deal; it's a hassle at best. To a girl born and raised in Texas, snow is *magical*. The giant snowflakes came down in enormous clumps, gleaming against the dark brick of the building my window faced, and it was lovely. And calming. I tried to open the window to stick my hand out but it was painted shut and I cursed silently. I watched the snow fall for an hour as I waited for my foot to stop bleeding and I wished it was light enough outside for me to go play in the snow. "*IT'S SNOWING, YOU GUYS,*" I tweeted to everyone in the world, who honestly didn't care.

And then, at four a.m. I decided that the only thing that would cure my insomnia/anxiety would be a long walk. In the snow. I pulled a coat on over my nightgown, slipped on my flats, and went downstairs. My foot was killing me as I tiptoed outside, nodding quietly to the confused man at the night desk, who looked puzzled to see me leave in my pajamas. Then I walked out into a New York night, which was muffled by snow, a thick white blanketing of powder that not a single person had put a step into. I could hear a drunk yelling for a cab down the street but it was comforting to not be the only person out in that weather. Sure, I was in my pajamas and I had been stabbed in the foot by arthritis, but at least I was mostly sober and not too far from a warm bed.

My foot ached. As I took a step the sharp pain shot all the way up to my spine. And that's when I just said, "*Oh fuck it,*" and carefully stepped out of my shoes into the gleaming white snow.

It was freezing, but the cold effortlessly numbed my feet and aching hands. I walked quietly, barefoot, to the end of the block, leaving my shoes behind to remind me how to find my way home. I stood at the end of the street, catching snow in my mouth, and laughed softly to myself as I realized that without my insomnia and anxiety and pain I'd never have been awake to see the city that never sleeps asleep and blanketed up for winter. I smiled and felt silly, but in the best possible way.

As I turned and looked back toward the hotel I noticed that my footprints leading out into the city were mismatched. One side was glistening, small and white. The other was misshapen from my limp and each heel was pooled with spots of bright red blood. It struck me as a metaphor for my life. One side light and magical. Always seeing the good. *Lucky.* The other side bloodied, stumbling. Never quite able to keep up.

It was like the Jesus-beach-footprint-in-the-sand poem, except with less Jesus and more bleeding.

It was my life, there in white and red. And I was grateful for it.

"*Um, miss?*"

It was the man from the front desk leaning tentatively out of the front door with a concerned look on his face.

"*Coming,*" I said. I felt a bit foolish and considered trying to clarify but then thought better of it. There was no way to explain to this stranger how my mental illness had just gifted me with a magical moment. I realized it would have sounded a bit crazy, but that made sense. After all, *I* was a bit crazy. And I didn't even have to pretend to be good at it.

I was a damn natural.

George Washington's Dildo

The First Argument I Had with Victor This Week

ME: Hey. Are you busy?

VICTOR: No. What's up?

ME: Are we . . . *fighting*?

VICTOR: Why? What did you do?

ME: I didn't do anything. I was just at my computer and then I remembered that you were talking to me in my office and then I realized you weren't there anymore.

VICTOR: That was like . . . *an hour ago.*

ME: I know. But I couldn't remember you leaving and I thought maybe you stormed out on me because I wasn't paying attention to you, but then I didn't notice because I wasn't paying attention.

VICTOR: *You don't remember me leaving?*

ME: No. It's like when you drive home but then you can't remember driving home once you get there.

VICTOR: Huh. *Yep, we're fighting.*

ME: Hmmm. Were we fighting before I brought all this up?

VICTOR: *Nope.*

ME: Well if it makes it any better I was coming in here to say that you were right to storm out because clearly I was *not* paying attention, and so technically I think you *have* to accept my apology. Especially since it's for a fight that never actually happened.

VICTOR: No.

ME: BUT I DIDN'T DO ANYTHING WRONG AND I'M APOLO-GIZING FOR A FIGHT WE NEVER EVEN HAD.

VICTOR: *You didn't even realize I wasn't in the room until an hour after I left.*

ME: Ah, but *you* didn't notice that *I* didn't notice. And *I'm* the one who brought that to your attention. So if anything you should be thanking me. I'm like the George Washington of marital fights.

VICTOR: Wh—

ME: Because he told on himself for chopping down that tree and everyone was all, "Good job, George!" and then that probably turned him into a tagger because the greatest praise he ever got was for vandalism.

VICTOR: *What are you talking about?*

ME: A tagger is a graffiti artist.

VICTOR: I KNOW WHAT A TAGGER IS. It's what kids call a vandal.

ME: "Kids"? Are you implying I'm childish?

VICTOR: Of course not. *You're the George Washington of marital aids.*

ME: Ew.

VICTOR: *You're the one who said it.*

ME: No. "Marital aids" are sex toys. You just called me George Washington's dildo.

VICTOR: I'm pretty positive I've *never* called anyone that.

ME: Well, *you implied it.*

VICTOR: Stop talking.

ME: I can't. The marriage books say you're never supposed to leave a fight unresolved.

VICTOR: FINE. WE'RE NOT FIGHTING.

ME: THEN WHY AM I APOLOGIZING?

VICTOR: I have no idea. Everything after George Washington's dildo was a blur.

ME: You can say that again.

VICTOR: No, actually. I *never* want to have to say that again.

ME: *Deal.*

VICTOR: Huh?

ME: I promise to never make you say anything about George Washington's dildo if *you* promise to stop getting mad at me about fights we aren't actually having.

VICTOR: Do you ever wish we had normal fights like normal couples?

ME: Never.

VICTOR: Huh. Me either.

Winner of the argument: Neither of us. Or possibly both. Hard to say.

I'm Not Psychotic. I Just Need to Get in Front of You in Line.

This year my doctor prescribed me antipsychotics.

"To . . . keep the psychotics away?" I asked, jokingly.

She was not joking.

She promised me that this did *not* mean I was psychotic but assured me that in small doses this drug—made for schizophrenics—could decrease the length of my depressive episodes if I used it as a sort of a side dish to go with my antidepressants.

So of course I took the drug. Drugs are magic. You take a pill and feel happy. You take another and feel less hungry. You take another pill and have minty breath. (That last pill was actually a Tic Tac, but you get the picture.)

There is nothing better than hearing that there is a drug that will fix a terrible problem, unless you also hear that the drug is for treating schizophrenia (or possibly that it kills fairies every time you take it).

Frankly, I think it's the word that scares me.

Antipsychotic.

I dare you to find a drug that will freak people out more when they're rifling through your medicine cabinet during parties. Unless maybe it's medicine for contagious explosive combustion of the urethra, but I don't count that because it doesn't exist (I hope). Surely the people naming antipsychotics could have come up with something less hurtful. After all, we don't call Viagra the "floppy-dick pill" and hardly any of us refer to anger-management therapy as "maybe-just-stop-being-such-an-asshole class." I honestly can't think of any drug that has more of a stigma than antipsychotics.

Truthfully though, there are some advantages to being on antipsychotics. First off, you can say you're on antipsychotics. This might seem silly but when you go to the pharmacy and you're standing in line with twenty germy people sneezing all over the place you can honestly say, "Would you mind if I went first? I have to pick up my antipsychotic meds and I REALLY needed them yesterday." This tactic also works for grocery lines, the DMV, and some buffets.

The second advantage of being on antipsychotics is that they can actually help. In the time I've been on them I've hurt myself less. I feel more stable. The blue men who live in my closet try to sell me fewer cookies and most of those squirrels plotting against me have disappeared. (That last sentence was a joke, but only people on mild antipsychotics will laugh at it because everyone else is afraid it's true. It's not. Squirrels are real and they don't disappear no matter how many pills you take. Frankly, I'm shocked at how often I have to explain this.)

Some people say that drugs are never the answer, and I respect their opinion, but sometimes drugs *are* the answer and I think you need to be flexible. In fact, if you ask those same people, "What was it that Nancy Reagan said you should always 'just say no' to?" they will all say, "Drugs," and then I'll say, "Correct. Drugs *are* the right answer." So technically we're both right. Then I point out that drugs are often very bad for you, and that you have to do your research first and realize that there's a difference between "drugs" and "medication." You can tell the difference because the first ones are ironically much cheaper and easier to get than the latter, and also because use of medicine requires constant doctor supervision, treatment, and blood work.

Being on medication for mental illness is not fun, nor is it easy, and no one I've ever known does it just for kicks. Kids don't buy black-market Prozac to take to raves. People don't use B_{12} shots as a gateway drug to heroin. The side effects and troubles with taking medication are very real and (if you have a chronic mental illness) are something you have to deal with for the rest of your life. Even if a drug is working for a while, it might stop working and you'll have to start all over again with something new, which can be incredibly frustrating and dis-heartening. And then you have to deal with the side effects of the new drug, which can include "feeling excessively stabby" when coupled with some asshole telling you that "your medication not working is just proof that you don't really need medication at all." I can't think of another type of illness where the sufferer is made to feel guilty and question their self-care when their medications need to be changed.

When I went on my first antidepressant it had the side effect of mak-ing me fixated on suicide (which is sort of the opposite of what you want). It's a rare side effect so I switched to something else that did work. Lots of concerned friends and family felt that the first medica-tion's failure was a clear sign that drugs were not the answer; if they were I would have been fixed. Clearly I wasn't as sick as I said I was if the medication didn't work for me. And that sort of makes sense, be-cause when you have cancer the doctor gives you the best medicine and if it doesn't shrink the tumor immediately then that's a pretty clear sign you were just faking it for attention. I mean, cancer is a seri-ous, often fatal disease we've spent billions of dollars studying and treat-ing so obviously a patient would never have to try multiple drugs, surgeries, radiation, etc., to find what will work specifically for them. And once the cancer sufferer is in remission they're set for life because once they've learned how to *not* have cancer they should be good. And if they let themselves get cancer again they can just do whatever they did last time. Once you find the right cancer medication you're pretty much immune from that disease forever. And if you get it again it's probably just a reaction to too much gluten or not praying correctly. Right?

Well, no. But that same, completely ridiculous reasoning is what people with mental illness often hear . . . not just from well-meaning friends, or people who were able to fix their own issues without medication, or people who don't understand that mental illness can be dangerous and even fatal if untreated . . . but also from someone much closer and more manipulative.

We hear it from ourselves.

We listen to the small voice in the back of our head that says, "This medication is taking money away from your family. This medication messes with your sex drive or your weight. This medication is for people with *real* problems. Not just people who feel sad. No one ever died from being sad." Except that they do. And when we see celebrities who fall victim to depression's lies we think to ourselves, "How in the world could they have killed themselves? They had everything." But they didn't. They didn't have a cure for an illness that convinced them they were better off dead.

Whenever I start to doubt if I'm worth the eternal trouble of medication and therapy, I remember those people who let the fog win. And I push myself to stay healthy. I remind myself that I'm not fighting against me . . . I'm fighting against a chemical imbalance . . . a tangible thing. I remind myself of the cunning untrustworthiness of the brain, both in the mentally ill and in the mentally stable. I remind myself that professional mountain climbers are often found naked and frozen to death, with their clothes folded neatly nearby because severe hypothermia can make a person feel confused and hot and convince you to do incredibly irrational things we'd never expect. Brains are like toddlers. They are wonderful and should be treasured, but that doesn't mean you should trust them to take care of you in an avalanche or process serotonin effectively.

I've never had a psychotic breakdown. I'm seldom delusional. I've never hallucinated anything that didn't come from too much of a drug I probably shouldn't have taken anyway. I'm just broken. But in a way that makes me . . . *me*. My drugs don't define me. I'm not psychotic. I'm not dangerous. The drugs I take are just a pinch of salt. A little seasoning in life, if you will. Your baked potatoes would be fine without it, but anyone will tell you that a pinch of salt can make all the difference. *I am your potatoes.* And I'm better with salt.

Maybe this is a bad analogy.

How about this . . .

My taking low-level antipsychotics is like using just enough rum to make a good slice of rum cake, but not using enough to get alcohol poisoning and choke to death on your own vomit. The first is medicinal. The second one is gross and unsanitary.

And I know some of you are saying that cake isn't medicinal. *Really? Cake isn't medicinal? Who's crazy now, asshole?* The whole world could be cured with enough cake and antipsychotics. Which actually makes sense because **you can't make a cake without salt, can you?**

Wait, *can* you make a cake without salt?

I actually have no idea. I don't know much about baking. I know there's something white in there. Maybe it's flour I'm thinking about. I just wrote "salt" because it brought all my metaphors back together. Sort of. Probably not. It's hard to tell.

I blame this whole chapter on the antipsychotics.[1]

---

1. And *this* is the third advantage to taking antipsychotics. You can blame all sorts of bullshit on them. It's like blaming it on your period, except it's a period *that never ends*. And no one ever questions you because you have a medical handicap. A scary, intimidating, possibly dangerous medical handicap. Plus, now you can use the handicapped bathrooms with no guilt. EVERYONE WINS.

Who wants cake?

Why Would I Want to Do More When I'm Already Doing So Well at Nothing?

Victor and I have different ideas about what we should do in our spare time. In *my* spare time I like to stare at shit. I mean, not literally. I like to stare at the TV, or the Internet, or a book, or cat videos. There's a lot of sitting very still and not moving involved. I suspect in a former life I was probably a statue because I am *profoundly* good at it.

Victor, on the other hand, spends *his* spare time creating new businesses, writing reference books, gleefully finding errors on financial forms, and telling me how I should spend my spare time.

In Victor's Type A world there should be no spare time. His motto is, "Time to lean, time to clean," except replace "lean" with "sleep" and replace "clean" with "build a multinational business and pull everything out of the closet with the intention of organizing it but not actually follow through and just leave it for your wife to sort out." *My* motto has always been "Time enjoyed is never wasted." Except replace "enjoyed" with "drunk" and "never wasted" with "never not a good idea."

I think it has something to do with the fields we work in. For most of our marriage Victor has been a workaholic entrepreneur or an executive of successful companies. He really enjoys it, which makes him dangerously questionable, or at least mildly sociopathic. He easily fills empty time with specific tasks that have a defined start and end. His e-mails are always answered with quick, smart, and often vaguely condescending directives that make people want to never e-mail him again, so he's always caught up with correspondence. My unopened e-mails often number into the thousands, and once every few months I'll panic at how far behind I am and send a form letter to everyone that reads: "Hello. I totally suck. I'm just now opening this. Do you still need me? I'm so sorry. I am *not* to be trusted. Hugs, me." Then I declare e-mail bankruptcy, delete everything, and start a whole new e-mail account and never *ever* go back to the last one. My old e-mail addresses are like bars I've been kicked out of and can never return to. It's a ridiculous and assholish system but I've found that it works for me and *I've never received a single complaint.* Victor says that's because it's impossible to receive a complaint on an account I never check again, but I suspect it's because everyone is equally behind and they appreciate my honesty.

My job is to write ridiculous things on my blog, in books, and on used napkins that get misplaced almost immediately. It's part of my job to be aware of the latest hedgehog-in-a-bathtub video. It's *research.* There's also a lot of behind-the-scenes work that non-right-brained people don't see happening. For example, when I have writer's block I sometimes have to "refill my creative cup." This is an actual phrase my shrink has used and I made her write it down so I could show Victor that I had a doctor's note explaining my behavior (but I lost the note in my stacks of used napkins and related flotsam so he just had to take my word for it, which he did not because he is sadly untrusting).

"Refilling your creative cup" means different things to different people, but to me it looks a lot like watching *Doctor Who* marathons or reading David Sedaris books while screaming, *"WHY DO YOU MAKE*

IT LOOK SO EASY?" Sometimes it looks like driving to pet stores so I can pull out all the ferrets from their bins and drape them over me to make them into tickly, freaked-out coats. Occasionally it looks like me drawing doodles of penises on the overdue tax forms Victor has passive-aggressively taped on my computer monitor.

In summation, I spend an *impressive* amount of time doing absolutely nothing. Like, I'm at pro level. Because *that's* how artistic genius works. And because I'm *very, very* lazy.

Now, some people will say that if you have writer's block you should just start writing anyway because then you'll at least accomplish *something*. However, I've never liked anything I've ever been forced to write so I'm pretty sure all that accomplishes is a bunch of shitty writing, and I already have enough of that even when real inspiration hits. Good writing cannot be forced. This is why you don't have any classic, beloved books filled with the begrudging and angry mandatory essays of students who didn't want to write them, and why you almost never see college dissertations go viral on Reddit. In other words, if you spent most of the morning reading Twitter and then scribbling weird, indecipherable notes to yourself on your arm then you are probably on the right track to becoming a successful artist. Or to being homeless. Those things aren't mutually exclusive.

You'd think after eighteen years of marriage Victor and I would be more accepting of each other's working styles, but no. Victor spent most of this morning directing several conference calls, yelling at plumbers, and rolling over our 401(k)s into something that sounded even more boring than 401(k)s. I'd stopped listening at that point.

I, on the other hand, spent most of the morning coming up with good names for cats that I don't currently have. My current favorite is "The President." It's an awesome name because you'd constantly find yourself saying things like, "The President will *not* stop sitting on my keyboard." Or "The President just threw up on the new rug." Or "I like sleeping with the President but why do I always wake up with his butt on my face?"

I tried to tell Victor about how awesome the President would be in bed on a cold night and he was like, "NO MORE CATS. YOU HAVE TOO MANY CATS ALREADY," but then I just stared at him and said, "Too bad. *Overruled.* You can't turn down a request from the President." He disagreed but I'm pretty sure that's considered treason. I called the pet store where I snuggle the ferrets to ask if they had any leads on patriotic-looking cats who need a new home, but they recognized my voice and informed me that the manager had just enacted a policy of "only one loose ferret at a time." And that's *ridiculous,* because the most you can possibly make with a single ferret is a small pillbox hat (which uses claws instead of bobby pins). I was a little upset and I may have said, "THIS IS OUTRAGEOUS. THE PRESIDENT *WILL NOT STAND FOR THESE KINDS OF CUTS.*" And then they asked what I was talking about and I considered explaining that ferret cuts were much worse than government budget cuts because *everyone* suffers when you cut ferrets. Especially the ferrets. But then I remembered that I hadn't adopted the President yet and I thought it might be inappropriate to throw around the weight of my nonexistent cat all willy-nilly. Victor agreed that it was extremely inappropriate, although not for the same reasons.

I told Victor that *not* having a cat named the President had already crippled me once today and that the President would probably get in all kinds of crazy shenanigans that I could write about. I argued that my buying the President was basically the equivalent of his buying office supplies, so it was fiscally irresponsible to *not* adopt a cat called the President. At this point Victor may have screamed, "YOU CANNOT HAVE ANY MORE CATS. I'M THE ONE THAT HAS TO CLEAN

UP AFTER THEM AND I'LL BE DAMNED IF I'M GOING TO SCOOP THE PRESIDENT'S SHIT TOO."

He paused and shook his head at his own questionable phrasing but I smiled contentedly because he'd just proven my point, as that was *exactly* the kind of argument that would be gold on my blog. In fact, the President has already given me four paragraphs in this book *and he doesn't even exist yet.* It's possible he might be the most productive President we've ever had.

Victor walked away before we could finish discussing the issue. So I wrote myself a reminder on the tax forms he'd taped to my monitor: "GET A LITTER BOX FOR THE PRESIDENT." I suspected the IRS would be confused (and possibly not in a good way) so I added, "I'm not referring to your boss. I totally voted for that guy. Please don't audit me. I'm kind to animals and small children. If anything, you should audit my husband, who thinks the President should just live in a cage rather than get adopted by my daughter, who would totally dress him up in old Cabbage Patch Kid clothes and snuggle him like crazy-cakes." Then Victor came back in, saw the now-vandalized tax papers, and just stared at me in disappointment. I explained that it would probably be better if he just did all my tax papers in the future. He claimed that that would be illegal and I told him that if the President were here he'd be just fine with it and that's basically the same as getting presidential approval on everything. Cats don't give a shit about stuff, so basically the President would automatically approve of everything we did by default. Except for maybe Victor's use of the Super Soaker to keep the cats off the kitchen counters. The President would probably *not* approve of that.

Case in point? Just this moment Victor walked in and asked what I was doing and I told him I was writing about how much he hates the President, and he started yelling at me about using my time more wisely. Frankly, it's not even that we disagree about my use of time. It's more about how completely far we are from agreeing about what would be a credible use of my time.

Actual things Victor has suggested I should do in my spare time:

- **Idea 1:** Open an art gallery.
- **Idea 2:** Open a comic book store.
- **Idea 3:** Open a restaurant.
- **Idea 4:** Anything that doesn't involve ferrets.

Actual things I'd consider doing in my spare time:

- **Idea 1:** Start a club for small monkeys. Set them up with people who like to have their hair played with. Note: There might be some technical problems because typically monkeys only pick out bugs in hair, and some people might be weird about getting insects dumped in their hair, but people who'd pay to have monkeys play with their hair are not entirely predictable, so it could still work. Or maybe we could just dump edible glitter in people's hair.

   That's where we'd make our money. *Selling edible monkey glitter.* I don't know how monkeys are with edible glitter but it's gotta be a step up from their current diet. I mean, *YOU EAT BUGS, MONKEYS. Stop being so goddamn pretentious.* Also, I have a real-life model to base this on because my dad's friend has a pet monkey, Amber, who likes to pick off scabs on people's scalps, so we call her Amber the Scab Monkey, which is a terrible name. Who names a monkey *Amber*? Total waste of a monkey. Also, I'm not sure how many people have scabs on their heads, but I suspect if you're letting monkeys dig around in your hair you're going to end up with scabs. This business builds itself.

- **Idea 2:** Adopt a stray cat and name it the President. Set it up with a Twitter account. Sell pardons from my cat that you can buy for whenever you forget your wife's birthday or for when you accidentally let too many ferrets loose in a store. Like, "I know you're still mad at me but I do have a pardon from the President. That's gotta count for something."
- **Idea 3:** Watch videos of goats doing funny things.

In the end, Victor and I both want the same thing—for me to get my shit together. That's where we find the common ground. And when Victor starts up again about opening an art gallery that sells comics and crepes I respond with some variation of what I always say: "It's a very good idea, Victor, but right now I'm just too involved with writing/catching up with TV/developing edible monkey glitter/the President. But maybe in my next life I'll do it."

And it could be true. Maybe in my next life I *will* open a successful business, and buy and sell stocks, and memorize my driver's license number, and do my taxes on time. *Or* maybe in my next life I'll open a deli that specializes in mashed potato sandwiches (mashed potatoes and tater tots stuffed inside warm potato bread) and spaghetti pies (no definition needed) and I'll have a big sign saying "The President Eats Here!" And he does, because cats fucking *love* spaghetti. And at least Victor won't be mad at me in my next life.

Unless, that is, in his next life he comes back as a customer. Then he'll shake his head a little confusedly as he steers his third wife away from the cat on the counter eating a spaghetti pie. But I bet Victor'll turn back once more to see a very happy woman handing a potato sandwich to her glittery monkey-waiter, and I imagine he'll feel a small pang of regret and sadness. Probably because he'll never know that potato sandwiches are fucking *delicious*.

PS: Victor just read this and he agreed that "mashed potato sandwiches *are* delicious" but stated that he'd more likely be looking back to see a woman covered in stolen ferrets getting arrested for not handing in her taxes on time because none of her glitter-eating monkeys loved her enough to make her do required paperwork.

I *really* hate it when he's right.

What I Say to My Shrink
vs. What I Mean

"I feel like I'm making some real progress."

I HAVEN'T STABBED ANYONE IN THE FACE IN WEEKS. SOMEONE GET ME SOME KINDA TROPHY. BUT NOT A BOWLING TROPHY. I ALREADY HAVE ONE OF THOSE.

"I've been having problems concentrating. I think I might have ADD."

I'VE BEEN WATCHING YOUTUBE VIDEOS OF KITTENS FALLING TOO MUCH WHEN I'M SUPPOSED TO BE WORKING AND IF MY EDITOR FINDS OUT I'M GOING TO NEED FOR YOU TO WRITE ME A DOCTOR'S NOTE EXPLAINING THAT IT'S A MEDICAL CONDITION.

"Your waiting room is *so* cheerful."

WHY DO YOU HAVE ALL THOSE CAT FANCY MAGAZINES IN THE LOBBY? ARE THOSE SOME SORT OF TRAP, OR IS IT JUST SOME SORT OF PROFILING?

"But I didn't look at those magazines because I'm not some kind of crazy cat lady."

I STOLE THE CENTERFOLD.

"Although I do, *of course*, love my pets as much as any normal person."

THE OTHER DAY I HAD INSOMNIA AND I MADE MY CATS A WATER BED OUT OF A ZIPLOC BAG AND A SHOEBOX. THEY POPPED IT WITH THEIR CLAWS AND THEY ALMOST DROWNED. THEN I TRIED TO PUT BABY SOCKS AROUND THEIR FEET BUT THEY KEPT PULLING THEM OFF SO I TRIED WRAPPING RUBBER BANDS AROUND THE SOCK HEMS AND THEN MY HUSBAND WOKE UP WHILE I WAS PINNING ONE OF THE CATS DOWN TO PUT THE SOCK ON HIM AND HE WAS ALL, "WHAT ARE YOU DOING? WHY ARE THESE CATS ALL WET?" AND I WAS LIKE, "I'M TRYING TO HELP THEM ENJOY WATER BEDS," AND THEN VICTOR MADE ME GO TO SLEEP. IT WAS A DISAPPOINTMENT TO EVERYONE INVOLVED.

"Who let all these squirrels in here?"

NO, SERIOUSLY. WHO LET ALL THESE SQUIRRELS IN HERE?

"I swear I saw two squirrels duck behind your receptionist's desk."

FOR REAL. THERE ARE SQUIRRELS INFILTRATING THE BUILDING.

"No? *Really?* Huh. Must've just been a trick of the light. Ha ha."

WHAT THE FUCK ARE YOU TRYING TO PULL, LADY? I TOTALLY JUST SAW THOSE SQUIRRELS.

"So, how are you?"

IS THIS SOME SORT OF TRICK? DID YOU PURPOSELY LET SQUIRRELS IN HERE TO SEE IF I'D PRETEND TO NOT SEE THEM JUST SO THAT YOU CAN SEE IF I'M PRETENDING NOT TO SEE THINGS THAT AREN'T THERE? BE-CAUSE THAT IS FUCKING SNEAKY AND UNETHICAL. AND PROBABLY A CRUEL USE OF SQUIRRELS.

"I've been well, thanks."

BETTER THAN THESE SQUIRRELS YOU'RE HOLDING HOSTAGE, AT LEAST.

"What's that? I seem 'distracted'?"

HOLY SHIT. WHAT IF THERE AREN'T ANY SQUIRRELS AND I'M JUST SEEING IMAGINARY SQUIRRELS? WHAT IF SQUIRRELS DON'T EVEN EXIST? IS THAT EVEN POSSIBLE?

"I'm *not* distracted."

DAMN IT. I PROBABLY NEED TO PROVE THERE ARE SQUIRRELS IN HERE OR ELSE THIS DOCTOR IS GOING TO THINK I'M REALLY INSANE. THIS IS THE LAST PLACE I NEED TO IMAGINE NONEXISTENT SQUIRRELS. MAYBE I SHOULD SMUGGLE SOME IN SO SHE SEES THEM TOO.

"Honestly, I'm doing *really* well."

WHERE COULD I GET SOME SQUIRRELS AT THIS TIME OF DAY?

"Sometimes when I'm staying in thin-walled hotel rooms I'll open up my laptop and play TV murder scenes really loudly to see if anyone ever calls the police to report a murder. No one ever does though. It's like people just don't care anymore."

MOTHERFUCKER. I CAN'T BELIEVE I JUST SAID THAT OUT LOUD.

"I can't believe I just said that out loud."

I BLAME THOSE FUCKING SQUIRRELS. WHICH MY SHRINK PROBABLY

SMUGGLED IN TO THROW ME OFF SO I'D ADMIT TO STILL NEEDING HER.

"Well played, Dr. Roberts. Well played, indeed."

PS: That was obviously a slightly hyperbolized account of how my psychiatrist achieves job security but last week I went in for my appointment after getting a call reminding me of an appointment I didn't even remember making. When I got there the nurse insisted that I didn't have an appointment and that no one had called me. And I stood there in the office wondering if I'd just imagined someone calling to tell me I needed psychiatric help, or if the office had intentionally called me so that I'd come in and question my sanity when I was told that I wasn't actually supposed to be there. It seemed like a highly questionable but also somewhat brilliant way to increase customer loyalty.

Then I walked outside the office and checked my phone and that's when I realized that it was my other doctor I had an appointment with and so I yelled, "Oh, shit!" and ran to my car so I wouldn't be late and then I looked back and saw the nurse staring after me in confused concern. It's almost like I showed up there just to show them how little progress I was making. *And* I was too frazzled to look at the cat magazines.

It was disappointing on all accounts.

LOOK AT THIS GIRAFFE

Last week a stranger showed up at my parents' house with an antique, six-foot, dead giraffe head in the back of his truck that he wanted to get rid of. This sounds *slightly* less weird when I explain that my dad is a professional taxidermist who has a reputation for trading dead animals for strange things. Or maybe it sounds weirder. Honestly, I'm not good at judging what our lives look like to normal people.

The stuffed giraffe was the head and neck, ending at the shoulder blades and mounted to stand on the floor like a strange, questionable hat rack with eyeballs. My father decided to pass because it was weird looking. But then he remembered that I like terrible, old taxidermy and this giraffe seemed exactly like the kind of fucked-up thing I'd love, so he called and said, "There's a guy here with a third of a dead giraffe in the back of his truck and it looks pretty messed up, so I thought of you."

I considered responding with "*Who is this?*" but it was perfectly obvious who it was and I wasn't sure if I should be insulted or perhaps flattered that my dad knew me so well.

"Which third?" I asked. He explained, and I asked him to buy it for me, but only if it died of natural causes and was cheap, and only if it was *truly* weird looking. "But 'funny and whimsical' weird," I explained. "Not 'sad and awkwardly depressing' weird."

"I'm not sure I can tell the difference," my dad replied. The love of taxidermy had not skipped a generation, but the evaluation of it certainly had.

Victor overheard part of the conversation and told me that I could **not** have a giraffe because we had no place to put it,[1] and I pointed out that it was only a third of a giraffe *and* that it was the most interesting third, so it was almost impossible to say no to. Victor then proved me wrong by saying "no" several times. He argued that we had no way to get the giraffe to our house but I explained that I could pick it up from my parents' home and put it in the passenger seat of our car. And then I could roll down the window so Monsieur Giraffe's head could stick out and then I'd even be able to use the HOV lane. Victor disagreed *because all of a sudden he knows everything about HOV regulations*, but it didn't really matter because my dad called back and said he couldn't get a good deal on the giraffe head so he passed. Victor was relieved, but I reminded him that my father is a terrific liar so there was still a small possibility that he'd bought the giraffe stalk himself and

---

1. Truthfully, we don't really have room for a giraffe head, but we do have an old, decorative English streetlight in our yard that needs replacing and I thought maybe I could put the giraffe head there and have him hold the handle of a hanging lantern in his mouth. I can picture him now, staring silently, as if telling potential burglars: "Just keep on driving, ya bastards. I've got this place well covered." Victor says it would more likely be saying, "Welcome, solicitors. *We'll buy fucking anything.*" He also pointed out that taxidermied animals rot in the rain so I made a note to ask my dad if he could drill a hole in the mouth so the giraffe could hold an umbrella over himself. Of course, then that would keep him from holding the lantern in his mouth because that would look ridiculously busy, but perhaps we could make his eyes light up like laser beams instead? Maybe something motion-activated. Because nothing says "welcome" like a surprise umbrella-wielding giraffe head staring at you with laser beams for eyes.

was fixing it up for me as some sort of weird Christmas present. That's the thing about my father. You never know when he's hiding a giant surprise giraffe head from you. I can't really tell if that's a good thing or a bad thing, but I'm leaning toward good.

Victor seemed concerned that a surprise giraffe might show up at any moment, but he didn't need to worry because my dad really did pass on the head, but oddly enough he ended up picking the head up from a local auction when the woman who won it hired him to fix the damage. He was shocked she'd paid double the asking price but when he was driving the giraffe back to his taxidermy shop another woman saw the giraffe's flowing mane and followed my dad home offering to pay double that price. The lady who bought it at auction refused because she'd fallen in love with him and my dad shook his head in bafflement. He called me that night and said in a hushed tone, "My God. *There's more of you.*"

But that's another story. Let's get back to the story of gift taxidermy. I'm quite good at giving gifts. Several years ago for our anniversary I gave Victor a giant metal chicken named Beyoncé. Then last year I surprised him with a live sloth, a loose wallaby, and a hedgehog in our living room. This year Victor decided to surprise me instead. And he did. First, because it was like a month away from our eighteenth anniversary, and second, because when I opened up the big box Victor had left on the kitchen floor, a giant bear attacked me. Mostly because my sleeve got hooked on the wooden frame that was securing the bear in the box and I got off-balance, and when I fell backward it rolled over on me and I was suddenly pinned by an unexpected bear in the middle of the kitchen.

This gift is especially sweet because 1) Victor does not like taxidermy and the fact that he bought me a bear head makes him the greatest husband ever, 2) he assured me that this bear died of natural causes, and 3) now I have a quarter of a bear to hide around the house.

Sometimes I hide him outside Victor's office so it looks like he's being eavesdropped on by a bear. Sometimes I stick his head quickly through the shrubbery outside our house so that people driving by will think they've seen a bear, because I like to add intrigue to other people's lives. Victor says it's because I have too much free time on my hands. I think it's because *I'm a giver.* It could be both.

No one knows where the other three-quarters of that bear are but I'm okay with having just the face, although I *did* mention that I would have liked for the bear to have arms because that way it could hug you when you were having a bad day. Victor argued that bears give terrible hugs because they're made of claws and teeth but he's wrong because everyone knows that bears give the best hugs. *That's why you call a good hug a "bear hug."* I didn't mention that to Victor though because it's probably not cool to look a gift bear in the mouth.

Instead I just started looking online for someone who was selling taxidermied bear hands from a bear that died of old age because I thought I could just nail them under the bear like he was coming through the wall. Or maybe I could glue him and the paws to a mirror like there was a bear magically coming out of the mirror and then Victor was all, "WHAT THE SHIT? You can't glue a bear to a mirror. That's fucking crazy. And also, *WHY IS THERE A BEAR IN MY BED?*" and I was like, "Because that one's *juuust right*," and Victor looked at me incredulously because apparently his mother never read him "Goldilocks." He glared at me and so I just sighed and said, "Because I was all out of horse and I know how much you like *The Godfather?*" Then he got mad that I was going to spend money on bear arms, and I was like, "*I have the right to bear arms, Victor,*" and then I realized what I'd said and we both started giggling for a bit. And *that* moment? That's the moment when I realized how incredibly lucky I am to have spent eighteen years with a man who can laugh at bad gun-control jokes while a severed bear head is lying on his pillow.

"His name is Claude," I said. "Get it? *Clawed?*"

I could tell he got it because I could see him rolling his eyes. Although he might have been rolling his eyes because Claude has no claws and he thought I was being ironic. I'm not actually sure if it's ironic or not. That Alanis Morissette song sort of fucked up irony for everyone.

"You really *do* love me, don't you?" I asked. "You bought me taxidermy. You are *literally* bearing your heart."

Victor scratched his head. "I don't think that's how 'literally' works. And that's not really the right use of the word 'bare' either."

And, well, maybe not . . . but I think that's how *love* works. Sometimes it means doing the washing up when it's not your mess, and sometimes it's driving to the airport three times in one week to pick up a loved one, and sometimes it's all unexpected bears and possible surprise giraffes. Probably not so much the last ones for most people, but then again, we're not most people.

And thank God for that.

PS: This is Claude. Please give him a hand. *(Two, preferably.)*

The Fear

Some stories aren't meant to be told.

There was too much blood, I remember thinking. I could feel it dripping down my neck and I ran to get a towel, applying pressure to the cuts along my scalp.

"You okay in there?" Victor asked quietly from the other side of the bathroom door.

I was fine. I was fine. I was . . . bleeding. Badly. And I felt . . . relief? The pressure in my head was gone. The pain in me was floating away, making room for a pain so much easier to bear. The panic was fading slowly, and I told Victor I was okay and that he could go back to bed, but I could already hear him fumbling with the lock on the bathroom door. He was an expert at picking this lock and I knew I

only had a few seconds before he'd be in. I shoved the bloody towel in
the cupboard and turned the sink on to wash my hands.

Too late.

Victor walked in, that look on his face. I could never quite place it.
Resigned. Angry. Scared? It was probably the look I'd have on my
face if I allowed myself to feel those things. But I didn't. Instead, I cut.
Not with a knife. I chose a weapon much more personal, and more
punishing. I chose me.

It wasn't really a secret anymore. Victor had known that I hurt myself for years. But it had never been this bad. I picked at my cuticles
until they bled, but so what? So do lots of people. I picked at scabs
when I was nervous. It's gross but not unusual. I pulled my hair. Out.
By the roots. And I couldn't stop until large handfuls were on my lap. I
scratched my scalp and forehead. Deeply. With nails specially filed
for slicing. Victor would grab at my hands while we lay in bed to keep
me from doing it, but I couldn't stop myself. Nor could I explain it.

Impulse control disorder. Trichotillomania. Dermatillomania.

That's what the shrink called it. She said it wasn't uncommon for
people like me with anxiety disorders and avoidant personality disorder. I thought she was wrong. I'm fine being labeled with an anxiety
disorder. *I'm* perfectly fine. It's just my anxiety that's in disarray. But
"personality disorder"? That meant . . . broken.

"But I'm not broken," I explained to my psychiatrist. "I just . . . I
just hurt . . . inside. And when I tear at the outside it makes me feel less
torn up on the inside."

She nodded, waiting.

"I don't want to die."

She waited.

"Really, I don't. It's not a lie. I'm *not* suicidal. I just feel like sometimes I can't keep myself from hurting me. It's like there's someone else
inside of me who needs to physically peel those bad thoughts out of my

head and there's no other way to get in there. The physical pain distracts me from the mental pain."

She waited.

"It sounds crazy when I say it out loud," I whispered. "Sometimes I think I might really be crazy."

"If you were crazy you wouldn't realize how crazy it sounds," she said gently but insistently. "You're recognizing a problem and you're getting help for it, the same way any sane person with a medical problem would."

My hands itched to pull at my hair but I forced them to lie on my lap. There was dried blood under my nails. "This is why they put people in straitjackets," I thought to myself, "to stop them from hurting themselves."

And then we started a very long process of behavioral therapy, of drugs and of meetings with doctors. I read books with twelve-step programs designed to stem unhealthy needs.

Sometimes the impulse ended with a twinge . . . just a thought that I needed to scratch or to hurt myself, and then I was able to stop myself by redirecting the thought. Sometimes it was harder and I'd wear rubber bands around my hands, snapping them against my wrists to mimic the pain of cutting without the risk of infection or worse. Some nights I'd find myself hunched over the kitchen sink, crying pathetically as I forced myself to squeeze handfuls of ice until it burned like I'd stuck my arm in a fire. And sometimes . . . I'd relapse. Those nights are dark. They shine like broken glass in my memory, as I flirted with danger and allowed myself to cut, and bleed, and shed pieces of this body that has so betrayed me.

Sometimes Victor finds me the next morning with bloody hands, or a thin spot in my hair that I'll have to comb over, and he asks me, "*Why can't you just stop?*" He asks me why I would victimize myself intentionally, and he looks at me as if he thinks I could actually explain.

I can't.

I can't even tell myself why I am this way. I just know that it's how I'm made . . . and maybe one day someone will crack open this head of mine and find out what's wrong in there . . . and also what is right.

Because it's both.

Without the dark there isn't light. Without the pain there is no relief. And I remind myself that I'm lucky to be able to feel such great sorrow, and also such great happiness. I can grab on to each moment of joy and live in those moments because I have seen the bright contrast from dark to light and back again. I am privileged to be able to recognize that the sound of laughter is a blessing and a song, and to realize that the bright hours spent with my family and friends are extraordinary treasures to be saved, because those same moments are a medicine, a balm. Those moments are a promise that life is worth fighting for, and that promise is what pulls me through when depression distorts reality and tries to convince me otherwise.

Maybe the scales that weigh everyone else's emotions don't work for me. Maybe my scales are greater. Or less. Maybe instead of a scale I've wandered off to one of those nowhere places where you wait. And maybe one day I'll be found, and someone will explain to me why I am the way that I am.

Or maybe not.

After all, some stories aren't meant to be told.

Skinterventions and Bangtox

I've never been much of one for cosmetic enhancements or additions. I don't understand the need to stuff yourself with Botox, or implants, or collagen injections; however, I can *completely* understand the urge to strip stuff away in the name of beauty. I am a sucker for PedEggs, getting the fat pummeled out of you with high-frequency radio waves, wraps that make you sweat out your toxins, and cleanses that make you shit out your colon. Somehow that all seems healthier to me. Or at least more likely to make me less of who I am. Which is probably pretty unhealthy, now that I think about it.

I think I may need to call my shrink to tell her I just had a breakthrough. *Hang on.*

Okay, I'm back. Turns out that my shrink sends all her calls to her answering service after ten p.m. and they were disappointingly unimpressed with my epiphany about why I have dermatillomania. Probably because they don't even know what dermatillomania is. In fact, even spell-check doesn't know what it is and when I asked it for suggestions it just said "*LEARN SPELLING.*" Which is both rude *and* unhelpful, spell-check. Dermatillomania is an impulse control disorder that makes you want to scratch your skin off. It flares up when I'm stressed out and I find myself scratching at any imperfections. I usually pick at my scalp until it won't stop bleeding, or at my thumb, which is now permanently deformed from years of self-damage. It's sort of shitty and I don't recommend it.

I've found healthier ways of dealing with this need to pick my skin off, like wrapping my fingers with tape, or coating my hair with coconut oil so it reminds me not to unconsciously scratch. I've also found not-so-healthy ways, like when I heard about "microdermabrasion," which I suspect is Latin for "I want to pull off your skin and turn it into a jacket." My dermatologist sent me an e-mail about it, saying something about how my new skin was suffocating underneath layers of my old, dead skin, and I suddenly felt like I was wearing a mask of dust mites and dirt. I needed to have this done immediately and I couldn't go alone.

"SO THERE'S THIS NEW THING I HEARD ABOUT WHERE THEY RIP YOUR SKIN OFF," I may have screamed over the phone to my friend Laura.

She was silent for a bit and so I explained, "*BECAUSE IT MAKES YOU PRETTIER.*"

She still seemed slightly unconvinced so I continued. "I got a coupon for this microdermabrasion thingie. As I understand it, they rip off your face skin to make you look nice. I don't know what they have against face skin but apparently it's very out of style. Much like pubic hair. And Gwyneth Paltrow."

"*What does everyone have against Gwyneth?*" Laura asked, slightly annoyed.

We'd gotten off track. Clearly I wasn't describing this right. I continued: "Laura, they rub your face off using *DIAMONDS*. It's like a giant FUCK-YOU to the homeless. Like, I'M USING DIAMONDS TO RIP MY OWN FACE OFF. That's how little I care for diamonds *or my face*. Except that personally I plan to *keep* my bloody diamond waste and strain it out like the miners do when they pan for gold. That way I get a pan full of diamonds *and* some face skin. IT'S ALMOST LIKE THE FACE RIPPERS ARE PAYING ME TO DO THIS. Plus, you get a skin consultation and analysis so basically you get your face ripped off *and* then they tell you how shitty you look. But that's the price of beauty. That and forty-five dollars with Groupon. Apparently."

"Wait a second," Laura replied. "So I'm paying to have someone rip off my face *and then* **shame** *me*? It's like this was *made* for women. COUNT ME IN."

"*Right?*" I said. "They'll probably bring people in off the street to laugh at us. It's gonna be like high school all over again. WHO SAYS NO TO THIS?"

Laura was in. "Sign me up. I'm going to hang up now before you convince me that being friends with you is *too* good for my self-esteem. Call me if something else medieval and torturous opens up. Like nipple waxing. Or bloodletting."

And that was all it took. Because we were broken women who were all about paying stupid amounts of money to protect our sensitive face skin until someone offered to burn it all off for even more money.

I'm not sure why women are often so vulnerable to every suggestion involving our faces but for me it's like I'm having an abusive relationship with my own head. I use nothing but soap and water until one of those mall beauticians stops me on my way to buy a pretzel to tell me how bad I look and convinces me to lavish my face with an expensive cream that makes me immediately break out, probably because my face is not used to being cared for and is panicking. Then I have to buy different expensive creams to fix the breakout. I'm told I need something to open up my pores so they can breathe, and the next week I'm assailed by shame-based commercials telling me that my pores are so big gophers have fallen into them, so I buy something for that too and suddenly I look like I have very fancy leprosy. Then my dermatologist says, "*What have you done to your skin?* Stop everything you're doing. Just use this cream to clear this all up." But when I put it in my medicine cabinet I realize it's the *exact same cream* that started this mess, but ten times as expensive because it came from my doctor. Then I'm like, "FUCK YOU, FACE. I'LL BURN YOU OFF WITH FRUIT ACIDS AND DIAMONDS."

In truth though, I was a bit concerned about the whole process. I remembered watching Slim Goodbody on TV, an odd white guy with a small Afro who wore a full-body leotard with the inside of the human body painted on it, which made him look as if he'd been flayed alive. He was like a terrible precursor to those Body Worlds corpses they show at museums-that-have-given-up-on-being-actual-museums, and I worried that I might end up looking like Slim Goodbody's estranged sister, Fatty Noskin.

The next day, Laura and I arrived at the clinic and immediately felt out of our element as we huddled together on the couch and gazed at women who looked as if they'd had fat sucked out of their clavicles and injected directly into their lips.

We signed a pamphlet that explained the risks but that also promised we'd end up with "thicker skin," which I think meant our faces would get huge and our feelings wouldn't get hurt as much. I felt conflicted. "So I'll *gain* inches . . . but on my face. I'm paying to get fat-faced." Laura looked at me uneasily and we considered running, but then a nurse came to bring us back to the exam room. She was sweet and nice and she looked like she was thirty-five but she said she was in her fifties. Laura assumed she was a poster child for the process. I assumed that she was a compulsive liar.

The nurse had each of us put her head into a glowing machine that took a series of pictures of our faces and then she used those pictures to scare the ever-loving shit out of us. She showed us sun damage and scarring, and then she showed us the picture that made me stand up and shout, "WHAT THE FUCK IS THAT?"

It was a colony of bacteria living on my face.

"Holy shit," I said, while peering in at the large green clusters across my nose and forehead. "There's an entire alien race camping out on my face. It's like a fucked-up version of *Horton Hears a Who!* EXCEPT THAT THE WHOS ARE SQUATTERS LIVING ON MY FACE."

"It's pretty normal," the nurse tried to assure me. "It's just bacteria."

I stared at the nurse. "THERE ARE LIVE CREATURES SQUATTING ON MY FACE AND YOU ARE GOING TO KILL THEM."

"*Well.* That's a . . . strange way to look at it," said the nurse uneasily. Apparently she'd had a lot of people grossed out by these pictures, but none had ever had an ethical crisis about them.

"EVACUATE, YOU GUYS!" I tried to yell at my own face. "GO TO THE NECK," I offered.

"Wait," I asked the nurse, "you aren't doing my neck, are you?"

"Oh, stop being such a hoarder," Laura said.

"I'm not a hoarder," I countered. *"I'm trying to stop a mass murder on my face."*

"No," she replied. "You're a face hoarder. You're hoarding bacteria on your face. We're going to have to have a skintervention."

I looked at the nurse, who seemed baffled and slightly unnerved (probably because of Laura's terrible pun). "Does PETA ever have a problem with this since you're killing all these tiny life forms?"

She shook her head. "I can honestly say I've never had *anyone* have a problem with this until now. They're *really* not good to have on your face. Your porphyrins are unhealthy and can—"

"What the shit?" I interrupted. "THEY'RE CALLED '*POOR FRIENDS*'? *You want me to murder my 'poor friends'?*"

"No. You're pronouncing it wrong. Honestly, it's just a routine cleaning."

"IT'S A *GENOCIDE*."

The nurse took a deep breath and tried to change the subject. "So, what would you *expect* to have happen as a result of this treatment?"

I paused and thought about it for a second. "I sort of expect to have my face ripped off and find John Travolta's underneath it. But just for the day. After that it wouldn't be funny anymore."

Laura had a much more normal reason why she wanted the treatment. "I want to get rid of some of these wrinkles, but I don't ever want to get Botox."

"Well, Botox *can* be very helpful," explained the nurse.

"I don't need Botox," Laura countered. "I got *Bangtox*. It's when you decide to get bangs to cover your forehead wrinkles. It totally works and no one injects poison in your face."

I nodded in agreement. "Yes. I would also like to avoid getting poison shot near my brain."

Laura concurred: "I need my brain. It's where I keep all my best stuff."

The nurse looked a little lost and did our treatments quickly. It was much like getting your teeth cleaned, but for your whole face.

The nurse reluctantly gave me the filter after she was done but there was hardly any face in it and pretty much no diamond dust. It wasn't even enough to pan for. So in the end I was left with a small vial of face dust filled with now-homeless Whos, an expensive face toothbrush, and hundreds of dollars' worth of what I assume is Vaseline.

I also ended up with a newfound appreciation of what my dermatillomania was doing to my face and I went an entire month without scratching it open. Mostly because I didn't want to disturb the "poor friends" who were probably valiantly trying to rebuild after the tragic act of God they'd just encountered.

Still, my face does feel very clean.

Clean and *terribly, terribly* lonely.

It's Like Your Pants Are
Bragging at Me

There are few things in the world that make me angrier than poverty, the lack of basic human civil rights, and the fact that most women's clothes don't have pockets. Obviously the first two are more pressing, but the pockets thing is pretty irritating too.

Victor claims girls don't need pockets because they have purses, so I had to explain, "No. We are forced into purses *because* we don't have pockets. Imagine if I ripped all of your pockets off of your sweet pocket-pants right now and you had to carry them around with you everywhere. You have like . . . *seven* pockets in those pants. Imagine carrying seven pockets with you at the carnival. You can't. You'd need a purse. Then you'd get on the Zipper and it'd be fine for a minute until your purse popped open and all of your stuff was being poltergeisted around the cage at you like you were a kitten in a dryer full of batteries, and then your phone gave you a black eye. This is all based on real life, by the way."

Victor seemed a bit taken aback but argued that "pocket-pants" don't exist and that *"they're called cargo pants."* But that's just semantics.

"You have pants with *multiple*, masculine purses all over them," I may have screamed. "Frankly, it's like your pants are bragging at me." Then Victor gave up, probably because he didn't want to look like he was taking his pants' side.

The closest equivalent women have to pocket-pants are pocketbooks and honestly that's just insulting. Pocketbooks aren't pockets *or* books. They're liars. Basically they're pockets you have to carry around with your hands until you get tired of it and give up and buy a purse to put it in. It's as if the clothing industry just came out of a bad breakup and was brainstorming during a bitter drunken rage and was all, "Hey, you know how girls hate carrying purses and they just use you to carry their lipstick and shit in your pocket and then they leave you for Brad? Let's make a purse in the shape of a pocket. But we'll make it too big to fit in a pocket so you have to buy *another* purse. AND WE'LL CALL IT A *POCKETBOOK*. THOSE BITCHES WILL NEVER SEE IT COMING *AND* THEY'LL PAY FOR IT." I might be overreacting but it feels like they did it on purpose. I don't even know Brad.

And yes, you might be thinking that girls can totally wear cargo pants if they want to, but I disagree. Skinny girls might be able to wear those things, but girls like me look like they're wearing pants with a bunch of purses stapled to them, and that's really the last thing you need when you're looking for something slimming in the plus-size section. In fact, most of the pockets you see on women's pants are just illusions made to taunt you. Or sometimes they really are pockets but they are intentionally sewn closed, as if to say, "I'm letting you have these pockets but I'm sewing them shut for your own good." And most of us leave them sewn shut because we'd rather look thin than have pockets.

Really the only way it would work is if the pockets in the pocket-pants made me look thinner *and* still held tons of stuff. I guess basically I want magic. In a size sixteen. I want my pockets to be like a TARDIS, or Mary Poppins's carpetbag. Also, why did Mary Poppins even need such a huge bag if it's magically designed to fit everything? Seriously. I'm guessing that Mary asked for a magic pocket and the wizards were like, "What, *like a dude?* Nah. *I don't think so, lady.* You'll get a purse." Those guys were motherfuckers. They were probably the same guys who were like, "So, let's get this straight . . . you need to magically travel long distances to find young children, and society says you're not allowed to wear anything other than dresses? *Got it.* FUCKING FLYING UMBRELLA." Thanks, wizards. I didn't think you could come up with a worse design than Wonder Woman's invisible jet, *but you did it.* Thank God cell phones didn't exist then because there would be a shit-ton of Mary Poppins up-skirt pics all over the Internet now. This is exactly why I don't trust wizards.

On the upside, yesterday I taped a Ziploc bag to the inside of my skirt so I'd have someplace to store my *everything-that-didn't-fit-in-my-bra* and it worked really well, so now I'm working on a cape made solely from stapled-together Ziploc bags. It'll be awesome because I'll be able to see all the stuff in my Ziploc pockets (unlike my purse, which just eats everything, like a tiny black hole). And it'll also double as a rain poncho. *And* I can put a stiletto knife and a "How to Stab People" pamphlet in it so assholes know not to fuck with me and I don't even have to pull it out and threaten them. *There is no downside to this.*

Long story short? I'm going to get super rich selling pocket-ponchos. (Which will be all-pockets-all-the-time, and also compact enough to be stuffed into a pocket so if you rip one pocket-poncho you can just pull a spare one out of the first.) And I will use that money to invest in magic, and overthrow those goddamn misogynistic wizards. Also, I just realized that men get stiletto knives and women get stiletto shoes. This whole thing is fucked.

Thanks for nothing, feminism.

Nice Bass

Sometimes people just need to get away from their ordinary life to escape and recuperate. Personally, I prefer to do that by locking myself in my bedroom with a bottle of rum, several books, and lots of questionable British TV, but most people prefer to leave home and go to a beach or something. Probably because *most* people don't end up on vacations where small gangs attempt to break into their hotel rooms at two o'clock in the morning.

Hang on. I'm getting ahead of myself.

Victor goes to Japan every year because he studies Japanese stuff. I'd be more descriptive but I tend to just blank out even more than usual when he starts talking in other languages. Regardless, he eventually decided that I needed to go with him at least once, even though I really hate traveling. I finally said okay, but only if my mom could watch our daughter because I didn't trust anyone else to stay with her. Hailey was seven at the time and was that strange combination of confidently independent and dangerously stupid that really only comes with young children and drunks, so I was hesitant to leave her. But I knew my mom was very responsible and would counter any instability caused by my entertainingly insane father, who gave me a giant hug when I came in to drop off Hailey. He sat down at the kitchen table and went back to casually inspecting the new order of glass eyeballs that had just arrived. He assured me that my worry about leaving Hailey was normal but unfounded and that vacations are what keep people healthy and sane. "Like, remember when I brought those ring-tails in a coffee can on vacation with us?" he asked.

Strangely, I did not.

"Why would you bring a bunch of ringtails on vacation?" I asked. My father seemed slightly offended and assured me that he'd never bring "a bunch" of ringtails on vacation and that it was just two, be-cause *"who brings a bunch of ringtails on vacation?"* A better ques-tion might be *"Who brings **any** ringtails on vacation?"* but I realized I already knew the answer.

"Well, they couldn't be trusted at home alone," my father continued. "The last time I did that they broke into the filing cabinets and made nests out of our taxes."

"Why don't I remember any of this?" I asked, and my mom casu-ally explained that I wasn't with them on that trip.

"So you took a bunch of lemurs on vacation *instead* of me?"

My mother looked at me like I was overreacting again. "Well, it wasn't an *either/or* situation."

"And ringtails aren't lemurs," my dad said, seeming vaguely dis-appointed that he was even having to explain this. "They're more like small raccoons. Like if a raccoon and a squirrel had a baby."

It was informative but it wasn't making it any easier to understand why anyone would choose to take a vacation with wild animals and not me.

"It certainly wasn't *my* idea to take them on a trip," my mom ex-plained, with a mild glare at my dad. "They were orphaned and your father was nursing them back to health until they were old enough to be let go. I didn't even know they were in the car with us until I saw the giant coffee can in the backseat."

"They lived in a coffee can," said my father. "They **needed** a vacation."

That was hard to argue with. Mostly because it was insane.

It did, however, make me hesitate a moment before leaving Hailey. But I figured that my sister and I (and the ringtails) had survived, so the odds were in her favor. Plus, Hailey loved the strange and unexpected madness of my parents' home. The year before she'd spent a week with her cousins learning noodling at my parents' house. For those of you who don't know what noodling is, you've probably lived a very sheltered life and you probably also don't keep baby ringtails in a coffee can. Noodling (aka hillbilly handfishing) is when you catch a catfish, but instead of using a fishing pole you just shove your hands into underwater holes that you're hoping might have fish in them rather than crocodiles, snakes, or bitey turtles. It's how people fish when they've run completely out of bait, dynamite, *and any common sense whatsoever.* There are stories of people being dragged to their death by giant catfish, which is a really shitty way to die. It's like being dragged to your death by mermaids, except instead of mermaids it's a fish that tastes like mud. My dad was smart enough to realize that teaching his grandkids to shove their hands in murky lake holes would be something my sister and I would find questionable, so he just brought home a bucket of live catfish, dumped them inside the back-yard canoe, and filled the boat up with water instead. It's sort of the exact opposite of how boats are supposed to work, but it was a safe way for the grandkids to practice catching Winston McFishface over and over. (Technically there were several fish there, but all catfish sort of look the same so they just named them all Winston McFishface.)

It's weird, but that's what my parents have instead of a trampoline—

you work with what you're given. Plus, the kids were happy and my dad assured me that all the Winston McFishfaces were eventually returned to the wild (which I suspect is code for "we ate them") and I suppose that's all that matters.

And that's what I tried to remind myself of when we were in Japan, but I still spent most of my time worrying about Hailey. The only time I finally stopped worrying was on day three when we took the bullet train to Kyoto. After severe jet lag, plus a lack of sleep, we finally fell into our hotel bed. I was so exhausted I didn't even get undressed but Victor managed to at least take off his shirt and jeans before falling fast asleep. A few hours later Victor heard a noise and shook me, whispering: "I think someone's breaking into our room."

I muttered, "Fine. Just tell them to keep the lights off," and turned over to go back to sleep as Victor groggily dragged himself out of bed to see that our door was slightly open and a pair of bolt cutters were being slid in to cut the top of the metal latch, which was the only thing keeping the intruders out. Victor is not someone to mess with even when he's in a cheerful mood, but waking grumpy, middle-of-the-night Victor up with a noisy robbery is like disturbing a bunch of hibernating bears so you can shoot Roman candles at their cubs while wearing Lady Gaga's meat dress.

Victor watched as the bolt cutters slid back through the door and he said, "Oh, hell no," and grabbed the bolt cutters and pulled hard. The person holding the bolt cutters was caught off guard and slammed into the other side of the door with a dull thud. Then Victor threw open the door and yelled, "WHAT IN THE SHIT IS GOING ON OUT HERE?" while angrily waving the bolt cutters at four skittish Asian people who gasped in horror and ran away down the hall as if they were being chased by Godzilla. It was possible they were just really bad burglars, or maybe they were just surprised to see a large, disheveled American man wearing only socks and a pair of novelty boxer shorts with a big fish across the rear that read "NICE BASS!" who was waving bolt cutters at them semi-menacingly. (I would pay *real* money for that surveillance tape as it's probably very popular on whatever the Japanese version of *America's Funniest Home Videos* is.) The possible-burglars disappeared down the stairwell so Victor walked back inside, shoved a chair under the doorknob, and fell right back asleep. He claims he told me a small gang was breaking in and apparently I said he was hallucinating ninjas. And I guess that doesn't make a lot of sense because ninjas probably would have been much more subtle, but it's not like *all* ninjas are automatically great at their job. *Someone* has to be the worst ninja in the class. That's just basic math.

The next morning I rolled over and said, "God, you were so out of it last night you thought people were breaking into our room," and then I laughed until Victor pointed to the bolt cutters on the floor, the half-cut lock, and a letter that had been slid under our door. The letter explained that the hotel manager wanted to talk to us as soon as possible about "the incident that occurred last night." We assumed that we were going to be arrested, but apparently the terrible ninjas who'd broken into our room were hotel staff who'd been convinced to pull out the bolt cutters after an angry guest insisted that he'd been locked out of his room. Turns out he had the wrong floor and he and his wife were two of the frightened people that Victor chased down the hall in his underwear while swinging bolt cutters at them. The manager was very apologetic about the whole misunderstanding and moved us to a larger room without a cut lock and with a toilet that was so complicated I couldn't even use it and I considered asking room service to just bring up a bucket.

Honestly, the toilets in Japan are intimidating as hell and I suspect we'll all be replaced by Japanese toilets in the future, because they can do pretty much anything you can do, but better. Like, one of the features of a fancy Japanese toilet is that the seat is warmed for you, which seems like it would be nice but it's just unsettling. It's as if someone else has just come off the toilet, but no one is there but you. It's like a ghost is haunting your toilet. No one wants that. It's like the opposite of those little strips that say, "Sanitized for your protection," that you have to break before you can use the motel toilet. Plus there are all sorts of other buttons and levers and pulleys and I'm pretty sure one of them launches nuclear bombs or calls the Pentagon. Here's a picture of just a few of the buttons on a Japanese toilet:

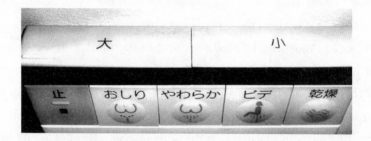

I'm not entirely sure what these are all for but I think the top one that looks like a stick figure is to notify people that you've found the Blair Witch, and I think the next one means "Poop won't go down.

Use your foot." I assume the orange button on the far left is for start-ing a war, and then there are two for washing your boobs for some rea-son, and then one about levitating on a fountain, and I think the last one is for ordering bacon? Frankly, I was too afraid to try out all of the but-tons because just sitting on it triggered something that made it break out into song. It was unsettling. Like, a pooping lullaby. Frankly, I think we've gone too far if you need someone to sing you to the toilet. In fact, I think the toilets were scarier than the whole rest of the trip, including our room being broken into by non-ninjas.

I was feeling bewildered about the whole thing so I called my mom to let her listen to the toilet sing and also to find out how Hailey was doing. When I talked to Hailey on the phone she assured me she was having an absolutely *brilliant* time and had spent the afternoon "wrap-ping rubber bands around Papaw's birds and then *throwing them into the air.*" Then she hung up because she has a short attention span and thought she saw a cloud that looked like someone she knew.

I called back later to ask my mom if Hailey was strapping poultry together in bird clumps and just chucking them in the air like ineffi-cient boomerangs, but Mom dismissed the idea and thought it was more likely that Hailey and my dad were clipping messages to the car-rier pigeons my dad was training* and then letting them go. Or possi-bly she was *really* fucking up the family chickens. Hard to tell with seven-year-olds. Also, hard to tell with my family. Regardless, I sus-pected that Hailey was having a better time than I was.

That's when I decided that from now on I'd stick to vacations that didn't have intimidating toilets and bad ninjas in them. Staycations, where I can actually relax and recuperate in my warm bed full of books and cats, and which don't require me to take vacation time to recover from my vacation time. My mom said I should probably also include "and no ringtails in coffee cans" in my new standards. She had a point. A weird one, but one that obviously needed to be made.

⊢—≺

*Interesting side note: My father is constantly trading, nursing, and releasing animals into the wild, so the limpy bobcat he had last week is usually a rescued peacock the next week and will be replaced with a three-legged iguana the next time you visit. However, it's been years and he still has dozens of carrier pigeons, who wiggle out of their enclosure and sit on their roof, staring pointedly at you and waiting to be fed. I was a little impressed with my dad's dedication but then I realized that you probably *can't* get rid of homing pigeons. They just keep coming back. It's like a horror movie with birds, which actually exists now that I think about it. It was probably written by someone who got tired of having homing pigeons. If you could sell them it'd actually be a pretty great pyramid scheme, but with pigeons instead of money. Except no one wants pigeons. Basically it's like having a child who never leaves home and shits everywhere, and then you're all, "Go. Be free!" And they're like, "Nah. We're fine here, thanks. Where's the food? Need me to pass a note?" My dad loves them though and keeps tying notes to their legs.

"Have you never heard of e-mail?" I asked him. "It's very fast and there's so much less bird flu and feces involved. Usually." But he just smiled and went back to mending the doggy door he'd made for the birds.

God knows who he's sending bird-delivered letters to. Who uses birds to pass notes? Is it Harry Potter? Because that's all I can think of. I hardly even respond to my e-mails and I don't have to wrestle a bird and tie a note around his foot in order to do it.

Victor pointed out that Daddy might be sending bird notes to me and that's just great because now I'm going to be staring down every bird to see if they have a letter for me, and that makes me look even crazier than normal. Plus, the letters will likely be chain letters telling me I have to send off six of my own pigeons with a message about Jesus or else I'll be cursed with . . . I don't know . . . something worse than having to strap letters to six birds, probably. *Thanks a lot, Daddy.* Expect to get a lot of homing pigeons back that just have "UNSUB-SCRIBE" written on them with a Sharpie.

It's Hard to Tell Which of Us
Is Mentally Ill

I've always been a fan of therapy. You spend an entire hour talking about yourself and someone has to fake being fascinated by the strange assemblage of minutiae that is you. I shop around for great therapists the way drug addicts shop around for doctors with loose prescription pads. I'm not looking for drugs. I'm looking for good actors. Or people so boring that my life actually seems interesting to them. Either way. I'm not picky.

I enjoy therapy so much that I am constantly trying to get Victor to go, but he won't. Finally I said that we were going to a marriage counselor so that way he'd *have* to go and I could watch. I was like a shrink voyeur. Victor was against it until I explained that a therapist is like a referee who could decide which of us was the most wrong in the recurring arguments we'd been having over and over for the last twenty years. Usually when we were in a fight I'd end up saying something like "If we were on *Jerry Springer* everyone would be booing you right now," but Victor doesn't watch *Jerry Springer* so instead I moved to, "If we were at a therapist's she'd be shaking her head at you in disappointment and throwing dollar bills at me in appreciation for my seemingly inhuman patience." She was like an imaginary friend who was always on my side and who also had more education than either of us. Eventually Victor called my bluff and set us up with a therapist himself, which was what I'd wanted until it actually became reality.

The shrink set it up so that Victor would go first and then I would come alone to talk the next week. This sounded perfectly reasonable until the moment Victor left for his appointment and then I immediately imagined every terrible secret he was telling her. I'd never even had a chance to charm this doctor with my (according to my last shrink's level of attention) fascinating tales of being me. And Victor was going to ruin my chances of her ever liking me by telling her about the surprise funeral I'd accidentally crashed last week.

It wasn't like a "surprise party" funeral. The funeral had been planned. The surprise really was on me. *Surprise! You're at a funeral!* It was the closest I'd ever been to a surprise party, but with more corpses than I would have expected.

In a nutshell, I stopped at a nearby cemetery because I love the quiet, but unfortunately I unwittingly pulled into the cemetery minutes after a funeral procession had pulled in. I would have driven off but the small cemetery road was full of mourners and parked cars, and a cemetery worker directing traffic motioned for me to park there and join them. Then I panicked and waved him off like, "Oh, no. I couldn't," but when I turned to reverse I saw a line of cars right behind me and that's when I realized I was fucked. Apparently the funeral procession had been separated by a red light and I'd managed to wedge myself right in the middle of it and that's how I found myself stuck in my car, accidentally held hostage by mourners.

I wanted to explain that I was just browsing but thought it would sound weird, so I just got out and went to the funeral, which was odd because I avoid most social occasions of people I know and love and here I was, willingly participating in the burial of a dead stranger. I was like the Patty Hearst of funerals. Plus, Victor kept calling me to see where I was but I couldn't answer my phone because I'm pretty sure it's poor etiquette to take a call in the middle of a funeral you weren't even invited to.

When I got back home Victor was all, "I'VE BEEN WORRIED SICK. WHERE HAVE YOU BEEN?" and I was like, "DON'T YELL AT ME. I WAS AT A SURPRISE FUNERAL AND I'M FEELING VERY VULNERABLE," and then he said I wasn't allowed to drive unsupervised anymore because apparently "normal people don't allow themselves to get abducted by funerals." It was exactly the sort of thing Victor would bring up in therapy without the proper context.

The entire next week I was a wreck. Victor refused to tell me what he'd talked about with the therapist and thought I was insane for even asking. He looked unconvinced when I told him that I'd stab him in the knee if he didn't tell me what he'd told her but I suspected he'd write this all down for his next session.

Finally it was time for me to go visit the therapist myself. She looked like the kind of shrink who would make you hold a speaking stick and play the "emotion bongos" but I didn't care because I immediately launched into a very long and random speech about how Victor was not to be trusted because *who gets mad at someone for attending a funeral?* Crazy people who want you to question your own sanity, *that's who.*

Then the therapist interrupted me to tell me that Victor had only said nice things about me and that it was obvious that he adored me. Then I accused her of being some sort of plant because a real psychiatrist would have picked up on the fact that Victor had obviously done this entire thing on purpose to make me think that I was *Gaslight* crazy. The bongo lady (I refused to refer to her as a doctor after that) revealed nothing but poised her pen to write in her pad of "shit that's wrong with people" as she asked a benign question. I've been to therapy enough to know the tricks and I was aware that shrinks never write something down when you've said something truly crazy because then you'll know it's crazy. Instead, they wait until they ask the next, easier question and then write down the notes. I assume it's to put you at ease but it's just the opposite for me because I want to call them out on it but then they'll add "paranoid" to my list of problems. So while she settled in to write down her notes I answered her easy blow-off question ("Do you like your job?") by saying:

"If I was a serial killer I'd leave a note on my victims saying, 'I only stab assholes, so just don't be a dick and you'll be fine. Hugs, Tiny Babies.' I think that's the best name for a serial killer because then the news anchor has to say, 'People across the nation are still terrified of Tiny Babies,' and 'Tiny Babies suspected of stabbing assholes. Police encourage you to remain calm and take standard safety precautions against Tiny Babies. Lock your doors and stop being such a jerk.' And the newspaper headlines would be like, 'TINY BABIES STILL AT LARGE. PROTECT YOURSELF FROM TINY BABIES.'"

I paused and looked over to see the therapist just staring at me in confusion and I felt bad because she'd probably already forgotten the last thing she needed to write and now would have to ask an even more benign question in order to capture all of the other stuff I'd just said. Luckily we were at the end of our session.

She didn't have a secretary so I paid her directly, which is always awkward because basically this is the person I'm choosing to divulge my deepest, darkest secrets to and then in the end I have to pay her $200 to make up for her having to listen to me. It's pretty much the most unhealthy relationship ever and one that probably needs therapy. It seems at the very least counterintuitive to see a shrink for low self-esteem and after an hour of their convincing you how worthwhile you are they end the session by telling you that you owe them a lot of money for that. I wonder if shrinks are ever so good that their low-self-esteem patient says, "Nope. Not this time, doc. My problems were so fascinating that this time I'm billing you." I'm not sure if a psychiatrist would consider this a success, but it seems like one to me.

I immediately went home and told Victor I didn't appreciate being punked like that and he seemed innocently baffled and then we got in a fight about how wrong it was for him to pretend that I was a nice person in therapy. That's when Victor said I had a problem and I realized that I was perhaps too crazy for therapy. Or at least, too crazy for couples therapy.

He was right. And that was the last time we ever saw that therapist. Instead, we just came up with some rules to get us through the rest of our marriage. Basically, I promised to stop leaving half-drunk cups of water all over the house and Victor promised to forgive me when I inevitably *still* left half-drunk cups all over the house. It was a weird arrangement, but we were both happy with it and sometimes you have to find what works for you.

Occasionally I'm tempted to stop by that marriage counselor's office and tell her that we're still happily married, but then I think that she probably really enjoys telling people that they have a great marriage compared to that crazy couple with the surprise-funeral story who never even got out of the first month of therapy without imploding. I suspect telling her that we were okay without therapy might fuck up her stories, so I leave it alone. *Because I'm a good person.*

At least, according to my new therapist.

I Left My Heart in San Francisco. (But Replace "San Francisco" with "Near the Lemur House" and Replace "Heart" with a Sad Question Mark.)

You know when you're walking to the trash can at the zoo and you're holding something important in one hand, and you have something you have to throw away in the other hand, and you're sort of distracted because you just realized the universal truth that *everything in the world either is or isn't pandas* and you're trying to decide if that's an important epiphany or not and it's so distracting that it's not until you're halfway back to the lemur house that you realize you're still holding the garbage in your hand and that you seem to have thrown your car keys in the trash?

And then you run back to the trash can to find your keys, but apparently they've sunk to the bottom and so you're bent over, hesitantly sifting through other people's garbage, and people are starting to stare and you want to explain that you're not crazy, except that would be disingenuous because you *are* mentally ill but it certainly wasn't your mental illness that caused you to throw your keys in the trash and you don't appreciate their assumption? And you consider explaining that but then you suspect you might seem even more unbalanced if you start yelling at total strangers about judging your mental illness while you're digging through the garbage can at the zoo?

And then you realize that you're going to have to use two hands to find your keys so you look for a place to set down what's in your other hand and then you realize that you're still holding the trash you went to throw away originally and that it probably looks to others like you were digging through the trash and were particularly happy to retrieve the mostly eaten funnel cake you just wanted to throw away before you got pulled into this mess?

And then you move to throw it in the garbage but you stop yourself because you realize if you put it in the trash you're just creating *more* stuff to sift through to find your keys, and so you stand there with one hand in the garbage while you stare indecisively at the funnel cake, which has stumped you?

And then your husband comes looking for you and is like, *"What in the hell are you doing? Why are you digging in the trash?"* and you say, "I'm looking for my keys," and he's like, *"Most women just store them in their purses,"* and you glare at him but he's still saying, "Seriously, stop that. You look like a lunatic," and you say, "I DROPPED MY KEYS IN HERE BECAUSE I THOUGHT THEY WERE FUNNEL CAKE SO CAN YOU JUST HELP ME?"

And then he stares at you with speechless, baffled concern and shakes his head incredulously as he pulls out the car keys that you'd apparently just left on the table at the lemur house? And you feel relieved for a second but then you look into the garbage and think, *"Then what did I throw in there?"* And you can't decide whether to keep looking because maybe it's important, but now you can't even say, "I'm digging through the trash looking for my keys," and instead you have to say, "I'm digging in the trash for something of mine that I just threw in there that I don't even know what it was"?

And no one can even help because they'd be all, "What does it look like?" and you'd have to say, "I HAVE NO IDEA. IT WILL BE A SURPRISE TO US ALL, I GUESS," but the crowd is getting larger and so instead you let your husband pull you away *and you never find out what it was you left in that trash can*, and it haunts you forever because you let some random strangers shame you into not rolling up your sleeves and dumping the garbage can out on the sidewalk so you could solve the mystery of what-was-I-looking-for?

And then all the way home you root through your purse, desperately looking for something missing, but nothing is and it drives you crazy not knowing what the hell it was you left behind in that trash? And then your husband mumbles that maybe it was your dignity, and he has a point but you explain that you remember it being heavy and substantial so it was obviously *not* your dignity, and you explain that the only reason you were distracted enough to throw away something that wasn't keys was that you'd just discovered a mind-blowing universal truth. But then he looks at you expectantly and your mind goes blank and you can't remember what it was[1] and now you've lost two important things that you don't know what they are?

Yeah.

That is how my whole week has been.

---

1. I did finally remember the universal truth (that everything in the world either *is* or *isn't* pandas) but when I told Victor he was like, "OH MY GOD, IT'S THREE O'CLOCK IN THE MORNING. WHY ARE YOU WAKING ME UP FOR THIS?" and I had to apologize because no one is prepared for that level of brain-melting epiphany when they're still half-asleep. The next morning though he still wasn't impressed and I tried to explain it but he insisted it was rubbish. I think I got the last laugh though because my epiphany was just quoted in a published book and that's pretty damn impressive.

Stock Up on Snow Globes. The Zombie Apocalypse Is Coming.

If you'd like to quickly round up a whole lot of assholes all in one spot I suggest going to the airport. In a normal environment I'd say that about 5 percent of any nearby population are assholes. FYI: another 2 percent are total bastards. Ten percent are fine but think they're better than you. Ten percent are awesome unless you push them too hard and then they get sort of stabby. Probably .0001 percent are serial killers or people who intentionally make pants too small. About 32 percent are awesome but secretly suspect that there's something very wrong with them (which there is, and that's why they're so awesome). Six percent are questioning the validity of this breakdown right now and want to see the raw data. But I'm not going to give it to them because this is not a book about statistics. Besides, 37 percent of all statistics are made up on the spot so I'm not sure what you're expecting from me.

As I was saying (before I was rudely interrupted by math), in a normal environment about 5 percent of the population are assholes. Go to an average airport and suddenly the asshole population leaps exponentially. You might disagree and point out that *you* never see any assholes in *your* airport, but that's usually a pretty good indication that you might be one of them. *Sorry.* I don't really blame you though as it seems to be out of your hands. And, believe me, I can relate. Whenever I have to do story problems I turn into a small, burrowing animal and I often find myself hiding in a cupboard, so I'm not judging you. Except that I sort of am because my hiding from math in cupboards hurts no one (except possibly the cupboards) whereas people being assholes on planes makes me want to poke them with large sticks.

It's such a strange phenomenon. People who (outside of airports) might normally hold open doors or stop cars for crossing ducklings will suddenly be fine with plowing down elderly women and kicking small children out of the way in order to get to their preassigned, horrifically cramped seats. They'll stand in crowds, circling the boarding lane and blocking other passengers who have earlier boarding tickets than them, and will glare at anyone who tries to walk around them. A few hours later you'll see these exact same people breathing heavily and glancing around with trapped-animal eyes, straining against their seat belt the moment the plane begins to descend, and they will immediately leap up as soon as the seat belt sign goes off in order to be first to aggressively stand in a line of people *who are not going anywhere for quite some time*. I always wonder about these people. I can only suspect that they must have some sort of weird standing-in-line fetish.

It's my personal opinion that airlines can do two things to make air travel better for everyone. The first is to have the people taking boarding tickets recognize the person who seems the most unreasonably determined to be sitting on the plane, hold up their arm, and joyfully announce over the loudspeaker: "YOU, SIR! You are our winner for most unaccountably and frantically eager to get on a plane *that will not leave until every single person is seated anyway*. Well done, you! Can you tell us how you feel now that you've won?" At best he'll realize he's being a bit douchey, laugh it off, and might calm the hell down from now on. At worst he'll start yelling and then everyone else gets a good show. Then give him a small medal and a mild tranquilizer. Plus a mild tranquilizer for the person who has to sit next to him. And, if you're handing them out, I'll take one too. In fact, mild tranquilizers for everyone!

(I apologize for the gender stereotyping, but in fairness it usually is a he. And he's usually in a business suit. And he often has triple-diamond status. And he's occasionally my husband.)

Frankly, if we all had tranquilizers, that would reduce the need for the second part of my plan to make air travel less awful. There's always that one person who is making a nuisance of themselves because they're furious their enormous bags don't fit, they're loudly muttering racist bullshit about people who aren't actually terrorists, or they've had too many tranquilizers and now they can't swallow correctly. (I've been there, but in my defense, I'd mixed up my antianxiety sedatives with my heartburn medication and so I'd like to think it was less that I was "drooly" and more that I was just slightly too generous with my saliva.) Regardless, I think it would serve everyone as a community if the flight attendants were able to whack one person (per flight) on the head with a piñata stick for being the stupidest damn person on the plane. It wouldn't hurt them permanently but if it happened to them more than once they'd probably get the picture *because HOW ELSE ARE THEY GOING TO LEARN?*

This would also be helpful because I think we're *all* a bit stressed and judgmental on planes and probably at one time or another each of us would get hit with the piñata stupid-stick, and it would be a good reminder to be more compassionate to others. Personally, I'm most likely to get whacked in the head because my anxiety disorder gets really bad on planes and so I end up panicking a bit. Usually I get on Twitter and tell everyone that I love them because that's about the time that my antianxiety pills kick in and they make me super sentimental and scared that I'm going to die. It's like taking ecstasy, but instead of having sex and going to a rave I just want someone to stroke my hair and sing me old Irish drinking songs. Unfortunately I always end up sitting next to people who don't know any drinking songs at all and spend their time making pie charts, which is pretty much the worst use of pie ever.

During my last book tour I flew constantly and it really fucked with my anxiety disorder, to the point where I eventually had a mild nervous breakdown, which they now refer to as "vital exhaustion" for some reason. My shrink suggested that if I was going to continue traveling so much that I could look into getting a service animal expressly trained to provide emotional support to people with anxiety disorders. I considered getting Hunter S. Thomcat trained, but then I remembered that he gets spontaneous nervous diarrhea every time he's in a moving car, and I'd imagine that holding a cat who seems to have explosive plane dysentery wouldn't necessarily *help* my anxiety so much as it would just give me something new (and horribly unsanitary) to be anxious about.

I called around to different service-animal specialists and spoke to a woman who told me that it's better to get an animal who has already been trained and has the right temperament. She also told me that cats aren't preferred emotional-support animals for anxiety disorder, but my cats hate dogs so I figured I was fucked, but then she told me that the Americans with Disabilities Act was recently interpreted as allowing "people with anxiety disorders to travel with an *emotional-support pony* on airlines." So basically *I could bring a goddamn pony on board with me.* I'm pretty sure a pony wouldn't fit under my seat or in my lap, but I rather liked the idea of a small medicinal horse standing in the aisle beside me while I braided his mane. Plus, Pony Danza would make a great pack animal and instead of bringing suitcases I could just put my extra clothes on him and that way I wouldn't have to pay to check a bag. Plus, the pony wouldn't get cold because it would be wearing my pajamas.

I tried to convince Victor that this was a win-win situation but he got all shitty about our having an indoor pony pet, even though I pointed out that it was for my mental illness. He responded that he had no doubt my mental illness was involved in a decision that would eventually conclude with a bunch of horses in bed with us. I reiterated that I only needed *one* medicinal pony but he argued that I'd eventually claim that the pony was lonely and then one day he'd come home to a houseful of ponies. I didn't respond because we both knew he was right. Besides, I'm pretty sure the girl who brings her horse on the plane is going to get hit with the piñata stupid-stick every flight and Victor's probably just saving me from myself. And from a concussion.

Truthfully though, ponies on planes are small change compared to some of the things I've seen. Like the time the lady sitting next to me listened to every single ringtone available on the highest volume possible in the thirty minutes we waited for everyone else to board. Or one time Victor was sitting in the quiet wooden-cubicle section of the President's Club, where professional people go to work on their laptops during layovers. There was an older man in Victor's row who had his headphones plugged into his laptop so he could watch *True Blood*, and out of nowhere he lunged toward the screen and screamed, "*LOOK OUT, SOOKIE!*" so loudly that Victor accidentally screamed a little too. Or the guy who was sitting two rows ahead of me one time who was *super* careful to hold his phone in such a way that no one around him would notice that he was watching hard-core porn on the plane. And probably no one *would* have noticed if he'd remembered to plug the earphones he was wearing into the phone jack but he didn't and so he groaned in frustration (I hope) and kept turning the volume up louder and louder until he realized the problem. Or the woman in front of me in the security line who asked if they would put her cat,

Dave, through the luggage X-ray machine because she wanted to see if he'd eaten a necklace. (What the fuck, Dave? Get it together.)

I have to admit that occasionally I'm the one causing the scene. Like the time I bought an antique basket in California but it wouldn't fit in my suitcase so I decided to carry it on like a purse, except that it was a basket made out of a dead armadillo and the handle was its tail and it didn't fit under the seat so I tried to hide him in my lap but the flight attendant was like, "Ma'am, you need to place your . . . uh . . . armadillo in the overhead compartment?" and I said, "I can just hold him. He's carry-on. And carrion." She made me stuff him under the seat but he wouldn't fit and I ended up sighing to my seatmate that I'd just chipped two nails on my armadillo and this is *exactly* why people hate to fly. I considered keeping a nail file in my armadillo for the future (tucking the file under one of his armored plates so it would fold down when you didn't need it) and it sounded like such a good idea that I thought you could probably add a cheese knife and a corkscrew and make a Swiss Army Armadillo. *A Swiss Army Dillo.* I made a note on my phone to create a Swiss Army Dillo but spell-check changed it to "Create a Swiss Army Dildo," which frankly just seems painful and excessive.

Victor believes that people turning into assholes is a new phenomenon, because flying twenty years ago was much easier and less stressful. I have to take his word on that one because my family always drove or camped on our vacations. This included a summer trip to Lost Maples (age nine), when we returned to my grandparents' camper after a morning of fishing to discover that a band of squirrels had chewed a hole through the cloth of the pop-up camper and shit *everywhere*. It was like a shit sprinkler had gone off in there and we were horrified but also grudgingly impressed. Perhaps the neighborhood squirrels were mad because they could see campers relieving themselves in the woods and were like, *"Really, asshole?* You just shit in my living room. Now *this* is happening in your living room. *I can do this all day, mother-fucker.*" Hard to say. Squirrels can be real conundrums.

Still, angry, shitty squirrels can't hold a candle to angry, shitty people in airports and if you've ever doubted this you've probably never seen a person refuse to switch seats so that a parent can sit with their very small child who was inexplicably assigned a seat on the opposite side of the plane. Once, in Chicago, I saw a man refuse to switch seats with a mother who'd bought a seat for her ten-month-old but hadn't been given a seat next to the baby. She asked the man who was assigned the seat beside her if he could sit in the same window seat a few rows away and he refused. "I'm sitting in the seat assigned to me *because those are the rules.* THIS IS MY SEAT," he grumped as he sat down huffily. What I really wanted was for that mother to stand up and say, "You know what? *Fine.* This is the baby's seat anyway. I'm two rows behind you guys. Have a good flight, baby. Hope you like screaming and urine, sir." Of course the surrounding passengers quickly gave up their seats to switch around before it ever came to that, which is sort of a shame because it would have been a just punishment. Sitting next to a crying, kicking baby on an airplane is not fun, and is *almost* as hellish as being the parent of a crying, kicking baby on an airplane, which is practically as terrible as *being* the crying, kicking baby on an airplane.

Last year CNN brought me on live TV to discuss a proposal to create "kid-free planes," and I explained if we were really going to start segregating passengers I'd prefer to ride in an "a-hole-free plane" because babies almost never ask you to join the Mile-High Club, or clip their toenails while in flight, or do any of a plethora of horrible things I've witnessed from others. The CNN anchor seemed slightly aghast that I'd said "a-hole" and "Mile-High Club" live on air, but they really should have expected it because several months earlier they asked me about "mommies and politics" and I explained (on air) that I don't usually write about either subject but that I thought it was a little condescending for anyone to call me "Mommy" unless they'd personally come out of my "lady garden." I also explained that I'd like political candidates to present their prep plans for the zombie apocalypse, or for the robot revolution, or for when the Internet becomes self-aware, because at least then the debates would be more interesting.

Surprisingly, CNN has not asked me on again. (Although I would like to note that I asked the woman on the pre-call if I could say "vagina" on TV and she said she thought I'd better not, so I said, "Well . . . can I say 'my lady garden'?" English was not her first language so she needed help on that one, yelling, "Is 'my lady garden' okay?" to the people near her, and she said that no one seemed to have a problem with it. Of course, it's possible that no one had a problem with it because there wasn't any context so no one knew that it was a euphemism, or maybe everyone in the office assumed that the woman was fishing for compliments about her lady garden. Regardless I think it all worked out for CNN because that clip ended up being the most popular video of the day and it was nice to be able to call my parents and proudly tell them, "My lady garden is going viral." In hindsight, that may have been a poor choice of phrasing.)

Victor travels at least weekly for business and thinks that increased security at airports is what's making people insane, because they seem to lose all sense of logic in the security line. One time Victor witnessed a guy carrying a *gallon* of homemade iced tea in his carry-on. The TSA agent pulled out the leaking jug and looked at it like it was a severed arm, and then said, "Sir, I *just* asked you if you had any liquids." Then the man testily replied, "*I don't. That's iced tea.*" The agent paused for a second, sighed, and explained that "iced tea is a liquid," to which the passenger condescendingly replied, "*No, dumb-ass. IT'S A BEVERAGE.*"

Then the TSA agent hit him with a piñata stick.

Or that's how it would have worked out in my world.

Everyone gets caught accidentally sneaking weird stuff through security sometimes though. Our friend Jason travels with us a lot and is forever bringing inappropriate things through airports. Last month Victor and Jason went to a conference in Vegas and Jason tried to bring through an industrial-sized jar of hair gel from Costco.

"*It was like something from a barber college,*" Victor told me later. "And security was like, '*Sir, you're like* **seventy-two ounces** *over the limit.*' Jason just shrugged, scooped out a big handful, and put it on his hair for later. It was like the size of a Crisco can. *You could have put both hands in there.*" I tried to convince Victor that Jason was probably doing this on purpose to fuck with him.

"Nope. He did the same thing in China last year. He told me he bought a bottle of wine and they wouldn't let him bring it on and so he angrily drank it in security so it wouldn't be wasted."

"Well," I said. "*That showed them.*"

"Yeah. It showed them what a drunk American looks like trying to put his shoes back on. And he did the same thing when we were in Mexico last year. *Remember when he bought two liters of hot sauce at the airport?*"

"Yeah, that was awesome," I said, nodding. "But I'm pretty sure we were all too drunk to remember we hadn't gone through security yet. Besides, isn't hot sauce a beverage?" Victor glared at me but I bet he was laughing on the inside.

But in a bring-this-whole-thing-full-circle sort of way, I'm starting to suspect that maybe the reason why people are jerks at airports is *because* of the zombie apocalypse.

I'll explain:

Have you ever noticed that all of the stuff on the posters of what you can't bring into the airport terminal is pretty much *exactly* the same stuff that would come in really handy if a zombie apocalypse broke out? Swords, guns, grenades, meat cleavers, fire, disinfectant, booze, chain saws: these are all things I'd want on me if there were a zombie epidemic in Terminal B. Basically, if we get attacked inside the airport we're all fucked, so maybe people are just scared because they've been disarmed. Even the phrasing of where you're headed (the "terminal") is another word for "approaching immediate death."

But on the plus side, airport security probably has a giant stash of brass knuckles and grenades and chain saws that they've confiscated from people, so we could probably still arm ourselves if necessary. (Side note: Can you even *buy* brass knuckles anymore? I'd be pissed if I had to give up my brass knuckles at the airport. Those things are pricey.)

I often take photos of the posters showing the prohibited items you can't take through security to use as an outline for preparing my own zombie prep kit and it's interesting how they subtly change from airport to airport. Some of them can be quite intimidating and are filled with items you wouldn't think you'd have to put on a sign, like machine guns and dynamite. Others focus more on having too much lotion. At our airport it says you can't bring in snow globes. Swear to God. *Snow globes.* Which seems weird. It's not like you're going to be attacked by a zombie and think, "JESUS. *If only I'd had my snow globe.*"

Victor recently looked over my ever-growing list entitled "Things-Not-Allowed-Through-Security-That-Would-Be-Good-to-Have-During-the-Zombie-Apocalypse" and thought it was questionable. "Why do you have booze on your list?" he asked.

"You think I'm going into the zombie apocalypse sober?" I shook my head. "*I don't think so.* Plus, alcohol is a good disinfectant."

"I'm pretty sure butterscotch schnapps isn't ideal for wounds." He knew me too well. "And what's this other stuff? *Water guns? Lacrosse sticks?* This is just a list of things you want to play with."

"*No,*" I explained, glaring in a way that said Victor was stupid. "They're weapons that don't need ammunition. You can use the lacrosse stick to keep the zombies at a distance and then you squirt them with acid."

"Acid . . . *which would melt the water gun,*" Victor replied.

"Ah," I said. "*Right.* Fine. Then we fill it with holy water in case of vampires."

"Vampires?"

I sighed at his ignorance. "Well, I think if zombies turn out to be real then all bets are off, Victor. In fact, I think I might need to start a whole new list labeled 'In-Case-of-Vampires.' *BECAUSE I'M A PLANNER.*"

Victor laughed and said I was getting a little defensive, but I'm pretty sure "defensive" is probably a good state of mind to be in when focused on prepping for monster attacks. Assholish and defensive. And unconcerned about babies, who will probably slow you down. And with piñata sticks you've sharpened into stakes in case of vampires. That's how you survive.

So I guess maybe the airport isn't always the worst place to be after all.

What I want you to know:
Dying is easy.
Comedy is hard.
Clinical depression is no fucking picnic.

When my last book came out I spent a lot of time avoiding people who wanted to interview me because I was afraid I'd say something wrong, or because I couldn't find pants. I decided that this time around I'd just include an entire section with questions and answers, which you can use if you have a story due or need a quote. This seems like an odd use of a chapter but it's nice because there are always things that you don't get around to writing about, and apologies that need to be made, and all of that fits in here.

I realize that it's weird that this appendix is in the middle of the book instead of at the end where appendixes are supposed to be, but it works better here, and *technically* your appendix is in the middle of your body so it sort of makes sense. Probably God had the same issue when Adam was like, "I don't want to sound ungrateful, but it sort of hurts when I walk. Is that *normal*? Is this thing on my foot a tumor?" And God was like, "It's not a tumor. That's your appendix. Appendixes go at the end. Read a book, dude." Then Adam was all, "*Really?* Because I don't want to second-guess you but it seems like a design flaw. Also that snake in the garden told me it doesn't even do anything." And God shook his head and muttered, "Jesus, that fucking snake is like TMZ." And then Adam was like, "Who's Jesus?" and God said, "No one yet. It's just an idea I'm throwing around." And then God zapped Adam's appendix off his foot and stuck it in Adam's midsection instead in case he decided to use it later. But the next day Adam probably asked for a girlfriend and God was like, "It's gonna cost you a rib," and Adam was all, "Don't I need those? Can't you just make her out of my appendix?" And the snake popped out and hissed, "Seriously, why are you so attached to this appendix idea? Don't those things occasionally explode for no reason whatsoever?" and God was like, "THIS IS NONE OF YOUR BUSINESS, JEFFERSON. I'M STARTING TO QUESTION WHY I EVEN MADE YOU." And Adam was like, "Wait . . . what? *They explode?*" And God was all, "I'M NOT NEGOTIATING WITH YOU, ADAM." And *that's* why appendixes go in the middle and should probably be removed.

I've asked Victor to play the role of interviewer because no one else is here except the cats, who are crap at sticking to the subject. (Victor is the one in bold who is not entirely happy about being dragged into this. I'm the one not in bold who isn't wearing pants.)

What am I even doing here?

You are pretending to be a reporter for prestigious publications. I need you to ask me interview questions so that other people can steal these quotes when I'm too weird to talk to them.

I have no idea what you want from me.

Luckily, I'm here to help. Start with a compliment. Something about my hair, maybe.

Okay. Is that your real hair?

Some of it. But it's rude to ask that.

Oh. Sorry.

It's fine. I forgive you. Just remember this act of kindness when you review my book. Also remember the word "revolutionary" and the phrase "buy a dozen copies for everyone you know."

Why would I review your book? I'm your husband.

You're supposed to be a reporter. *My God. You are terrible at role-playing.*

Fine. It seems like by this point in a book about depression you would have explained what depression is.

It's hard to define.

Well, this is a book, *so maybe try*.

Fine.

Depression is like . . . it's like when you meticulously scroll up through hundreds of pages in a Word document to find a specific paragraph you need to fix, and then you try to type but it automatically takes you right back down to the bottom because you forgot to place your cursor where you wanted to type. And then you bang your head against the desk because you just totally lost your place and then your boss walks in while you have your head planted on your desk and you see her shoes behind you so you immediately say, "I'm not sleeping. I was just banging my head against the desk because I fucked something up."

Hmm.

Wait. No. That's not it. Depression is like . . . when you don't have any scissors to cut that thick plastic safety tie off the new scissors that you just bought because you couldn't find your scissors. And then you just say, "Fuck it," and try everything else in the world to get the scissors to open, but all you have are plastic butter knives and they aren't doing anything, so you stand in the kitchen holding scissors that you can't use because you can't find scissors and then you get frustrated and throw the scissors in the garbage disposal and sleep on the couch for a week. And that's what depression is like.

So . . . ?

No. Hang on.

Depression is like . . . when you don't want cheese anymore. *Even though it's cheese.*

I want to be helpful but I don't know if that means that I should ask you to elaborate or tell you to stop elaborating.

Okay. Let me rephrase. Sometimes being crazy is a demon. And sometimes the demon is me.

And I visit quiet sidewalks and loud parties and dark movies, and a small demon looks out at the world with me. Sometimes it sleeps. Sometimes it plays. Sometimes it laughs with me. Sometimes it tries to kill me. But it's always with me.

I suppose we're all possessed in some way. Some of us with dependence on pills or wine. Others through sex or gambling. Some of us through self-destruction or anger or fear. And some of us just carry around our tiny demon as he wreaks havoc in our mind, tearing open old dusty trunks of bad memories and leaving the remnants spread everywhere. Wearing the skins of people we've hurt. Wearing the skins of people we've loved. And sometimes, when it's worst, wearing our skins. These times are the hardest. When you can see yourself confined to your bed because you have no strength or will to leave. When you find yourself yelling at someone you love because they want to help but can't. When you wake up in a gutter after trying to drink or smoke or dance away the ache—or the lack thereof. Those times when you are more demon than you are you.

I don't always believe in God. But I believe in demons.

My psychiatrist always says, "But if you believe there are demons, then it follows that there could be a God. It's like . . . believing in dwarves but not in Cyclopses."

I consider pointing out that I've met several dwarves in my life and almost no Cyclopes, but I get what she's saying. There can't be dark without light. There can't be a devil without the God who created him. There can't be good without bad.

And there can't be me without my demon.

I think I'm okay with that.

Or maybe it's my demon that is.

It's hard to tell.

My psychiatrist told me that when things get rough I should consider my battle with mental illness as if I were "exorcising a demon" and I was like, "Well, no wonder I'm failing so miserably. I'm *shit* at exercising."

Then she called me out for deflecting with humor, and explained: "You are exorcising a demon. It's not something you can do alone. Some people do it with a priest and holy water. Some do it with faith. Some do it with chemicals and therapy. No matter what, it's hard."

"And usually people end up with vomit on them," I replied.

I'm seeing more of a connection. I wonder if I'm the priest in this scenario. I hope not because he almost always dies just when he thinks everything is fine. This analogy is starting to creep me out.

Did you just break into an essay in the middle of our interview?

I did. Sorry. But you're the interviewer so technically it's your fault for not reining me in.

Sure. Blame the victim. I don't have depression but I've seen you struggle with it. What advice do you have for people who are currently looking for help?

Every mental illness is different because every person is different. There aren't any easy cures but there are so many tools available now that people are finally starting to talk about it. You have to figure out how to *survive* depression, which is really not easy because when you're depressed you're more exhausted than you've ever been in your life and your brain is lying to you and you feel unworthy of the time and energy (which you often don't even have) needed to get help. That's why you have to rely on friends and family and strangers to help you when you can't help yourself.

Lots of people think that they're a failure if their first or second or eighth cure for depression or anxiety doesn't work the way they wanted. But an illness is an illness. It's not your fault if the medication or therapy you're given to treat your mental illness doesn't work perfectly, or it worked for a while but then stopped working. You aren't a math problem. *You're a person.* What works for you won't always work for me (and vice versa) but I do believe that there's a treatment out there for everyone if you give yourself the time and patience to find it.

Additionally, psychiatrists are always changing shit, so even they don't know exactly what's going on. A mental disorder might be reclassified into a phobia. A phobia might be reclassified as a disorder. In fact, I asked my shrink to read this book and fix everything that's now outdated but it'll just be outdated again next week when *The Big Book of Crazy* is updated again. She agreed that it's hard to keep up with it all but pointed out that it's called *The Diagnostic and Statistical Manual of Mental Disorders.* In my defense, I'm bored with that name and I think they'd sell more copies if they used my title. Or maybe *Game of Thrones, Part 14.*

Here's what I find helpful: Sunlight, antidepressants, and antianxiety drugs, vitamin B shots, walking, letting myself be depressed when I need to be, drinking water, watching *Doctor Who*, reading, telling my husband when I need someone to watch me, making a mix tape of songs that make me feel better and not allowing myself to listen to the stuff I want to listen to but that I know will make me worse. I talk to people on Twitter when I'm afraid to be out in the world. When I can't be an active mom, I snuggle with my daughter and watch TV with her or ask her to read to me. I replace the moments when I feel I should be at a PTA meeting with a memory I hope she'll treasure of us hiding under a blanket fort with the cats. I remind myself that depression lies and that I can't trust my own critical judgment when I'm sick. And if things get really bad I call the suicide hotline. I'm not suicidal, but I've called several times before to be talked down from hurting myself. They help. They listen. They've been there. They give advice. They tell you that you aren't crazy. Or, sometimes, they tell you that you are crazy, but in a good way. A way that makes you special.

Okay. What *doesn't* help when you're depressed?

Everyone is different so the best thing you can do is to ask the person you're dealing with what they need.

Like, some people prescribe God for depression or self-harm, and I think that can be really helpful for people who aren't me. Some claim that depression can be "prayed away" or is caused when you don't have enough God in your life. I tried God once but it didn't work well so I cut the dose by a third and just had "Go." *Go where?* I asked. No one answered. Probably because I didn't have enough God in my life. Someone else told me that capitulating to my depression made me seem ungrateful because Jesus died so that I wouldn't have to suffer, but frankly Jesus seemed to have more than his fair share of bullshit in his life too. That guy got nailed *to death*. I bet people walking past Jesus were like, "Wow. That guy should have had more God in his life." Or maybe they just sent him those e-mails that say, "Let Go and Let God," or "God listens to knee-mail." Probably not though because e-mail wasn't popular yet, but I think that's for the best because there is *nothing* more annoying than having someone tell you that everything would be fine if you were just a better pray-er. Or if you just smiled more, or stopped drinking Diet Coke.

I *can* tell you that "Just cheer up" is almost universally looked at as the most unhelpful depression cure ever. It's pretty much the equivalent of telling someone who just had their legs amputated to "just walk it off." Some people don't understand that for a lot of us, mental illness is a severe chemical imbalance rather just having "a case of the Mondays." Those same well-meaning people will tell me that I'm keeping myself from recovering because I really "just need to cheer up and smile." That's when I consider chopping off their arms and then blaming them for not picking up their severed arms so they can take them to the hospital to get reattached.

"Just pick them up and take them to get fixed. *IT'S NOT THAT HARD, SARAH. I pick up stuff all the time. We all do.* No, I'm not going to help you because you have to learn to do this for yourself. I won't always be around to help you, you know. I'm sure you could do it if you just tried. *Honestly, it's like you don't even **want** to have arms.*"

Granted, it's not a *perfect* analogy because you don't usually lose your arms due to involuntary chemical imbalances. Except that if I cut off your arms because of my mental illness then *technically* a chemical imbalance *did* lead to your arms falling off, so it's dangerous for everyone. I guess my point here is that we *all* suffer when mental illness is not taken seriously.

How do you deal with people who don't understand depression?

Sometimes people say, "How can you feel bad for yourself when people are starving in Greenland?" and I'm like, "I dunno. Talent?"

And you can't win because you're given the same guilt when you feel good. "How can you laugh when people are starving in Greenland?" Again, *I don't know*. I don't ask starving people in Greenland how they can laugh when people in Sweden are cancerous and missing hands. (I don't know if that's right about Sweden or Greenland. I don't keep up with geography.) The point is, sometimes shitty things happen, and sometimes they don't. My rule is "Enjoy the non-shitty things now because shitty things are coming." And vice versa. This is just basic life 101. Your family member is sick. Your dog needs to go out. You find a lump. People tell you to stop eating gluten. That stuff never stops, so go with the flow and don't apologize for starving people. Unless you're the one starving people. Then you should totally apologize.

Right. Apologize if you're starving someone. This is all good stuff.

Right? Oh, I need you to ask me the question on this card because I'm sure it'll be pertinent.

Okay. **This seems fairly unethical, but whatever. "A lot of people have been critical about this book, because of [fill in the blank with whatever people are currently mad at me about]. What's your response?"**

That is an *excellent* question.

Well, you wrote it.

Fair enough. But back to the question . . . First of all, I apologize for that thing I did. It was *incredibly* stupid and I was young and probably drugged. This seems a bit inauthentic since I don't know precisely what you're referring to but I can assure you that there is at least one thing in this book I will think is ridiculously awful within a few years. This is a real issue that I struggle with.

It's tempting to start each sentence with an apology or disclaimer.

To preface everything with "In my life I've found" so that people can't yell at me for being wrong (I often am) or misinformed (sure) or overly emotional (HOW *DARE* YOU). But this is a book about my life so I have to simply hope that unsaid disclaimer is just implied. This is my life, and my observations of it, and they change as I change. That's one of the frightening things about writing a book that no one ever tells you. You have to pin down your thoughts and opinions and then they exist on a page, ungrowing, *forever*. You may convince yourself that *you* were never stupid or coarse or ignorant but one day you reread your seventh-grade diary and rediscover the person who one day becomes you, and you vacillate between wanting to hug this unfinished, confused stranger and wanting to shake some damn sense into her. In fact, if you read this book and hated something I wrote, chances are I probably hate it too. Like my grandmother always said, "Your opinions are valid and important. Unless it's some stupid bullshit you're being shitty about, in which case you can just go fuck yourself."

I'm pretty sure neither of your grandmothers ever said that.

Well, I'm paraphrasing, but still . . .

Someone once said that if you make something no one hates, no one will ever love it either, and that's true. The same goes for art, writing, and people. *Especially people.* In fact, most of my favorite people are dangerously fucked up but you'd never guess it because we've either become adept at hiding it or we've learned to bare it so honestly that it becomes the new normal. There's a quote from *The Breakfast Club* that goes "We're all pretty bizarre. Some of us are just better at hiding it." I have it on a poster but I took a Sharpie to it and scratched out the word "hiding" because it reminds me that there's a certain pride and freedom that comes from wearing your unique bizarreness like a badge of honor.

None of us are immune to feelings of failure. Brené Brown has been my friend for more years than I can count and she's violently successful. She's a Ph.D. who hangs out with Oprah and writes bestselling books about authenticity and vulnerability and being daring. She is the very definition of "having your shit together." But I know that I can call her up at midnight and say, "I'm super scared that I'm fucking everything up." And she'll say, "Same here. There's a lot of that going around. What's wrong with us?" Then we'll talk it out and in the end we'll feel better that we both feel shitty because we each respect the other and if we *both* feel like failures then all bets are off and probably *everyone* feels like this. Then I tell Brené that her fear of failure is a good thing because no one can write helpful books about honest emotions if they're already perfect, so technically feeling fucked up is just the first step to her next bestseller. Then she reminds me that my entire livelihood is based on my mortifying myself so if I suddenly got sane I'd become unemployed. She's right. But I'm still afraid that I've written something awful in this book so I've decided that I will *intentionally* make a mistake in here on purpose; just be prepared. And now I can relax because if I fuck something up I can just explain that *that* was my intentional mistake and ten points to you for finding it. Brené says this is a fine idea so technically I think that means I can intentionally fuck shit up *as prescribed by a doctor.*

That's weird. You sound paranoid.

You only think it's weird because you've never accidentally written something offensive. I write intentionally offensive stuff all the time and I'm prepared to take the heat on that, but I'm always afraid of writing or saying something that I have no clue is awful. (Like, one time I wrote that a friend had welched on a bet and spell-check was like, "That's not a word. Did you mean to say 'Welsh'?" and I was all, "*Jesus, spell-check.* That's a bit racist, isn't it? I write about someone not paying their debt and you're all, '*I bet it was the Welsh.*' Sort your-self out, spell-check." So then I looked it up online and read that the suspected origin of the phrase "welch on a bet" is an offensive dispar-agement "on account of the alleged dishonesty of the Welsh." I didn't even know that was a thing. It's like when little kids would say, "My sister got a bigger piece of pie so now I feel gypped." When I got older I found out "gyp" is a derogatory term for "Gypsy" so I nipped that in the bud. But the best replacement the dictionary offered was "flimflam" and it just sounds ridiculous to say, "Your dessert is bigger. I feel flim-flammed." No one is taking that complaint seriously. Instead I just end up feeling bitter about pie and saying nothing. And also now I'm wor-ried that the word "flimflam" is somehow offensive to the Flemish.

You've overthought this.

Well, I have an anxiety disorder. *This is what it's like in my head all the time.*

I'm also worried that writing about struggling with my weight is going to piss people off because society is *already* overly focused on appearance and I'm not helping by talking about how I feel fat some-times. And I also worry that I might get skinny accidentally and then people who see me on tour will be pissed because they won't realize that my weight fluctuates by sixty pounds depending on how sick, tired, or depressed I am. And I'll have to carry around unflattering pictures of me as evidence and bring affidavits from my doctor who continually tells me I need to lose weight until I get incredibly sick or too depressed to eat for a week and then he's like, "You look great! But why are you in the ER again?"

I'm sensitive about my weight, but overall I love who I am and I pre-fer my curves because when I'm fatter my wrinkles disappear. No one ever tells you that but when you're older and you suddenly get skinny you *also* suddenly age five years because your fat isn't filling out all of your wrinkles anymore. I sometimes get hassled for using the term "fat" but I also use the term "crazy" to describe myself and I'm fine with that because I'm taking those words back. I'm also taking "sexy" back because, frankly, Justin Timberlake has had it too long and he doesn't even need it. And I'm taking "flustrated" because that's not a real word. Stop using it.

Long story short, I am often crazy and sometimes overweight. It's not always ideal but it makes me who I am. *Literally.* Plus, I won't have to feel bad for eating too many egg rolls because if I suddenly get skinny that's going to be hard to explain. That's why I had cheesecake last night. *Because it's part of my craft.*

Is there ever a line you don't cross in your writing?

I'm relatively filterless but I do have boundaries. When my last book came out everyone I wrote about got to read it before it went to press and they were all given full permission to take out anything they wanted. To their great credit they were cool with everything and in fact were the first people to say, "Hey, I have pictures of your dad's Armadillo Racing Championship ring, and of the pet raccoons wearing shorts that lived in our house. Do you want those?"

I do have boundaries. I don't tell stories that I think a mean fourteen-year-old girl could use against Hailey one day. I don't write about anything I'm currently fighting with someone about or anything where I'm not the biggest butt of the joke. There are a lot of stories that I don't write because they aren't mine to tell, but I think telling my stories helps to encourage putting other stories out there. When I first started writing, my father was very quiet about his own struggles, but after seeing the response of people who've read my stories, he's much more open. And that's a wonderful thing. When we share our struggles we let others know it's okay to share theirs. And suddenly we realize that the things we were ashamed of are the same things everyone deals with at one time or another. We are so much less alone than we think.

Do you ever worry that you'll pass on your mental illness to Hailey?

I used to worry, but she's ten now and I can see that she doesn't have the same anxiety issues I had at her age. It's possible she'll struggle with mental illness and if so I'll try to understand, and probably fail, and try again until I get it right. It would almost be easier if she had the same issues I have because I could help her and teach her the tools I've learned, but she's who she was born to be.

My sister and I were raised exactly the same way and we could not be more different. One of her daughters is more like me and my daughter is more like her. It's baffling for all of us. But it's not our fault. We're born the way we are. One of the best things you can do as a parent is to realize that your child is *nothing* like you, and *everything* like you.

You get asked to do lots of speaking and TV. Do you feel famous?

I just cleaned up cat vomit. I feel queasy.

Let me rephrase. Does it ever feel like everyone wants a piece of you?

Like they're pissed and want to fight me?

What?

You mean like, "*Hey, asshole, you want a piece of me?*"

No. Not like that at all.

Or did you mean they *literally* want a piece of me? Like they need my kidneys? Or they just want to dismember me? Because that still seems like people are mad at me. You don't usually want to dismember people you like. I think you've confused "famous" with "despised."

I meant, like, a *metaphoric* piece of you.

Oh. Right. Sorry. These questions are making me paranoid and then I get defensive.

Yeah. I can see that.

WHAT THE HELL DOES THAT MEAN? *YOU WANT A PIECE OF ME?*

And *now* I see why you don't do interviews.

Honestly, I'm doing it for the good of humanity. Someone should get me a medal.

I can't think of any more questions.

I can't think of any more answers.

We make a good team.

Amen, mister.

I'm Turning into a Zombie
One Organ at a Time

Last year my friend Laura woke up when her husband was tapping on her head at two a.m., but when she tried to wave him off she realized that he was fast asleep and on the other side of the bed. That's when she put her hand up to her head and felt something warm and moving. She thought it was her son's guinea pig so she turned on a light and found a live possum on her pillow that was chewing off part of her hair to make a nest. She screamed and the possum hissed angrily and ran into the living room and she made her husband go after it even though he was certain she'd just dreamed it. She was all, "*REALLY? AM I DREAMING ALL THIS SLOBBERY HAIR ON MY PIL-LOW?*" Then the possum charged and they had a full-out possum battle in the living room, which did *not* end well for the possum. But don't feel *too* bad for it, because of the entire wild kingdom, Texas possums are the dickiest animals ever. My dad made me raise an orphaned possum when I was ten and every time I fed it, it hissed and glared at me like it wanted me to die in a fire. It was a very imaginative, bitey possum and also a total douche-canoe. Eventually it was old enough to be set free but a few months later it came back to our house and died on the porch. Probably out of spite. It's hard to tell with possums.

Laura's possum hair story always struck me as being one of the worst ways to wake up at two a.m. until the day when I woke up at that exact same time and found that my right arm had been ripped off and replaced with bees. Or at least, that's what it felt like. And I lay there for a second, thinking that I was certainly dying and that if a possum *had* chewed off my arm I would probably bleed out within minutes and that this was exactly the sort of way I would die. I considered nudging Victor softly so that his last moments with me would be romantic and tender but then my chest spasmed and I may have involuntarily punched him in the neck as hard as I could. Luckily for him, that wasn't very hard (as I was fragile and dying) and so he groggily asked, "Christ. Did you just punch me in the neck?" and I screamed, "A POSSUM JUST ATE OFF MY ARM," and *that's* probably the worst way to wake up ever.

I felt certain I was near death and Victor switched on the lights and pointed out that there was no blood and that I was probably just having a charley horse in my chest, which I'm pretty sure is not a real thing. I gasped for breath and told Victor that I was having a heart attack. Then he pointed out that I was clutching the wrong side of my chest for it to be my heart and that's when I realized that I was probably having a heart attack so bad that my heart was trying to run away. Or maybe my right boob was exploding. I tried to explain this to Victor but he was too busy yelling at me to calm down and so I explained that I needed to go to the hospital, except what came out was, "I'VE SWALLOWED A LEPRECHAUN AND IT'S EATING ITS WAY OUT OF MY CHEST." This is when Victor assumed I'd had some sort of stroke and he got Hailey and me in the car as quickly as possible.

Hailey was still mostly asleep so I tried to stay quiet so I wouldn't scare her. Victor kept telling me to breathe, and I told him that I already knew how to breathe *and why do people even say that because it's not like people just forget to breathe.* He pointed out that perhaps people do and maybe that's why people die all the time, and then another spasm hit me and I bit through my lip and passed out. When I came to there were police lights flashing and Victor was in the process of getting arrested for speeding. But then he explained that he was speeding because his wife was having a heart attack and the cops came to my door, looked at me, and called for an ambulance. Then they proceeded to yell at Victor for stupidly driving so fast when he could have just called for an ambulance but in his defense, he wasn't thinking straight and he'd just been punched in the neck by a woman who claimed to have a leprechaun inside her.

The ambulance arrived and the EMTs tried to get me to walk to the gurney but my entire body was shutting down and I couldn't stand up straight from what I just assumed was spontaneous retroactive scoliosis. The next twenty minutes were a blur, but I remember looking at my feet as the ambulance careened down the road and thinking that I should totally tweet a picture of this. Then I realized I hurt too much to use Twitter and that's when I knew I was dying.

The EMT strapped monitors to my heart and took my vitals and then told the driver to make it quicker. Then he said, "Sweetheart, are you allergic to nitroglycerin? Because I need to give you some," and that seemed really bizarre because I clearly remember that episode of *Little House on the Prairie* when the wheat crop failed and Pa had to take that job driving a wagon of highly explosive nitroglycerin and almost blew his balls off. Then the EMT asked again and I said, "I'm allergic to exploding," and he looked at me funny and told the driver to speed up again. Probably he thought I was hallucinating because he didn't watch enough *Little House on the Prairie*. Regardless, he made me hold nitroglycerin under my tongue and it tasted a lot like pain, but that sort of made sense since I was letting an explosive melt in my mouth like a poisonous Jolly Rancher.

Moments later I was being whisked into the emergency room while a horde of doctors tried to ascertain what was wrong with me. "Patient complained of severe chest pains. Blood pressure is elevated," the EMT said.

"And I ate explosives," I whispered, but no one was listening because they were too busy pulling my shirt off and doing an EKG, which apparently told the doctor that my heart was perfectly fine and that I probably had gas. I was relieved that I wasn't having a heart attack but I was pretty sure I was still dying and so I screamed, "MAKE IT STOP OR I'LL CUT YOU," right as Victor rushed into the room.

"She's not good with pain," he explained as the doctor backed away from the gurney. Then the doctor nodded and ordered something diluted to give to me. I told him I wanted the full strength and then he explained that he'd actually said "Dilaudid" and that this was a major pain reliever. A few excruciating minutes later a nurse injected me with the Dilaudid[1] and then the pain abated and I decided not to set fire to the hospital after all. In fact, I felt so grateful that I thought I should make up for my poor behavior by sharing a bit of trivia.

"Did you know," I asked no one in particular, "that sharks are attracted to urine?"

"She'll be a bit high for a while," the nurse said to Victor.

"So no matter how scared you are," I continued, "DO NOT URINATE."

"And *that's* how you can tell the drugs are working," said the nurse.

---

1. Spell-check keeps trying to tell me that "Dilaudid" is not a word and that most likely the word I'm looking for is "deluded." *I don't appreciate what you're implying, spell-check.*

"No," Victor sighed. "It's actually not. This is your tip. She does this at restaurants too."

I tried to protest but I was a bit too nauseous to point out that I only do it when we have excellent service or when the waiter refills my Diet Coke without my having to ask for it.

Then I blinked and we were home. I might have been high. Also, I was a little mortified that I'd mistaken gas for a heart attack but I trusted the doctor and was relieved that it would never happen again.

Until two weeks later when it totally happened again.

This time I was certain I was dying but I was calm enough to let Victor drive me to the hospital at a normal rate of speed because in spite of the fact that I hurt more than when I was in labor, I was pretty sure the doctor was just going to tell me I needed to fart really bad. We arrived and they recognized me immediately because apparently I have that sort of face, or maybe because most people don't give out valuable shark advice for services rendered.

I calmly explained that this was not gas and that it felt like I was having labor pains in my chest and that possibly I'd developed an extra vagina and needed to push. No one believed me and so I screamed, "I HURT AND YOU'RE SUPPOSED TO FIX ME SO GIVE ME DILAUDID," and then Victor told me to stop talking because I looked like a drug seeker. I explained that that was very astute of him because I *was* a drug seeker and I was seeking drugs to make my invisible chest vagina stop being such an asshole. Then he explained that "drug seeker" is medical code for addicts who come into the hospital looking for a fix and that screaming the actual name of the drug that I wanted was not helping my case. Luckily there was a doctor there who did a ton of blood work while I was screaming and realized that there was something wrong and that I was probably passing a gallstone. They gave me drugs and told me to see a gallbladder specialist to make sure the stone had passed. I told them that hamsters can only blink one eye at a time. I considered this a fair trade but they billed my insurance company anyway.

I went to see a group of gallbladder specialists but they all said that it was better to not do surgery because maybe I wouldn't have another attack, but I always find that removing body parts that want to kill you is a good thing so they referred me to Dr. Morales, who was known for taking out gallbladders like crazy. Maybe he collects them. Hard to know. What I did know though was that Dr. Morales didn't have a normal office and instead just used one from the nearby colon and rectal surgery clinic, which was disconcerting for a number of reasons. First, because I was pretty sure I didn't want my gallbladder removed rectally, and second, because the pictures in the waiting room were of asses. Literally.

Dr. Morales was over eighty, spoke English only when he had to, and had been doing gallbladder removal since before my mom was alive. He was odd but brilliant, and after a look at my chart he told me that my gallbladder was lingering and was diseased. I explained that it wasn't really "lingering" so much as it was "loitering" and that I wanted it removed. I wondered if you could file a restraining order against your gallbladder for loitering since it's not wanted and it's also trying to kill you. Then you could call the police and have your gallbladder removed and never have to pay for it because it was creating a public nuisance. Unless you have to pay the police to remove people who are public nuisances. I don't know. Frankly, I've never actually been on the complaining side of that scenario.

Dr. Morales said he'd fill me full of carbon dioxide or carbon monoxide (whichever one is not poisonous) and yank out my gallbladder through a hole in my belly button, but when I asked if I could keep my gallstones (so I could make a necklace out of them) he said that he couldn't do that because the new regulations are assholes, and he said that he couldn't even give people who'd been shot the bullets he dug out of them because they're considered "medical waste" once they've been pulled out of your body. This seems a bit hypocritical because my daughter came out of my body and they totally let me take her home. And some people even bring home their placenta and make their family eat it (seriously . . . that's a thing) and no one ever complains about that. (Except for the people who have to eat placenta, probably.) I explained that I was pretty sure that wearing my gallstones was less offensive than making your family unwittingly eat your placenta and Dr. Morales agreed with me and said he'd totally had this same argument a dozen times, which seems like an odd argument to have more than once. He did, however, agree to take lots of pictures and share them with me. My friend Maile offered to come take pictures of the surgery, and I almost took her up on it because she's an amazing photographer. But then I remembered hearing that after the surgery the doctor pushes all of the leftover carbon-whatever gas out of your belly button. I don't think I'd want anyone to witness me forcibly farting out of my own belly button, because if people are really your friends this is exactly the sort of shit you should want to protect them from. Like it says in the Bible, *being a friend means never having to witness farting belly buttons.* Or something. I might be misremembering.

As I waited in the hospital room for the surgery to commence I was a bit worried because you always hear horror stories about people getting things left in them or having the wrong body part removed. "What if I wake up and have a penis?" I asked the nurse.

She assured me that wouldn't happen. She said that it was a normal fear and that often she sees people write "NOT THIS LEG" on their good leg when they're in for knee surgery. I considered doing that, but everywhere. Small notes all over my body saying things like: "No, not there." "You're getting warmer." "What the shit are you doing? I need that." "Don't fuck with that. That's mine." But Victor wouldn't give me a Sharpie because he said I couldn't be trusted when I was fully sober, much less high on pain drugs.

So instead I pulled out my lucky nipple. (Side note: On book tour once a woman brought me a fake nipple that she makes for people who want bigger nipples or are recovering from a mastectomy. It looks amazingly realistic and I often wear it peeking out of my shirt to see if people will tell me I have a nip slip. If they do I remove the nipple and thank them for being decent. It's an excellent way to single out the awesome people. Also, if I'm at a bar and the bartender won't look at me I'll put the nipple on my forehead because it always gets people's attention.) I stuck my lucky nipple to my stomach and when the nurse came back in I said, "I think I'm having some sort of allergic reaction. Is this supposed to be there?" as I pointed at the very realistic stomach nipple that wasn't there a few minutes ago when she'd begun prepping me for surgery. To her credit, she was not surprised at all, which makes me think that there are more people than you think growing extra nipples and also that she's probably not the most observant nurse ever.

They eventually wheeled me in and the surgery was probably very surgical but I don't remember it because I was high. The recovery was a bit painful because my gallbladder was more infected than expected but it was also somewhat entertaining for people who weren't me.

"I need drugs," I moaned to Victor from my hospital bed.

He looked at his watch. "Not for another twenty minutes."

"Why do you hate me?"

"I don't hate you," he said as he looked back down at his magazine. "I just don't want you to overdose on morphine."

"Fine," I said. "Distract me then."

"Okay. This magazine says that you can tell what you should do with your life if you just take away all thoughts of risks. So what would you do if you knew you couldn't fail?"

"I'd be a Pegasus."

"That's not really how this works."

"I'd be a brown Pegasus though, because if you were a white Pegasus you'd be hounded by Lisa Frank fans and nine-year-olds. And black Pegasuses are just as bad because they're all badass and heavy metal bands would probably want to kidnap them. But no one wants a shabby brown Pegasus. I could just flap around the neighborhood and no one would really care. And maybe I'd wish for back herpes so that people wouldn't hassle me for rides."

Victor looked back at his magazine. "I'm not going to talk to you if you're not taking this seriously."

"I *am* taking this seriously," I said. "I'd be a rumpled, brown Pegasus with back herpes if I knew I couldn't fail."

"That's not how this works," Victor said. "It's supposed to teach you what you really want in life."

"That *is* what I want."

"PICK SOMETHING REAL."

"Fine," I huffed. I thought for a few seconds. "Then I guess I choose failing. I'd choose to fail but I *couldn't* fail so that would create a wormhole or some sort of paradox and then the whole world would explode."

Victor raised an eyebrow. "You're going to blow up the world because you didn't get your way? Don't you think you're overreacting a bit?"

"I think I need more morphine."

"I think this conversation proves you've had enough."

I crossed my arms. "I'm going to tell the nurse that you're mean to me and won't let me have back herpes or drugs."

Victor looked back at his magazine. "Good luck with that."

I looked at the "on duty" chart in my room and was very confused about the fact that there was a nurse assigned to my room whose name was "Labya" and I couldn't stop myself from wondering if it was actually pronounced like "labia" or if it was more of a short "a" like "LAH-bee-yuh."

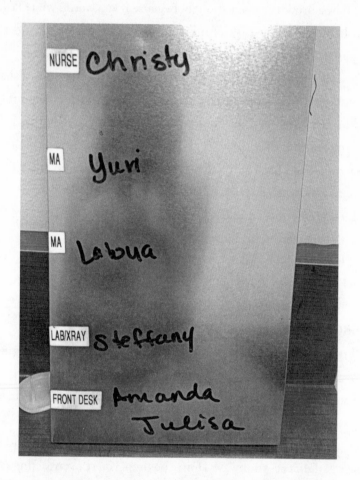

When the nurse came back to give me a shot in my ass cheek I figured all social pretenses were gone and so I said, "I just have to ask . . . is it pronounced 'Lay-bee-uh' or 'Lah-bee-uh'?" and she shook her head in confusion, saying, "I thought you were here because of your gallbladder."

"No," I explained. "I mean, on the menu. Is that Labia?"

And she asked, "You're asking me if *labia is on the menu*?"

Victor sank into his chair and tried to pretend he wasn't there.

I explained that I wasn't hitting on her and that I was referring to the chart on the desk and then she stared at it and then at me with a furrowed, confused brow, probably because she was now offended that I wasn't hitting on her.

Then she took a deep breath and said . . . "*Latoya*. That says *Latoya*."

And I looked closer and it totally did say Latoya. But in my defense, it looked liked "Labia" from a distance. Much like tacos. Or Georgia O'Keeffe paintings.

Then Dr. Morales came in and showed me pictures of my gross, removed gallbladder, which was filled with stones, and he said it was really good that we did the surgery because my gallbladder was mostly dead and was beginning to affect my other body parts because it had started to gangrene.

"Gangrene?" I asked. "I didn't even know that was still a thing. It's like I'm on the Oregon Trail all over again." Then Victor pointed out that I was thinking of dysentery and Dr. Morales was like, "*You had dysentery on the Oregon Trail? None of this is in your chart.*"

I said, "I'm guessing you didn't play a lot of educational computer games when you were a kid?" and he said that they didn't have computer games when he was a kid and I explained that that's why he probably never got dysentery in a video game.

Dr. Morales shook his head. "Sounds unsanitary. Just where were you putting those games?" I explained that that wasn't really what I meant and I redirected the conversation to my zombie gallbladder.

Victor tried to argue that my gallbladder was not zombified but I disagreed. It was slightly alive but mostly dead and was infecting everything it touched. It was literally the living dead. That's kind of the very definition of a zombie. So basically I was turning into a zombie one organ at a time. And I had a bunch of tubes in me to drain out all the bad stuff, which was shitty because I had to keep them in for a week. When I went home the cats thought that the tubes coming out of my stomach were great cat toys and kept batting at them and trying to hang on them. It's funny until your pain pills wear off. I don't recommend it for recovery.

Victor said he wasn't surprised that my ordinary gallbladder surgery—that he'd had as an outpatient—had turned into weeks of hassle because my body is known for being as complicated and weird as I am. But I'm not the only one with weird body parts. For example, Victor insists that he has "internal ear flaps," which is just ridiculous. When I go underwater I always end up with an ear infection and then Victor blames me because I don't close my ear flaps. And he's right because *they don't exist.* He disagrees and claims my ear flaps are just weak. He says his ear flaps are almost superhuman. "I use them to drown out your crazy so they get a lot of practice." I don't believe in ear flaps, but if I did have them I probably lost them when I was little and I got so many ear infections my eardrums burst. My mom would always try to cure them the old-fashioned way, by pouring olive oil in my ear and putting a cotton ball in it. The first time I tried olive oil in a restaurant I was like, "This tastes like ear ointment," and that's because it was ear ointment. This is why I don't like olives or olive oil. Because they taste like ear infections.

A week after surgery my friend Maile drove me to the ass clinic to have my surgical tubes removed. Dr. Morales was in rare form and started talking about catacombs and the mounting national debt and he closed the small talk by saying, "We're doomed. End of days. Thank God I'm dying soon so I won't have to witness it like you will." This is all true and not an exaggeration at all. He said it very cheerfully though. The man has a *hell* of a bedside manner.

Finally Dr. Morales clapped his hands as if to signal that the small talk was over and he told Maile to *pin me to the table.* Maile looked at him for a second to see if he was joking but he explained that I had to be pinned to the table by someone so that I wouldn't punch him when he yanked the tubes out of my stomach. So she shrugged good-naturedly and totally pinned me to the table. This is the sign of a good friend. Or a terrible one. Maybe both.

Then the doctor unstitched me and yanked, and it felt as if I'd accidentally gotten a jump rope wrapped around my liver. Or like if I was one of those dolls that talks when you pull the string on her back. And the thing that I said was: "*Ughaaah.*" Which roughly translates to "So now I know what a yo-yo feels like and also why you think your patients want to punch you."

As we were driving home Maile said, "You know, this shit could only happen to you. It's like you manifested the *exact* kind of crazy, fantastic doctor to fit your life. I would never believe it if I weren't there." And, yes, that's sort of how my whole life has been.

Cats Are Selfish Yawners and They're Totally Getting Away with It

The Fourth Argument I Had with Victor This Week

ME: I was just thinking that when I see other people yawn I yawn because it's contagious, but when I see cats yawn it never makes me yawn.

VICTOR: You know, you don't actually have to tell me everything that pops into your head.

ME: So then I went on the Internet to find out why that is and apparently we yawn when other people yawn because we see them getting lots of delicious air and our brain is all, "FUCK, THAT LOOKS DELICIOUS. GRAB SOME QUICK BEFORE THAT BITCH TAKES IT ALL."

VICTOR: So you yawn because you're selfish. Got it.

ME: Not just *me. Everyone* yawns because they're selfish. But I think we don't yawn when we see cats yawn because they have such little mouths that we don't feel threatened about them taking our air. And also—did you ever notice that cats don't make that sucking-in Hoover-y noise when they yawn?

VICTOR: The what?

ME: You know. When a normal person yawns you hear this loud intake of air, like a tire going flat but in reverse. But when cats yawn they don't make any noises at all. Why is that?

VICTOR: You're asking me why cats don't yawn properly?

ME: Is it because they aren't *actually* yawning and they're really just stretching their cheek muscles, or is it that they've learned how not to make the gaspy "I'm-stealing-all-the-good-air-and-leaving-you-with-carbon-dioxide" noise so that we won't gulp down all the air after they yawn?

VICTOR: I don't even know where you're going with this.

ME: I'm just saying, are cats *not* yawning audibly because they want all the air to themselves?

VICTOR: Stop. Stop talking.

ME: You can just tell me if you don't know. I DON'T KNOW EITHER, VICTOR. There's nothing to be ashamed of here.

VICTOR: I think we're gonna have to agree to disagree on that.

Winner: Cats. Because they're getting a shit-ton of oxygen and no one is challenging them on it.

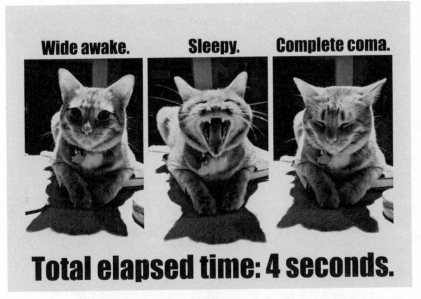

Hunter S. Thomcat devouring all of your lovely oxygen and
totally not feeling bad about it at all.

Koalas Are Full of Chlamydia

"So apparently I'm *really* leaving for the Australian outback tomorrow," I said to the storm trooper beside me. His look was one of surprise. Or horror. Honestly, it's hard to tell what a storm trooper is thinking even if you've been married to him for seventeen years. I blame the helmet.

"You can't even find your way around *the mall* without asking for help," Victor responded with mild disbelief, unconsciously gripping his firearm made of PVC pipe. "This whole trip is the most ridiculous thing I've ever heard of."

"You bought a used movie-grade storm trooper costume so that you could join a troop of strangers who visit sick kids in hospitals. *You don't even like healthy kids.* I'm pretty sure you're not in any position to judge what's ridiculous."

He shook his head, still baffled that I was going through with this. But he was right. I was fucked.

⋆

It was Halloween and I was spending what might be my last night alive in America chasing after a nine-year-old, sugar-riddled zombie Red Riding Hood while my storm trooper husband hopped through the neighborhood with us. At the last minute I'd surprised him by dressing up as Darth Vader so that when he was suited up I could jump out and scream, "Victor . . . I am your . . . boss!" He was not amused. I tried the death grip but he refused to lean backward in the invisible choke. It was probably because after I got Victor dressed in his *twenty-seven-piece outfit* he found that he was unable to sit, lean, bend over, or even put on his own shoes without help. It's really not that different from how most women feel after getting Spanxed up on date night, but as a man, he was utterly out of his element. He was like a knight, but wearing PVC and a unitard instead of a suit of armor. Honestly, if the rebels knew what *I* knew, they would have just pushed all the storm troopers over like dominoes, leaving them to awkwardly rock like turtles who've accidentally rolled over on their backs. I suspect the storm troopers' wives (who obviously had to help them completely dress and undress every day) went into their marriages knowing that they were likely going to be young widows. It's sad, but I'm betting the dark side had good life insurance plans. The dark side always seemed very organized and vaguely Republican.

This whole Australia-trip thing had started a month ago when my friend Laura asked if I'd come with her on a trip sponsored by the People Who Want You to Go to Australia. I said no because I'm the only person in the world who hates to travel, and because I knew that everything in Australia wants to kill you as violently and painfully as possible. Laura sighed and told me to keep an open mind, and in my defense, it's very hard to keep saying no to the person who once voluntarily chased off vultures with a shovel and helped you dig up a decomposing corpse in the scorching Texas heat of your backyard. I'd explain that last sentence but it's all in my first book. Go buy that and read it.

It's probably on sale. I'll wait. Also, pick up some doughnuts. You look too thin. Eat something.

Done? *Excellent.* Back to the story.

The whole Australia thing was a "do stuff on your life list" event sponsored by Tourism Australia, so we'd get a free trip as long as we wrote about it later. I reminded Laura that the very first thing on my life list *is to never write a fucking life list.* She then reminded me that I was being cynical, again, and pointed out that it was basically a free ticket to do *anything that we wanted* as long as it was on our life list.

"Really?" I asked skeptically. "Can I box a kangaroo?"

Laura stared at me. "Do you *want* to box a kangaroo?"

"Well, no. Not really," I admitted. "But I'd like to know that I have *the option.* Except I don't want any kangaroos to get hurt. So maybe . . . pudding wrestling with kangaroos? Is that a thing?"

"The problem is, I don't think kangaroos are naturally that fighty."

"No," I replied vehemently, "kangaroos are mean bastards who totally box each other in the wild. If anything, we're making it safer for everyone by putting mittens on their hands. They also smoke cigars while they're doing it, so they're polluting the environment too. Kangaroos don't give a shit about secondhand smoke."

Laura raised an eyebrow.

"Seriously. I saw it on a cartoon from the fifties."

She sighed deeply. "Everything you know about Australia you learned from cartoons. This is *exactly* why you need to go. Did you know there's a town in Australia full of ghosts and possibly lots of serial killers?"

I perked up. "We should go there."

"Is it on your life list?"

"Well it is *now*," I muttered, somewhat accusingly. "Can we go hold koalas while dressed in full koala costumes? And would you be more likely to say yes if I tell you I already have the costumes?"

Laura stared at me. "You have *two* koala costumes?"

"Well, yes. You need a backup in case one's dirty."

Laura: "Huh."

"*I'm kidding*," I said. "But I do have one koala costume and one panda costume. And they're both sort of bears, so that should count." Laura didn't respond, but that was probably because she was thinking that koalas aren't actually bears. Technically pandas seem more like giant raccoons than bears, so I suspect she decided not to bring it up because she's good at picking her battles.

Laura suggested that we take a sleeper train through Australia since I hated to fly, and I grudgingly admitted that I *had* always wanted to go on the Orient Express, but that I'd sort of consider it a wasted opportunity if a murder didn't happen. It's not that I'm particularly bloodthirsty, it's just that I have standards and it seems like it's not the full sleeper-train experience if there isn't a murder provided. I considered that if I wrote it down on my life list then Australia would be forced to provide a murder for me, but then I worried that they'd be all about "enabling and supporting" and would instead make *me* responsible for planning the murder, and I can't even organize my sock drawer, much less a murder. Laura seemed concerned that I was putting too much thought into this possible murder, but I think that's just because she's a professional event planner and this stuff is second nature to her. Laura needs to realize that not *everyone* is born with the natural organizational skills she has. If they were then there would be festive murders happening all the time. Ones with hors d'oeuvres, and charitable donations, and chocolate fountains, and mason jars with paper straws, and souvenir bags with human ears in them. Laura looked at me oddly when I said that but I think it's just because she can't take compliments well. Or maybe because human-ear party bags are "so 2011." I don't really know. I am *terrible* at keeping up with trends.

I said no to Australia about eight billion times until Laura finally said, "You are *always* going on about forcing yourself to be FURI-OUSLY HAPPY and pushing past your comfort level to really live life. *Well, this is one of those times, sister, so buckle up, buttercup, and get your work visa.*" She raised her voice, screaming victoriously (and slightly intimidatingly): "WE'RE GONNA SEE THE WILD SIDE, BITCHES."

And so I said yes. And Australia said yes. And my therapist said I'd need extra therapy sessions. And the woman scheduling our itinerary said, "I'll set everything up and tell you what you're going to be doing less than twelve hours before you actually leave the States." And she did.

The trip was to be based on life goals we wanted to tick off our bucket list and so Laura and I started putting together goals that we actually wanted to accomplish but that we'd probably never do if we were paying for it on our own. Mostly because we're cheap bastards and terrible at booking hotels.

My original list read as follows:

1. Lick David Tennant's face.
2. Ride a golden unicorn.
3. Wish for more wishes.

Laura pointed out that life lists weren't the same as genie wishes and made me start again.

I revised it to "Ride on camels," and "Watch giant-cockroach races," and "See where *The Hobbit* was filmed," but then Australia was like, "That's New Zealand. *Again*, New Zealand is not in Australia so please stop asking." So then I just added "Put New Zealand inside Australia so I can see hobbits" to my life list.

"I think they kind of have to do it now," I explained to Laura. "It's like I'm Alan Rickman in *Die Hard* and Australia is the baffled hostage negotiator. I think I could probably ask them to bring me a dump truck filled with live slow lorises and a young Sean Connery and they'd have to do it. I AM DRUNK WITH POWER." Laura suspected I was also drunk with wine slushees. Technically we were both right.

I considered that it was entirely possible that this whole setup was a trick and that I would get there and be forced to spend a week trapped at some sort of terrible time-share meeting. Or maybe that it was a sting to arrest me for unpaid parking tickets. But it was also possible I'd be riding camels in Middle Earth and that seemed worth the risk. After all, it's NewStralia. *Anything could happen.*

("NewStralia" is the name I made up for when they come to their senses and drop New Zealand onto Australia. You're welcome, Australian tourism board. I'm giving you that one for free.)

People warned us that everything in Australia wants to kill you, but I think they're overreacting. Australia doesn't want to kill you. It's more like an exclusive club for people who care very little about being alive. Australia is really a lot like Texas if Texas were mad at you and drunk and maybe had a knife. Like, in Australia they have dangerous funnel(-web) spiders. In Texas we have funnel cakes. I don't know what funnel spiders are but they sound significantly less delicious than fried cake. They're probably equally bad for you though.

People warned us of "drop bears"—mythical bears that fall out of the trees and eat you and you're supposed to put forks in your hair to scare them away from your head. I'm not sure why Australia feels the need to make up deadly creatures when they're already crawling with them. It's probably to identify the tourists by all the forks in their hair. We do that in Texas with snipe hunts, but you usually end up finding something to shoot anyway so no one's really mad when they find out that snipes are made up. Then again, watching for trees and putting forks in your hair is probably a good thing as it keeps out the flying foxes. Those are real, by the way. Enormous mega-bats with five-foot wingspans, which live in the park and are better named "enormous rats with wings that can envelop you."

We actually saw some flying foxes around Darling Harbour, which seems an unfortunate name. I don't like a place that randomly gives itself a compliment. A helpful Australian tried to tell me it was named after a guy whose last name was Darling but I wasn't having it. "I don't love it," I explained. *"It insists on itself."* The man nodded noncommittally, deciding it was better not to argue with a strange foreigner dressed in a full-body koala costume because it was cold and she didn't bring a coat.

But I'm getting ahead of myself.

Laura and I thought about leaving traps all over Australia (cardboard boxes propped up by sticks with babies inside of them) to see if we could catch dingoes but then Laura pointed out that it was probably BYOB (Bring Your Own Baby) and I never even remember to pack phone chargers, so we just crossed that one out. We asked if Greg from *The Wiggles* could drive us around in the Big Red Car and the Australian tourism board seemed a little hesitant so instead we decided to make things easier for them by keeping it simple.

Goal Number 1: Hug a Koala While Dressed as a Koala

I planned to dress as a koala so that koalas would know what it's like to be held by a koala because turnabout is fair play. Except, honestly, they probably just want you to put them down. People are constantly picking them up without asking first. Koalas are the new dwarves. Just because they're smaller than you, it doesn't give you the right to pick them up without asking. But that doesn't mean I don't want to go to a reserve where there are tons of them and rake them up in a pile and jump on them like they're a furry leaf pile. (Koalas, that is. Not dwarves.) Not that I would jump on piles of koalas *or* dwarves. Sometimes we're made from the stuff that we want to do but don't actually follow through on. Like when someone is an asshole and you want to burn down their garage, but then you don't because it's illegal and also because you can't find the matches. I'm made from a lot of unfulfilled arson. And un-jumped-on koala piles.

I told Laura that I was tempted to make a koala fall in love with me so I that could sneak it home in my backpack, but she pointed out that I didn't even bring a backpack. I am a terrible planner.

"Maybe I should dress like a eucalyptus tree because they really like to hang on them and it'll put them at ease," I said. "And then I'll rub Vicks VapoRub all over me because I think menthol and eucalyptus are pretty much the same thing. And I'll give them menthol cigarettes to smoke. Those fucking koalas are going to *love* me."

Laura agreed. "I read that they're all slothy and out of it because the eucalyptus they eat is full of poisons and so they spend their whole lives trying to digest toxins. They probably *do* want saving. They eat toxic shit all day. Someone needs to give them a steak to chew on."

"Or some pound cake and a multivitamin," I added.

"Plus, tons of them have chlamydia. Luckily koala chlamydia is not contagious to people though," Laura added.

"Huh. Does it feel like human chlamydia?" I asked.

"I dunno. I've never had human chlamydia," she replied.

Laura can be a real braggart sometimes.

The more I considered it, the more I realized how much I have in common with these koalas. We're both immunocompromised, lightly diseased, exhausted, and full of toxins. I'm totally a koala.

"I'm more of a kangaroo," Laura replied after a moment of thought. "I'm laid-back until you push me a bit too far and then I'll split your stomach open and walk away while you bleed to death."

"And that's why I keep on your good side," I said. "I'm also a Hufflepuff because I'm lactose intolerant and I get distracted by birds."

Laura didn't respond, but in her defense, it was a lot to take in.

My hopes of smuggling a live koala out of the country were significantly dampened though when it took the koala wranglers two weeks just to approve my koala costume because they were afraid that the fleecy costume would terrify and startle the koalas. It finally got approved, but then when we got to the Sydney zoo we were told that we were not on the list and were certainly not going to be holding any of their koalas. Possibly the koala costume threw them off. I explained that we'd specifically been told we could come here to snuggle koalas and that my outfit had been approved weeks in advance and they looked at me in a way that made me think that they'd called security. (I am *way* too familiar with that look.) We pulled out our paperwork and they sighed in relief when they told us that we'd come to the wrong place and that we wanted the Wild Life Sydney Zoo, which is not the same thing as the Sydney zoo.

"Just how many zoos do you people need?" I asked.

"They only recently started calling themselves a zoo, so it's confusing to people," the clerk explained. "Catch the bus back and ask the driver to take you to the aquarium."

"Awesome," Laura said. "We're going to hold a bunch of aquatic koalas. I didn't even know those existed."

"They *don't* exist," replied the clerk.

"Great," I replied. "Then we get to hold a bunch of drowned koalas. This isn't *quite* the day I expected."

Thirty minutes later we made it to the right spot and found that the zoo was part of an aquarium and wax museum conglomerate and was nice but fairly tiny compared to the zoo we'd just been thrown out of. We found our way to a koala enclosement. (Spell-check says "koala enclosement" isn't a real thing and it wants me to change it to "koala enslavement." Clearly spell-check feels *very* strongly about koalas in captivity. Victor says "enclosement" is not a real word, but I just put it in a book so it's a real word now, Victor.)

I told the people working there that I was there to hold a koala and they looked at me as if I'd said I was there to hack the limbs off tiny babies. Turns out it's been illegal to hold a koala in that particular part of Australia for years, but I wasn't giving up because they'd already approved my costume so they must've known we were there to nuzzle koalas. They called management and found that I was actually only approved to *wear* the koala costume while staring at the koalas.

I tried to politely argue my way into holding them but they told me that even David Hasselhoff had only been allowed to stand near them and that's when I gave up, because if the Hoff can't love on a koala I sure as hell wasn't going to get to. And I suppose they had good reason to be protective of their koalas since clearly someone had given a great number of them chlamydia. But then again if they're all rampant with chlamydia already it's not like they're going to get *more* chlamydia. If anything they should be concerned about their koalas giving *me* chlamydia, but I was willing to take that chance because I really wanted to say I'd held a koala and also because I was pretty sure there were shots to cure chlamydia now. Surprisingly, this argument only baffled the koala keepers but they were very sweet and apologetic for the disappointment and did agree to let me go into the enclosure to photobomb a koala.

Not *quite* as romantic as I was hoping for, but at least the koala wasn't overly panicked when he saw me. He looks terrified, doesn't he? Answer: No, he doesn't. *Because he's fucking asleep.* I suspected they were all high on quaaludes and I was a little jealous. I probably could have drawn a Sharpie mustache on him and he still would've stayed in whatever crazy fever dream koalas have.

I think the lesson here is that you shouldn't get your hopes up about holding koalas, but technically they smell weird and tons of them have chlamydia so maybe this was the universe's way of saving me from myself. Or from chlamydia.

(Note: I have several friends who went to the parts of Australia where you can still hold a koala and they all said that it was sweet but that the koalas are very heavy and a bit stinkier than you'd expect. They suggested that if you really want to hold a koala but can't, just get a furry pillowcase and fill it with lightly used cat litter. Or tie a bunch of sedated raccoons together. Or maybe hold a dead koala. I probably should have asked, "Do you have any koalas that are already dead from the shock of being cuddled? Because we're fine with that. We're not picky. *Unlike these fucking koalas.*" I'm sure that would've gone over well. Now that I think about it, it's possible that the sleeping koalas at the enclosure weren't even sleeping. They were probably taxidermied and they just hot-glued them to a branch. That's probably why you can't even pet them. Because hot glue melts in Australia because it's broiling so often. And that's why you can't jostle dead koalas on trees. They'll just fall right off the trees and then the jig is up.)

Goal Number 2: See the World's Biggest Something

Australia has a love for big things, like the Big Prawn (thirty feet) or the Big Slurpee (thirty-six feet). I wanted to see the Big Banana (forty-three feet). Laura didn't even know that there was such a thing but once she heard about it she wanted to go too. Unfortunately, we were in the wrong part of Australia for most of the Big Things, but we heard rumors on the Internet of a Big Potato, which would only take us a day to find. And so we rented a car so we could drive *many, many* hours so that we could see Australia's Big Potato. Except it isn't actually a potato. It's a cement sculpture in the shape of a potato. It's right by a gas station and when we asked locals where to find it they all said, *"What? You mean the big turd?"*

Apparently it's lovingly(?) referred to as a big turd. A big turd potato. *A poturdo.*

It was awesome. I'm not even being sarcastic about this. Just look at it.

(*Courtesy of Laura Mayes*)

It took the two of us working in tandem just to drive to the Poturdo because Australia is filled with roundabouts and everyone drives on the wrong side of the road. In the end we decided to split up the work and I feverishly watched the GPS and yelled, "Left! Right! ROUNDABOUT!" while Laura white-knuckledly followed my instructions and glared at people daring to easily drive on the wrong side of the road. Roundabouts presented the most difficulties. Instead of red lights and yield signs, everyone just drives in a circle until they find the place where they want out. I'm sure there have got to be some sort of rules to this but we didn't know them and so we'd just drive in with our windows down, pointing and screaming, "WE'RE GOING THAT WAY SO PLEASE DON'T HIT US," to the people in nearby cars. A pile of dogs could have driven better than us.

We never used our blinker properly because in Australia the knob you think is going to be your blinker is the knob that turns on the windshield wiper. So we had almost no driving skills and a windshield wiper that was constantly on *for no reason at all*. I bet rental places in Australia can probably tell when Americans have rented their cars because their windshield wipers always need to be replaced.

Additionally, everything is measured in klicks and meters and liters and neither Laura nor I knew how to convert metric to imperial so when the GPS would show that we needed to turn in two kilometers I'd say, "Be prepared to turn in two minutes or two hours. I don't know which." Laura looked at me with frustration but she never learned it either so she couldn't say much.

"There's too much math on this vacation," I complained like a whiny American. "I've gone thirty-nine years without learning the metric system and I'm not gonna pussy out now. If I did it'd be like admitting to Ms. Johnson that I *would* have to use this one day."

Laura nodded in agreement.

"Fuck it," I said. "From now on I'm just going to measure everything in babies. Lengthwise. Everyone knows how long a baby is so it's totally universal. The math people will probably be mad about having to convert everything though. This is probably how God felt when people stopped measuring arks in cubits."

"Or measuring arks at all," Laura replied.

We eventually drove into the bush, where we were expected to camp for the night. "This place is very bushy," I said, using words to describe things.

"Super bushy," Laura replied. "*The bushiest.*"

I felt sure Australia would be grateful they'd sent such wordsmiths on this trip.

When we arrived at the campsite we realized it was less "camping" and more "glamping," or glamorous camping. The tent was already set up for us and there was an outdoor bathtub and mosquito nets. There was also a lodge nearby that offered fancy food, booze, hot tea, and plugs to recharge our stuff. We met up with Ben (whose name might actually be Ben—or it might be something else), whose family owned and operated the campground. He had dinner with us. It was avocado ice cream with popcorn and Tabasco-sauce soup. (*"There's a lotta weird shit happening all at once here."*—Laura on Australian cuisine. *"What's in my mouth?"*—Me on the same thing.)

Ben told us about a costume party he'd been to last week where he'd dressed up as a vagina and the guy who was with him dressed up as tweezers to go with the vagina. It was then that I started to suspect that Ben didn't know how vaginas work. Then he exclaimed, "No, wait, not a tweezer. That other thing. Um . . . a . . . a SPECULUM!" Then the other diners jumped a bit and stared at us. With jealousy I suspect.

Ben assured us that our fear of sleeping in the bush was unfounded. His exact words were "No worries, mates. She'll be apples," which is apparently Australian for "Calm your ass down." I asked if there were any rhinos nearby and explained that everything I knew about the bush I learned from watching *The Gods Must Be Crazy* when I was in second grade. Then Ben pointed out that that movie was about the bush of Botswana, so basically everything I know about Australia is Botswana.

We explained that our fear of the bush was primarily of possums because they like to make wigs out of Laura's hair. Ben hesitantly admitted that it might not *all* be apples because we were assigned to sleep in something named "Possum Tent," but he did assure us that Australia's possums were adorable and not the angry, giant-teethed, hissing menaces that we had in Texas.

Just in case you think I'm overreacting, this is an American possum on his best behavior. (*Courtesy of Andrew Kantor*)

"One caution though," he said. "*Absolutely no food in your tent* because that will attract wild animals."

"Yes." I paused. "But Laura and I are *made* of meat."

Ben assured us that we'd be fine and sweetly added, "Please don't murder our possums. Ours are well behaved and won't eat your face off." Ben gave us what he called "a torch" but what we called a tiny keychain flashlight that seemed to have a short in it because it kept turning off as Laura and I walked through the dense bush, alone and shivering. Then we turned directly onto a path with A GIANT POS-SUM IN THE MIDDLE OF IT. Laura was so scared she screamed out, "AMANDA!" which was weird because *who the hell is Amanda*? Later she said she just screamed out a nonsensical phrase made from pure fear and too many vowels but I suspect she has unresolved issues with this Amanda person. Either way, that's when the flashlight went out and we were stuck in complete darkness with the sound of an animal scurrying either toward us or away from us. "PROTECT YOUR HAIR," I yelled, and I considered covering her hair with my hands but I was afraid she might think my hands were possums and knife me. Laura's awesome, but she's a bit of a loose cannon when it comes to hair possums. But then the flashlight came back on and the possum was gone. I considered telling Laura it was probably just a ghost pos-sum but I worried that might make her more freaked out.

We finally got to our tent, and we put on the kangaroo and koala costumes I'd packed because it was unexpectedly freezing and also because we thought if wild animals got in during the night they'd think we were one of them and wouldn't eat us. I'm not ashamed to say that at one point we made *Blair Witch*-esque videos saying good-bye to our families in case we didn't make it. I *am* ashamed to say that I tried to distract Laura with tales I'd heard the day before during a dolphin-watching trip. Sadly, all I'd really learned is that dolphins are super rapey. True story. I don't know why anyone wants to swim with them. Spell-check is trying to cover it up by saying "rapey" isn't a word, but it is. Male dolphins can go into murderous rages out of sexual frustration and will even gang-rape female dolphins at times. Laura looked at me like I'd gone insane and I realized I'd just been talking about scary Australian animals again, but I pointed out that it's not as if a land dol-phin was likely to come accost us in our tent. At least not this far in-land. Probably.

"Please stop talking about rapey dolphins," Laura said.

"*Got it*," I replied, changing the subject to something lighter. "The dolphin tour also pointed out a private island that no one is allowed on because there are penguins there who need to be protected, according to scientists. Seems sort of suspect though . . . penguins in Australia that no one is allowed to see? I think the scientists are lying and just want their own private island. That's probably how the Cullens got theirs."

"Or, maybe just stop talking in general," Laura suggested.

And so I did.

The next morning I chased a family of wild kangaroos toward Laura while she was taking a bath outside of our tent. I did this out of friendship. Sometimes you have to explain these things. *Apparently.*

Goal Number 3: Investigate If Australian Toilets Really Do Flush Backward

I totally tried this but all of the toilets in Australia are low flow so basically the water just disappears and then comes back. Sorry if you're disappointed. I assure you, you are not alone. But in a way, that's good because if toilets really flushed backward you'd get shot in the face with toilet water every time you flushed, like a violently angry bidet. Also, apparently Australia thought this goal was too ludicrous to take seriously and instead decided to send us to the outback to see more interesting things.

We were to be in the outback for several days, which seemed very wild and exciting until I actually read about the outback on the plane ride there and realized that it was basically just rocks and desert. It looks a lot like West Texas if West Texas went on for a billion miles and you took out all the beer barns and people and replaced them with deadly snakes that want to murder you.

The only *real* difference between West Texas and the outback is the pride Australians have in their rocks. And they *should* be proud. There are *enormous* rocks in Australia and we were on our way to see the second-largest one in the world, Uluru. I saw it as we flew over it toward the airport (which was built specifically to let people fly in and look at a big rock). I turned to Laura. "Hey . . . There's that big rock." I nodded toward the plane window.

Laura leaned over to see it. "Huh. That *is* a big rock." She nodded somewhat impressedly, the same way you would if you saw a monkey do the Macarena on YouTube, and then she flipped desperately through

our guidebook to see if there were any bars in the outback. "So now what do we do for the *rest* of our three days here?"

I shouldn't have doubted Australia though, because when we looked closer at our itinerary we found that we'd be doing a *lot* in the outback. Like looking at other, almost-as-big-but-not-*quite*-as-big-as-Uluru rocks. Or eating while listening to the rocks. And walking around the rocks. And taking a sunrise tour of the rocks, and a separate sunset tour of the rocks. And buying pictures of the rocks.

We did not have high hopes for this leg of the journey.

I suspected we were being unfair though, because the guidebooks all said that Uluru was astounding and that the subtle light changes on the rock turned it into a whole new rock each time the sun moved. I assumed the people writing those guidebooks were on LSD, because I once said the exact same thing about biscuits when I was really high.

Turns out that the guidebooks were right. Uluru was pretty amazing. It's the second-largest monolith in the world and I didn't ask what a monolith is but my guess is that it's Latin for "big-ass rock." Our hiking guide drove us to Uluru from the resort, which was a small cluster of low-end-to-high-end hotels you could choose to stay in if you didn't want to sleep outside and be gnawed on by dingoes. The dingo gnawing wasn't specifically in the hotel brochures but I think it was implied. "No dingo nibbling here, probably. Running tap water on demand." Something like that. The small airport, the resort, and some tents we never saw were about the only things for hours so there was no escape, but we found out that our medium-priced hotel was quite lovely and offered a full bar so we were fine. Also, the room we were in had an interesting carpet that was supposed to remind us of ancient red-bottomed creeks but instead the blood-colored stain running through the brown carpet looked a lot like a murder victim had been dragged across the room and thrown off the balcony. But in a pretty way.

Our guide was a very sweet and knowledgeable woman who was
eager to share the cultural magic of Uluru, which is now owned by
the Aboriginal people who originally owned it back before white people
showed up and said, "You have no concept of ownership? Lovely! We
own all of this now. But never mind that. How are you? Can we escort
you somewhere else and treat you like shit for a while?" It's a very long
and sordid history that is only now beginning to be rectified (includ-

ing giving Uluru back and paying the local indigenous people to let tours take place) but it basically boils down to the same principle around the world, which is that white people suck and should not be allowed to discover anything that's already been discovered by the people who've lived there since the world began. On behalf of white people I'd like to offer an extremely late but completely sincere "I'm so very sorry for our being assholes. We're learning. Also, I've heard a few stories about some of you guys eating some of us in Tasmania, but I can assure you there are no hard feelings. We'd probably eat us too if there was enough money in it." I don't have any pictures of the lovely Aboriginal people I met because they think it traps their spirit, and if they're correct then Facebook is basically creating a living hell. Which is really not that surprising, now that I say it out loud.

Our guide, whom I'll call Jessica because I'm a terrible journalist and I don't write down names, drove us (plus an older American couple and a young Danish girl) the short distance to the base of Uluru, where she began explaining that the part of the rock we see is "just the tip" (high five if you giggled there) and that the majority of the rock is still underground. Jessica used a stick to trace out in the red sand what Uluru actually looked like: the long shaft hidden, rising slowly upward until just the tip penetrated the surface. I stared at Laura with wide eyes and she stared back at me as we realized our guide had totally inadvertently drawn a penis on the ground that all of us were looking at in amazement. I got a quick photo of it but it doesn't really show up in black and white, plus our guide was in the process of stomping it out. But if you'd like a color picture of a young woman stomping on a penis on the ground, I can deliver. Not that you would want that. I'd like to think that no one really wants that.

We were sent to explore the desert and find out what might want to murder us. After an hour of heat we suspected it was Jessica, who kept pointing out new rocks. It was the same rock. I was no fool. Except that I was out in the desert on a forced walk, seeing imaginary snakes in every twig, so all bets were off.

I never saw any live snakes but apparently Australia is lousy with them, and they have so many that even the lizards are snakes. Please note: If you're a lizard but you don't have legs, you are a snake. That's how snakes work.

"I am not a snake."
This snake is a dirty liar.

It's never *not* snake season in Australia. In Texas in the winter we at least get a break from the scorpions when they all seem to disappear. I assume they must be hibernating with bears, which is sort of terrifying because imagine waking up a cranky bear and he's dripping with angry scorpions. That would be the worst thing ever and, *now that I think about it*, is probably something that totally exists in Australia.

Laura and I started our walk around the big rock and it was quite enjoyable except for the flies, which followed you in hordes, like an angry entourage intent on setting up house in your nostrils. I just pinched my nose closed at one point and then I accidentally ate two flies. You'd think that would teach the other flies to avoid me, but no. These were stupid, reckless flies following stupid, reckless tourists. We pretty much belonged together.

Uluru was quite cool and a bit mysterious. Laura and I both heard chanting, which we assumed was piped in, but which Jessica assured us was all in our heads. She suspected we were drunk. We weren't, but we appreciated the suggestion and quickly located a pub. We found out that getting drunk in Australia is referred to as "putting on the wobbly boot" and "getting off your face" until you do the "Technicolor yawn," which I think is the funnest euphemism for vomiting *ever*.

We also learned how to pronounce things with an Australian accent. For example, if you say "Good eye, might" it sounds like "Good day, mate." Also, "Raise up lights" = "razor blades" and "Dee yoon un-duh" = "Down under." Basically you just clench your teeth like you have TMJ. And drop a lot of "R"s haphazardly. Honestly, Australia is just wasting a lot of its "R"s. It's a little idiculous.

Goal Number 4: Find Out If Kangaroos Really Have Three Vaginas

Did you know that kangaroos have three vaginas? Because they totally do and that's probably why they're always hitting each other. They probably have PMS every damn day of the week. But on the plus side, kangaroos have plenty of places to smuggle things because they have so many holes in their bodies. In fact, they're so full of holes it's sort of shocking that all the kangaroo doesn't just leak out.

Interestingly, female kangaroos have three vaginas, but male kangaroos only have a two-pronged penis. It's like they've started a Darwinian game of one-upmanship and the girls are winning. (Fascinating factoid: Kangaroos also drool on themselves to keep cool [because nothing looks cooler than a drooling kangaroo] but that's helpful to know because when you see them drooling at the mouth it doesn't necessarily mean that they have rabies. It just means they're hot [hot referring to their temperature, not sexiness]. If you find drooling kangaroos sexy you probably need help.)

I wanted to ask the Wild Life Sydney Zoo about whether kangaroos actually do have three vaginas, but they wouldn't even let me touch their koalas so I thought a gynecological exam on a kangaroo was probably out of the question. And also I didn't have my forceps with me. Instead, Laura and I drove into the bush and looked for real, wild kangaroos so I could peer up their bums when they leaned over. I couldn't see anything through the fur, although one of the kangaroos did get an erection. It was pink and not attractive. At least not to me. But then, I'm not a kangaroo. Although I *did* dress like one to put them at ease. Here's a picture of me showing a kangaroo a picture of himself. He was unimpressed. Kangaroos don't understand selfies.

I gave up on my idea of looking at vaginas and I just decided to **be** a kangaroo **better** than a kangaroo.
(*Courtesy of Laura Mayes*)

Nailed it. (*Courtesy of Laura Mayes*)

We also *ate* kangaroo, which I feel a bit bad about. Partially because they're so cute and partially because they taste terrible. Well, maybe not *terrible*, but they taste a lot like blood, because if not served very rare, kangaroo becomes tough as shoe leather. This always seemed a strange analogy to me because when are people eating shoe leather? How do they know what it tastes like? Why not purse leather or pants leather?

Australia is a very strange country because you spend days running around trying to find wild kangaroos so you can see their majesty and then you eat them on a pizza an hour later. Bloody, vampire-friendly pizza. People in Australia really seemed to like kangaroo meat, but the only time I ever had it and didn't hate it was when it was served sliced very thin and drizzled in something alcoholic. I think I only liked it more then because there was so much *less* of it than usual. If they'd sliced it so thin that I could read through it I suspect I'd have liked it even more, and I probably would have even asked for seconds if they'd just waved a fork of kangaroo juice near my lips. Or maybe not. I'm not much of a foodie.

Goal Number 5: Boomerang

We had the opportunity to learn to throw spears in the outback but it was always scheduled right after we'd been drinking. Technically everything was scheduled right after we'd been drinking, but it *was* the outback. There's not a lot to do other than get drunk. I tried a plastic boomerang that was sitting in a bin outside the gift shop but it failed to return and then I realized I'd basically just tossed unpaid merchandise as far as I could throw it. I considered going to get it but then I was concerned that when I picked it up it would be considered shoplifting and it seemed like that would have a stiffer penalty than just throwing merchandise into the desert. So instead I just went inside the gift shop to see if anyone would say anything to me. No one did. Probably because it happens all the time. You can't just leave boomerangs out in the open and expect people not to throw them. It's like Australian entrapment. I thought about paying for the boomerang but then I considered that it didn't come back when I threw it so it was probably broken anyway. If anything I was doing unpaid boomerang testing. Laura didn't entirely agree and thought perhaps my technique was bad, but she'd been in the bathroom at the time so she wasn't really allowed to judge. "Honestly," I said, "boomerangs are made to make people feel inadequate and unloved. They're supposed to come back but they never do. Boomerangs are like bad, disloyal dogs or hot ex-boyfriends who your mom assures you will return after they realize they've made a terrible mistake in leaving you but they totally don't."

"I'm pretty sure boomerangs work," she said, "I've seen them on TV."

"And I've seen cartoon cats eat an entire pan of lasagna in one bite, but that doesn't mean that you wouldn't kill a real-life cat if you force-fed him that much cheese. Trust me. Boomerangs don't work unless you throw them up."

Laura stared at me. "Well, there's your problem."

"No, I mean in the air. Not vomit them up," I explained.

"Ah." She nodded. "I was wondering how that would help."

"*Everything* is a boomerang if you throw it straight up in the air," I explained.

"Not blimps," she countered, with surprising speed considering the number of drinks she'd had.

"Touché," I replied. "I always forget blimps."

Goal Number 6: Just Get Out the Damn House

This sounds absolutely ridiculous; however, leaving my house was the single hardest part of the whole weird trip. For someone who stays home for weeks at a time and struggles to even have a conversation with the UPS guy, saying yes to leaving my safe place was an achievement. And it was worth it. Sometimes you have to force yourself to leave your house even though every introverted bone in your body wants to secede and make you into a human jellyfish. But I pushed through. And it was amazing. And horrifying. And back to amazing. And weird. And baffling. And fantastic.

We saw dangerous blowholes and hopped with wallabies down the beach and played in tide pools and learned Aboriginal dot painting in the outback and snuggled with camels in the desert. Then we watched six Shakespearean actors simultaneously vomit onstage at the Sydney Opera House. (It was on the small stage though. It was only like, three hundred babies long.)

And it was good.

But I still want to lick David Tennant's face.[1] Get to work on that, England. Australia's in the lead here.

---

1. Or share air with him in an elevator. Or pat his hair while he's sleeping. Whatever. I'm not picky.

Voodoo Vagina

Last week my friend (Kim) mailed me one of her homemade, educational felted vaginas (with a small, felted baby inside of it so children can understand where babies come from). My first thought was that I no longer want to understand where babies come from. My second thought was, "Wait . . . is this pubic hair real? Because if it is I think I need to wash my hands. Also, isn't that how voodoo dolls are made? I think if you add human hair to a doll it becomes a voodoo doll so logically wouldn't that make this a voodoo vagina? WHAT IS EVEN HAPPENING HERE?"

(Courtesy of oneclassymotha.com)

I left the vagina on my desk while I went to get my camera to take a picture of it (because no one would ever believe that I'd gotten a voodoo vagina in the mail and they'd be all, "Pics or it didn't happen") but when I got back to my desk MY VAGINA WAS MISSING. I mean not *my* vagina. The gifted vagina. (Not that *my* vagina isn't gifted. It's fine. *This isn't a contest.*)

I was instantly reminded of a story I heard when I was little, about a severed human hand that came to life and gave you wishes but murdered people while doing it. I always thought there could be nothing creepier than a severed hand running around the neighborhood murdering people, until I was faced with the notion that a lone voodoo vagina was skittering around my house. Except that the vagina was oval shaped and had no fingers so it'd have to roll, I guess. Which made it slightly less creepy, but only slightly.

Then I remembered that Hailey was home and I didn't want her to find a random voodoo vagina lying in wait because I'm a good mother, so I had to ask Victor for help "because someone sent me a vagina in the mail but it wandered off while I went to go get a camera and might be on a murderous rampage now." He assumed I'd been drinking, but probably just because he knows how hard it is for me to ask for help.

I clarified that it was an arts-and-crafts vagina designed to show how babies are born but that I think it did have real pubic hair on it and that's why it probably came to life and ran away before I could photograph my friend's vagina. Then Victor shook his head, but instead of shutting his door he came out and helped me go vagina hunting because honestly *when else are you going to have the opportunity to do that?*

Fifteen minutes later we discovered the missing vagina halfway up the stairs, where the cat was chewing on it. I was a little grossed out, but more just concerned about my friend, because if it *was* a voodoo vagina she'd probably just fallen crotch-first into a chipper-shredder.

I had a closer look and realized it was that plastic doll hair you can buy in bags from craft stores and I felt a bit relieved, but Victor said I couldn't keep the vagina even if it wasn't made from pubic hair. This seemed a waste of a perfectly good vagina, but then I noticed that the cat had really torn it up quite a bit and had gnawed off the felt baby's head and so I figured it was a lost cause.

I was worried that the cat had eaten the baby's head and would have a digestive block, but then later we found the head in the toilet. It wasn't really a surprise because that cat loves to carry small things around and then drop them in the toilet. Cat toys, Polly Pockets, Barbie doll heads, lipsticks. They all end up in the toilet if you don't keep the lid shut. It's like her own personal wishing well. I have no idea what the hell she thought she was going to get in return for a baby's head she'd ripped out of a vagina, but regardless she seemed optimistic and mewled sweetly, rubbing against my legs as I peered down into the toilet. I flushed, delivering her small sacrifice to whatever toilet god she was praying to. God knows what she wished for. Probably more felt vaginas.

PS: For some reason people seem to leave this chapter with more questions than they had before they started so let me reiterate that Kim makes these felt, baby-filled vaginas as an educational tool for young children. She calls them Beaver Babies and they now feature "new and improved pubic hair." You can also use them as really gross wallets if you want people to never steal change from you.

PPS: I didn't make a single "pussy" joke in this chapter. Someone get me a damn medal.

The World Needs to Go on a Diet. Literally.

Yesterday my doctor said that I need to lose about twenty pounds to be at "a healthy weight." I really didn't appreciate it because I'd already had quite enough fat-shaming from a dressing room that week. This sounds ridiculous unless you're a woman and then you're probably nodding because you know the struggle.

All dressing rooms are just small cubes of vulnerability with mirrors to help multiply the shame. The worst dressing rooms are the ones that are missing doors for some reason. It's like a nightmare, but real. There was a store in the mall when I was in junior high (back before malls got sad and dangerous) that had open, non-doored dressing stalls that were located all around the edge of the room with a big empty square in the middle, so every other person in the dressing room could witness you not realizing that there was a zipper, or see you with the dress stuck over your head, or sweatily struggling to pull a pair of too-small pants over your hips as you heard an unfortunate ripping sound and hoped that people thought it was just gas.

Even in regular, private dressing rooms clerks inevitably come to your door right when you're most entangled in something and say, "Can I help?" And you say, "*Nope. Doing great!*" in that shaky, high, fake voice that you hope says that you totally *don't* have a shirt stuck around your shoulders. And you know the salesclerks are probably watching you on camera and know that you're stuck, which makes it even more embarrassing. My guess is that several stores probably have entire blooper reels of me falling and breaking things.

I feel almost as bad when I take eight things into a fitting room and none of them fit but I don't want to tell the fitting room attendant that, because "None of these worked" feels like code for "Sorry. I'm fatter than I thought I was." Instead, I give her all but one outfit, which I then put back myself when no one is looking. *Because apparently the opinion of a total stranger who hands plastic numbers to people all day matters to me.* I've tried saying, "These didn't work for me," because then it's like you're putting the blame on the clothes. Like, *these clothes just weren't even trying.* But the downside is that the clerk might offer to help and that's worse because then they start bringing you stuff they think you'd like and it's *never* the right size and by not buying the clothes they suggested it's like you're rejecting them too. It's better though than those stores that only go up to a size ten and I just have to pretend that I came in to look at the scarves and jewelry with all the other curvy women who feel insulted too. Usually it's only an *accidental* insulting, but sometimes it's intentional, like the time the clerk looked at me like I was the Michelin Man and said, "*I don't think we carry your size.*" It felt shitty and *Pretty Woman*-esque, so I explained that I was just there to buy clothes for stray, homeless dogs, because I like to put them in outfits that are warm but not nice enough to steal from a dog. That shut her right up.

I try to love myself exactly the way I am, but it's hard to not feel a *bit* crappy when your doctor is focused on "health" and all that bullshit.

And yes, I might be slightly overweight but I'm pretty sure this isn't entirely *my* fault. It's the world's fault.

Technically, if I were farther away from the center of the Earth then I'd be subjected to less gravity and then I would weigh less. So I'm not really fat. I'm just not high enough. Victor says I sound pretty high already but I suspect he's just being insulting.

But the simple fact is, there's no such thing as *real* weight. Only mass. Weight depends entirely upon the gravity of wherever you are, which is why if you weigh yourself on the top of Mount Everest you'd be closer to outer space and you would weigh slightly less than you would at home. But you'd have to lug a scale up to the top of Mount Everest to prove it, which would suck. Honestly, they should just leave a scale up there for people. Although, maybe they already have one, because who's going to drag a scale back down Mount Everest? That would be crazy. Frankly, I never understood why people climb that thing in the first place, but if there's a scale up there telling you that you're skinnier than you think then I guess I can see the draw. I'd ~~hike~~ helicopter up a mountain for a scale that says I need to eat more. Or for a magic bean that turns me into Jennifer Lawrence. Or for a nice basket of cheeses. Preferably cheddars.

Regardless, on the moon I weigh about as much as a large toaster, so using that logic I'm not overweight. I'm simply *overgravitated*. Spell-check says that I *can't* be "overgravitated" because that isn't a real word and suggested that I probably meant to say that I'm "*overly aggravating.*" Victor says spell-check has a point.

Spell-check and Victor are both dead to me.

Perhaps if people are so concerned with obesity they should just work on making the Earth have less mass so there's less gravity. "*I* need to go on a diet, Dr. Ryker? *I don't think so. I think maybe the fucking **planet** needs to go on a diet.*" Victor says this is a clear case of "deflection" and I agree because I assume "deflection" is something scientific used to deflect mass from Earth and, thus, make us all lighter. Victor says he thinks I don't know what "deflection" means. I think Victor doesn't know what "being supportive" means. (It means letting me lean on him a little when I'm standing on the bathroom scale.) I think this is all pretty commonsense. Victor says it's not at all.

Fuck it. Someone get me a scale.

And a mountain.

And a helicopter.

And some cheeses.

Crazy Like a Reverse Fox

The One Billionth Argument I Had with Victor This Week

Victor accused me of being insane, but really I'm crazy like a fox. But a crazy fox. Not a normal fox that acts crazy but really isn't.

Victor says the whole point of the phrase "crazy like a fox" is pointing out that foxes aren't crazy. But I explained that I'm like a reverse fox. People think I'm crazy and then they realize it's all just a game and I'm super clever. And then they spend a little more time and realize that no, I'm just crazy, but I'm also really lucky because shit still seems to work out for me. I'm crazy like a fox that really has gone insane. Those are the most dangerous foxen.

"I don't think you're listening to me," he said. And then he said something else but I didn't hear it because I was too busy being mad about his accusations. I mean, can you believe this guy? And then I realized that he'd stopped talking and was waiting for a response and I assumed he must've apologized so I said, "I forgive you. But don't let it happen again." Then he yelled some more, probably because he wasn't used to someone being that gracious. He seemed confused, and in my experience, that always makes a man angry at himself.

Some men are like dormant volcanoes, always ready to explode with anger. And also always ready to ejaculate everywhere with little warning. Plus they're often crusty. Metaphorically, I mean. You don't want a man who is literally crusty ejaculating on you. That would be a safety hazard and is probably how plague is spread. But my original point is that some seemingly quiet men anger easily. (Sorry. That metaphor got away from me a bit. I'd fix it but this is what editors are for.)

Winner: Everyone who isn't my editor. Also, foxen, because no one knows what the hell is going on with them so no one expects anything special from them. Lucky little bastards.

An Essay on Parsley, Wasabi, Cream Cheese, and Soup

(Side note: I had writer's block so I got very drunk and when I sobered up I found that I'd written an essay on parsley, wasabi, cream cheese, and soup. I assure you, I was just as bewildered as you, but I decided to leave it in because at this point drunk me writes much better than sober me. She is *such* an asshole.)

Parsley

I'm not a fan.

No one ever really eats it and it just ends up on plates as a sort of symbolic bookmark that says you're going to pay 25 percent more for this meal than expected. I don't even think it's edible and I'm pretty sure melted parsley is how plastic is made. In fact, I suspect there are actually no more than one thousand pieces of parsley in the world and chefs just keep reusing them over and over.

Maybe it keeps showing up on our plates because we don't eat it. Perhaps chefs are continuing to serve it night after night as punishment, much like when your mom served you the reheated lima beans you refused to eat for three straight evenings until you finally forced them down and then vomited on your plate, ruining lima beans for everyone in the vicinity.

It's not our fault though. From our earliest night out we're taught two things: That's butter, not ice cream. And that's parsley, don't eat it.

Although, now that I think about it, you hardly ever see parsley anymore. Maybe it's because we eat less American food nowadays. Instead, parsley has been replaced by that huge mound of wasabi served with the tiniest sushi roll.

Wasabi

You never finish it.

No one ever finishes it.

Have you ever seen anyone ask for a refill on wasabi? *No.* It always ends up back in the kitchen with the chef, where he probably just adds it back to the huge Play-Doh ball on the counter.

It's probably made of parsley.

Cream Cheese

If cream cheese is cream made out of cheese then why isn't face cream made out of face?

Or wait. Maybe it is.

Maybe I'm just slathering new bits of face skin into my wrinkles. Which is pretty brilliant. They probably get the skin from the microdermabrasion places and recycled Bioré skin strips. What a bunch of tricky bastards. Stripping off our own skin and then selling it back to us. It's almost as insulting as pulling fat out of your ass and injecting it into your lips. Which is totally a real thing that exists and is a pretty good sign that civilization is collapsing. This is exactly why I'm not a fan of forced kissing of your great-aunt. You might be *literally* kissing her ass. Sort of. I'm not really sure what "literally" means in this scenario. Is it still literally your ass if your ass is in your lips? These are the things they never teach you in journalism school.

Soup

I once went to a dinner party where waiters walked around with canapés, which I think is French for "hors d'oeuvres." Which is also French, now that I think about it. Apparently the French are really into small food, which sort of makes sense because they're very thin. That girl in *Amélie* is so tiny I could fit her in my vagina. *Not that I would.* I would have said "pocket" but I don't have a pocket in this dress. But I *do* have a vagina and that's sort of like a pocket, although not one you should store paper money in. Or coins, probably. I guess it depends on how strong your vaginal muscles are. More power to you if you can keep a roll of nickels up there. *My hat is off to you, my friend.*

But enough about your braggy, powerful vagina. I was talking about canapés. I can never eat them because I'm dangerously lactose intolerant and I'm always afraid there will be some sort of cream hidden in there that will send me to the hospital, but what sucks is that the waiters keep walking around asking you over and over if you want a canapé *now* even though I just said two minutes ago that I couldn't eat them, and now it's like they're just taunting me with food I can't have. I recently fixed that problem though because I realized that the secret to not having to continually say no to delicious food is to loudly say, "No. Sorry, I can't eat that BECAUSE DIARRHEA." It's jarring for the people around you, but I've found that most waiters continually ask if you want food not because they really want you to eat, but because they've zoned out or are high (I'm basing that on my personal experience in food service so stop judging me. Unless you're judging me for being high, in which case, *fair game*) and they've already forgotten who said no. But *no one* forgets diarrhea. "BECAUSE DIARRHEA" will make *all* the waiters perk up and avoid you completely. So will a lot of the people at dinner parties, but those are the risks of diarrhea.

One time I was at a patio party where I heard they were handing out *soup* as an hors d'oeuvre and I wondered how that was even possible and then I saw that the waiters were walking around handing out large, flat-bottomed spoons filled with a single bite of soup. Personally I think that whole concept is kinda fucked up regardless of who you are and what you're allergic to. Soup given to you one spoonful at a time by people in fancy tuxedos is *pretty much* the definition of "overprivileged what-the-fuckery" and I'm pretty sure it was invented by intoxicated food-service people who thought it would be funny to see if people would actually fall for such shenanigans. I suspect the next step is crackers that have been premoistened by your waiter's saliva and then fed to you from his mouth into yours like you're a baby bird. In fact, by the time this book is out, spit crackers will probably be the next big thing, and I want it noted that *I called it.*

And it wasn't even *warm* soup that they were serving. It was gazpacho, which I tried once and is basically what you call tomato soup once it's gone so cold that you just give up and try to pass it off as a nonalcoholic, tomato Bellini. Or a melty soup-Popsicle. *A soupsicle.* Still, everyone at the party tried it because no one wants to admit that gazpacho tastes like partially melted tomato ice cream. The problem was that by the time they swallowed their spoonful of soupsicle the waiter was gone, causing all of them to stand in their elegant attire while awkwardly holding a dirty spoon like a terrible, unwanted accessory. Some people laid their empty spoons on windowsills or on the ground when they thought no one was looking, but most just looked with quiet desperation for a waiter who might never return and were forced to hold the

spoons at their sides, seemingly pretending that the spoons were cigarettes or small fancy dogs.

I saw one woman look around expectantly for a minute and when
she realized no one was coming back for the spoon she just shrugged
and tossed it in the pool. It seemed slightly bitchy, but you have to respect that level of *I-have-no-fucks-left-to-give-about-silverware-that-
doesn't-even-belong-to-me*. With that one spoon drop she told everyone
at the party, "If *you* aren't going to take care of your shit then *I'm* sure
as hell not going to take responsibility for it."

That's when I decided I adored that woman *and* her attitude. I'd
probably feel differently if I was a foundling left on her doorstep, but I
was not. I was a woman who had just seen another woman pass the spoon
test, *a test I didn't even know existed and that no one else had studied for.*
And it was then that I vowed to *never* take personal responsibility for
other people's spoons/attitudes/stupidity, because frankly I have enough
to worry about with my own shit. I suspect this is one of those life lessons
that no one ever really gets to use, but still, I'm ready.

Just *try* to hand me a spoon.

PS: I just read my friend Karen this chapter and she liked it very much
but she interrupted me at one point and said, "**Hang on.** You can't say
you would put the girl from *Amélie* in your vagina," and I said, "I agree. I
said I *could*. Not that I *would*. She'd suffocate in there and she's France's
national treasure." Then Karen said, "You need to take out the vagina,"
and I was all, "In public? I almost never take out my vagina in public.
Are you drunk right now?" and she said, "Jenny, seriously, you have
to cut out your vagina part," and I flinched a little at her wording but then
she explained that I should take out the vaginas because men read my
books too and I said, "Karen, men *love* vaginas. They can't get enough of
them. And even men who don't prefer them came from them. Vaginas are
like home. A sort of clammy one." Then she flinched at my phrasing and

pointed out that not all men love vagina stories and that her father was going to read this book and might get a bit offended and so I told her that I'd add a small note apologizing to her father for my vagina. It is *shocking* how often I have to do this. I suspect it's just one of those things writers get used to.

PPS: I'm so, so sorry about my vagina. It's weird how often I have to say that. Honestly, I should just put it on a T-shirt.

And Then I Got Three Dead Cats in the Mail

*Conversation I had with my friend Maile. (It's pronounced Miley. Like Miley Cyrus. Except that she had the name before Miley Cyrus. She would like me to point that out. She was born **way** before Miley Cyrus was. She would like me to take out that last sentence.)*

ME: Guess what I got in the mail yesterday?

MAILE: Something gross.

ME: *OH MY GOD, HOW DID YOU DO THAT?*

MAILE: I'm psychic. *Plus, I've met you.* So, what did you get in the mail yesterday?

ME: A bunch of dead cats.

MAILE: Hmm. Taxidermied?

ME: No.

MAILE: Oh. *Fuck.*

ME: *Right?*

MAILE: You got some dead, rotting cats in the mail?

ME: Well, they aren't rotting. All of the insides were squished out so they're like cat . . . *sleeves?*

MAILE: Who would send you cat sleeves?

ME: There was no note. They were just in a grocery sack.

MAILE: *And the mystery deepens.*

ME: I *did* have an e-mail conversation last month with this woman who said she had some cat skins she wanted to send me but—

MAILE: And the mystery is solved. *Because it was never a mystery to begin with.* It was just you not giving me enough information. Because you are terrible at telling stories.

ME: Well, not exactly, because the lady said that she had these totally ethically achieved dead cats—

MAILE: *Stop.* That's not a thing.

ME: No, seriously. She said that she worked at this vet hospital but when they had cats that were already run over or had to be put down because they were cancerous they would have all of these dead cats left over that no one ever claimed and they didn't want to just *waste them* so they sold the insides to vet schools—so they could dissect them—but then they had all this fur left over, so they tanned them and used them as packaging material when they needed to mail stuff.

MAILE: They used dead cats as packing peanuts? That's disgusting. What were they shipping . . . *human torsos?*

ME: Technically it's sort of eco-green in kind of the grossest way ever. Anyway, she said she wanted to make me some kitten mittens because of the time that I wrote about them.

MAILE: Wait . . . why would kittens need mittens?

ME: No. Mittens *made out of kittens.* You know. For the homeless.

MAILE: I already regret asking this, but . . . *what in the fuck are you talking about?*

ME: A couple of years ago I came up with this idea to repurpose used breast pumps to suck dead kittens inside out because then . . . TA-DA! . . . *fur-lined mittens for homeless people.* I told my friend Kregg about it and he was all, "That's . . . weird," and I'm all, "*It's weird that no one's ever thought of it before.* Because no one wants dead kittens *or* used breast pumps so this way we'd be keeping them both out of the landfills **and** we'd be helping the homeless. *It's practically carbon zero!*" And then Kregg mentioned something about PETA and firebombs and I was all, "I'd only use kittens that were already dead from noncommunicable diseases, *Kregg.* I wouldn't just go around haphazardly turning *live* kittens inside out. I'm not a monster, for

God's sake." Frankly I'm a little insulted I even had to clarify that. I'm
doing this to help the homeless. Not for my own *personal* kitten-mitten
collection. I mean, I live in Texas. I don't even *need* mittens.

MAILE: Wow. You are so . . . altruistic.

ME: *Exactly.* So I was expecting a pair of ethically made kitten mittens
in the mail, but then I just got these skinned, untailored cats instead . . .
and *here's the weird thing* . . . there are three of them.

MAILE: The weird thing about you getting a bunch of dead cats in the
mail is the number of them?

ME: Yes, because I have two hands . . . *and three cats to put on them.*
What is that implying?

MAILE: Maybe they're supposed to be leg warmers.

ME: I don't have three legs, Maile.

MAILE: Maybe it's two leg warmers and a penis cozy.

ME: I don't have a—ARE YOU EVEN LISTENING TO ME?

MAILE: *Are you listening to yourself?* You want to use dead kittens for
leg warmers. I shouldn't be the one getting defensive here.

ME: Touché.

MAILE: How do you even get "ethically skinned" cats?

ME: Well, there's more than one way to skin a cat.

MAILE: I'm going to pretend you never said that.

ME: Are you kidding? I've been waiting this whole conversation to use that joke.

MAILE: I know. And I'm still your friend in spite of it.

ME: OH MY GOD. It just dawned on me. I have three cats and I have three ethically skinned dead cats. HALLOWEEN COSTUMES FOR CATS.

MAILE: Who could go as . . . ?

ME: . . . Different cats?

MAILE: That's a *terrible* costume.

ME: The skins are long and thin. Maybe I could use them as wine koozies.

MAILE: And there was no note?

ME: Nope. Just three dead cats in a grocery sack.

MAILE: Canvas or plastic?

ME: Plastic.

MAILE: Well *that's* no good for the environment. I'm pretty sure that woman was lying to you and she's just trying to hide her crimes against humanity.

ME: Technically they're crimes against cats. *Catmanity.*

MAILE: I don't think that's a word. It sounds like what you'd get if you crossbred a cat and a manatee.

ME: OR? *IF YOU PUT A CAT SUIT ON A SMALL MANATEE.*

MAILE: I think you're looking for clues that aren't there.

ME: I HAVE A BAG FULL OF DEAD CATS. I CAN'T BE EX-PECTED TO THINK LOGICALLY. *Do you think that woman was thinking logically when she sent me a box of dead cats?* You've got to *think* like a serial killer to *catch* a serial killer, Maile.

MAILE: You think she's a serial killer?

ME: No. It was a bad analogy. I just meant you have to think like a cat skinner to figure out why you have three cat skins in your garage.

MAILE: Why are they in your garage?

ME: I should keep them in the house? Way to scare the shit out of my cats, bad cat mom. That would be like if you brought home the skins of young children and let your kids see them. Although the cats might take me more seriously when I tell them to stop peeing on the couch if they saw a skinned cat lying around. *OH MY GOD, I could totally put one on the couch that Ferris Mewler keeps peeing on and then I'd be like, "YEAH, FERRIS. THAT'S WHAT HAPPENED TO THE LAST CAT WHO PEED HERE."*

MAILE: Is that why your cat keeps glaring at me? Am I sitting on the pee couch?

ME: Just because you mark it doesn't mean that you own it, Ferris. Stop with the glaring.

MAILE: Ew.

ME: Don't worry. It's been cleaned. And I know what you're thinking. You're thinking that Ferris would be like, "All the cats are accounted for and I've lived here since the beginning of time. I'm not falling for that," but here's the deal: *cats have terrible memories.* Ferris can't even remember where the litter box is. *Apparently.*

MAILE: Actually I'm just thinking that I'd like to move to another couch.

PS: I just went into the garage to find the dead-cat skins so I could include a photo in the book but now I CAN'T FIND THEM. I told Victor I lost some cats in the garage and he was all, *"You lost our cats in the garage?"* and I was like, "Of course not. How could I lose all three of our cats in the garage? That would make me an irresponsible mother. These cats are already dead." Then Victor and I had a fight about whether it was *more* or *less* irresponsible to lose dead cats, and I won because THESE MOTHERFUCKERS AREN'T GETTING ANY LESS DEAD, VICTOR. Then I called our maid service and told them that instead of cleaning the bathrooms this month I'd prefer for them to just go through our garage and look for dead cats and then the manager called me to tell me that "Merry Maids doesn't look for dead cats." They also don't do windows. I'm not even sure why we have maid service anymore.

Things I May Have Accidentally Said During Uncomfortable Silences

When I worked in human resources we used a technique to get people to admit when they'd fucked up, and it worked so well that people would often confess to things that might not even have been true.

Here's how it works:

You invite the person in, and after having them sit down you just stare at them expectantly and force yourself to say nothing. Most non-sociopaths have problems with awkward silences and they will fill those silences with incriminating details about whatever it is they assume they're in HR for. I'm not sure if this technique has a name but I called it "Making-out-with-Alan-Rickman-in-my-mind" because that's what I usually did during the awkward silences. Regardless, Alan Rickman and I solved a *lot* of cold cases in HR.

This same technique is used in homicide investigations and by a number of psychiatrists, including my own. I suspect my shrink uses it to get me to admit repressed memories or abuse, but I'm just naturally mentally ill and so instead I end up with rambling non sequiturs that do nothing but affirm that I am not in a psychiatrist's office by accident.

Things I May Have Found Myself Saying to My Psychiatrist After Brief Awkward Pauses

"I'm having one of those weeks where I just want to rip off my clothes and lie in the street. Is that a medical condition? Because it feels like it."

"I can taste things with my eyes. Stuff like eye ointment, I mean. I don't taste solid food with my eyeballs. *That would be crazy.* But I probably could if I wanted to. Shit. *What a terrible superpower.*"

"I need to find a skilled arsonist. I don't necessarily want to burn anything down. I just want to have the option. I need an arsonist on retainer. I'm pretty sure that's legal as long as I don't use it."

"Yesterday I found out that Barack Obama isn't *actually* on Twitter. Honestly, I feel betrayed. This is like when Clinton fucked that girl with a cigar. Except worse."

"My primary thoughts during the holidays are 'Stab. Stab. Stab. Run away.'"

"I'm mad at everyone who never told me about House of Pies."

"I spent last night cleaning up nine-year-old vomit. The vomit of a nine-year-old, that is. Not vomit that's nine years old. I'm not *that* bad at housekeeping."

"I'm having one of those rare days where I love people and all of the amazing wonder they're capable of and if someone fucks that up for me I will stab them right in the face."

"Victor hates Christmas. He says that the problem with nativity scenes is that there aren't enough samurais in them."

"I finished the Bible last night. Spoiler alert: Jesus doesn't make it. Or maybe he does, now that I think about it. I may have stopped reading too soon. In my defense though it was getting really depressing. Honestly, that book is my Waterloo. But I guess *technically* Jesus didn't die. He just faked it. Or maybe it was a dream sequence. Or possibly he's a zombie or something? But it's confusing because Jesus died for our sins but God didn't accept his death, so does that mean that our sins are still all outstanding? And when I say 'outstanding' I mean that they're like . . . still on the books. Not like 'AWESOME! THOSE SINS ARE OUTSTANDING!' Some people think stuff like that is sacrilegious but I'm pretty sure Jesus would think this shit was hilarious. Plus we could bond over how shitty it is to have your birthday so close to Christmas."

"I hate it when it's too hot for a blanket because I have this phobia that I'll float up onto the ceiling without it and then I'll get chopped up by the ceiling fan. That's totally normal, right?"

"I mispronounced my own middle name until I was twenty-two. It's Leigh. I pronounced it 'Leia.' *Like the princess.* I also purposely mispronounced my last name from sixth grade on because it was Dusek and the Czech pronunciation had it start with 'Douche.' I might "have gotten away with it but my sister and my mom (the lunch lady) pronounced it correctly. I told everyone at school that they just had lisps."

"I saw Anne Frank trending on Twitter and I thought she'd died. *Again.* Turns out it was the person who found her diary that died.

She's fine. And by 'fine' I mean 'still dead.' Not that I think that it's fine that she's dead. I just think it's fine that she's not back from the dead. No one needs an Anne Frank zombie."

"On the way in here I saw a cloud that looked like a skull. My first thought? *Death Eaters.*"

"How am I feeling? I'm sort of in the mood to feel righteously indignant but I don't have anything worth getting indignant about. I guess I'm mad that people aren't stupider when I need them to be."

"Is it normal to regret *not* making a sex tape back when you were younger and your boobs still pointed vaguely at the ceiling when you were lying on your back? Because I feel like no one ever talks about that."

"Why do they call them 'map colors' instead of 'colored pencils'? *Who colors maps? Who buys black-and-white maps?* Why doesn't anyone ever answer my questions?"

To her credit, my psychiatrist almost never seems shocked or surprised and usually just follows up with a calm "And how does that make you feel?" or "Tell me more." To her discredit, she's probably just thinking about making out with Alan Rickman and isn't paying any attention to what I'm saying at all. I've considered testing this by admitting to murdering my neighbors and burying them in my basement, but I haven't actually done this because a tiny part of my mind is worried that maybe I *have* murdered my neighbors and buried them in my basement. It's doubtful though because I don't even have a basement, so it would be easy to prove my innocence if my doctor was actually listening. Unless I really do have a basement and I've just repressed it to save my brain from remembering all the dead people I've buried there. So basically I can't test my doctor to see if she's imagining Alan Rickman naked because it's possible that the basement I don't have is filled with people I don't remember murdering. And this is exactly the kind of thing that I should bring up in therapy. Right after I make sure we don't have a basement.

My Skeleton Is Potaterrific

When I was in junior high most of the girls in my class were focused on the Three P's: popular, pretty, and petite. It was obvious I had no chance at succeeding at any of these so I considered creating my own Three P's. I'd inadvertently cornered the market on "peculiar" but I couldn't think of any other good "P" words.

My mom suggested "papillose," which means "possessing nipples," but I thought this was aiming rather low, even for me. She offered up "palmiped" (web-footed) and said if my dad glued my toes together in his taxidermy shop no one would ever suspect it was fake. Probably because most people don't intentionally fake having webbed toes. She also offered "pecorous" (full of cows) and "potaterrific," which isn't even a real word but "is great fun to say." (And it is. Say it. *Potaterrific.* It's awesome.) Then I gave up, but not before making a mental note that my mom is fairly unhelpful at superficial popularity advice, and incredibly dangerous at Scrabble.

When I was in eighth grade all of the popular girls in my class had an exclusive slumber party weekend, and a few weeks later they all ended up with scabies. If you don't know what scabies are you should just stop reading here because it's so gross you're going to want to burn your house down. Scabies are tiny creatures that burrow under your skin, lay eggs, and set up camp *inside your flesh.* They make lice look like a summer breeze, and the same infection in animals causes mange. You'd think all the cool kids getting infested with flesh-eating parasites would be a great equalizer, but most of them wore it as an outward sign of having attended an exclusive event where the party favors happened to be real-life cooties. Suddenly bug infestations were the new friendship bracelet and some people even took to *pretending* to have scabies in order to fit in with the cool kids. People were *literally* bragging about internal bug infestations THAT THEY *DIDN'T. EVEN. HAVE.*

And that's when I realized that popularity is a big bunch of bullshit.

Recognizing that popularity is sometimes the equivalent of human mange sort of cured me from wanting it. But I still struggled with the other P's: petite and pretty. I'm okay to look at but there's nothing particularly striking about me. Growing up, my little sister was golden haired and blue eyed, and perfect strangers always said she looked "angelic" and jokingly threatened to kidnap her. (Which is a weird joke and one that you people need to stop making. It's on par with "I just want to eat you up," which is a lot like "Just looking at you is turning me into a raging cannibal." Please stop that. It's creepy.) I, on the other hand, was continually being told, "You look *just* like your father" (a large, intimidating, and heavily bearded man usually covered in blood).

The thing I hear most often now is *"Don't I know you?"*

You don't.

I just have that kind of face. This was especially shitty in college when I was forever being mistaken for another girl on campus who apparently looked just like me and had a similar first name. I never met her but she was apparently quite well-known, and strangers would smile and wave and ask me if I had a cigarette. I'd explain, "That's not me. I don't even smoke. You're thinking of another girl who looks just like me," and then the stranger would think I was fucking with him or was just really selfish with my cigarettes. I was sometimes a little jealous of this other, more dangerous me who was always getting high fives for stealing frat mascots and winning at drinking games while the real me was buried deep in the library. But then the other me started sleeping with married men and selling drugs. I wanted to find other-me, shake her, and say, "You have to stop this. *This isn't us*," but I never ran into her. I did, however, run into several angry, accusing people whom she'd wronged and who never believed that I wasn't me, and I sort of resented my doppelgänger for pulling me into her mess. Eventually I decided to take matters into my own hands, telling strangers who insisted they'd had a drunken hookup with me that they should get tested for a particularly virulent strain of herpes. Random people would stop me on the sidewalk to quietly ask if I was "holding" and I'd tell them that new regulations stated that I had to inform them that I *may or may not* be an undercover cop and then I'd ask them exactly what they wanted. "*YOU HAVE TO TALK LOUDLY SO THAT THE MICROPHONE PICKS IT UP*," I'd enunciate slowly, pointing to my chest as they quickly walked away. I heard that the other me moved the next semester (possibly because of those baffling herpes/undercover cop rumors she may have kept hearing about herself) and I never saw her, which was sad because it would have been interesting to see if the other me looked as nondescript as I do. Although now that I think about it, I probably saw other-me all the time and just never even noticed her.

I try not to get caught up in appearance issues though because my grandmother always used to say, "It's what's inside that counts." And that's probably true because with my luck my best feature would be hidden *deep, deep* inside my body. I suspect my best feature is my skeleton, which is a shame because it might be the most elegant and hauntingly graceful skeleton ever but I'll never get complimented on it while I'm still fleshy enough to appreciate it. That's why I'd like people to say "Nice skeleton" to me now. Just give me the benefit of the doubt, you know?

I've started handing out similar compliments to strangers, but not about their skeletons, because that would seem disingenuous or even sarcastic since I'm already pretty sure I have the sexiest skeleton ever. It's dead sexy. See what I just did there? I credit my skeleton with that joke. Clever *and* beautiful. No, instead I say things like "I'd wager you have an exquisite pancreas." Or "I bet your tendons are *fantastic*." People are usually so overwhelmed that they move away very quickly or tell me they don't have any money on them. No one is ever prepared to accept compliments from strangers about their internal organs, which just goes to show how seldom we compliment them.

Souls are sort of the exception to the rule here. People are always complimenting "old souls" or "beautiful souls" or "unblemished souls," but that seems like a cop-out because souls are totally invisible and never end up in bathing suit competitions. Still, people are super-focused on souls, always trying to win them over for their particular god or sacrificing them to volcanoes or gambling them to win golden fiddles from the devil. I mean, souls are fine but they're a bit overrated. Like clavicles. Or the ability to roll your tongue. They're important but we're ignoring a lot of other parts that are probably just as compliment-worthy and sexy because we're too busy complimenting firm pecs and thin waists and untarnished souls. Branch out a little, is all I'm saying. It couldn't hurt. I bet your small intestines are *adorable*.

Of course, now that I've written about how awesome my insides are I realize I've just made my eventual skeleton incredibly tantalizing to grave robbers and so now I'm going to have to make booby traps to protect my dead body. Like maybe I should plan to get buried in a coffin full of glitter because that way if anyone in the future digs me up they'll be like, "What the fuck? Is that *glitter*? That shit *never* goes away. Fuck that noise. Let's just rob the guy next to her." (*Sorry, Victor.*) That's how I'd keep grave robbers out. And if I get cremated I'll have the undertaker leave my ashes way at the bottom of my glitter-filled coffin so even if someone does decide to dig in they won't find me until they're beard-deep in glitter. And then there'll be a note in my ashes that says, "*AND THAT'S WHAT HAPPENS WHEN YOU ROB GRAVES, MOTHERFUCKER.*" Or maybe I'll put a smaller coffin in my coffin and a smaller one in there and it'll keep going like Russian nesting dolls and in the smallest coffin would be a sealed envelope covered in tiny specks and a slip of paper that says, "*Congratulations. Now you've got scabies.*" It'll be like when your parents give you the biggest present at Christmas but you unwrap it and there's a smaller present inside and that keeps happening until you have a mountain of wrapping paper, some new socks, and a lot of unresolved anger. And that's exactly what it's going to be like when people try to disturb my corpse. Except instead of new socks they'll get glitter and scabies. *Worst. Christmas. Ever.*

I've tried many torturous techniques to make my outsides fit the ridiculous standards society has set but it never ends well because my body lives in reality and it's a reality that has too much cheese in it.

"I blame Photoshop," my friend Maile once told me. "I use Photoshop to make my waist smaller and my neck longer and then I feel like I need to make those things happen in real life so that people on the Internet don't see me tagged in a non-touched-up picture and say, '*Oh my God, what happened to you?*' And then I have to pretend I've been in a fire or something."

"Photoshop is a terrible enabler," I agreed. "I always make myself thinner and my hair less awful if I publish my picture online. And then I want to Photoshop someone else's upper arms over mine, and soften my knee cellulite, and Photoshop a less-covered-in-cat-fur outfit onto me. It would be easier to just say 'Fuck it' and Photoshop a cat falling out of a window on top of my body and then be like, 'Yep. Perfect selfie. This shit is done. *PUBLISH.*'"

I shared my grandmother's platitude about what's inside counting more than what's outside and Maile raised her eyebrows in appraisal. "I never thought of it that way," she said. "Maybe my uterus is *stunning.*"

"I bet it's magnificent. You've made some of my favorite people in there."

Maile nodded. "I should do a live webcam of my uterus and call it *What's Up Maile?*"

I wasn't sure it would play on prime time but it'd probably be more redeeming than the Kardashians.

I'd recently been to a spa that offered wrinkle removals but I'd just read that some places use dead people's donated skin to fill in wrinkles, which is insulting because it's like saying, "You look so awful that we think injecting dead people into your face might be an improvement." Although now that I'm thinking about it, I bet the donated skin is only helpful when it's pulled off of a young and still collagen-filled corpse, which seems a little like bathing in the blood of virgins, but with less blood and more injections.

Where does the skin come from? What if it's penis skin? Or ball-sack skin? No one wants the skin of someone's nut sack injected into their lip wrinkles. In fact, when I see heavily cosmetically altered people my first thought is "I wonder how much of their face is genitals?" My second thought is that they probably got their corpse skin from grave robbers. That's why I told Victor to leave a warning in my coffin of scabie-glitter telling potential robbers not to inject my corpse into rich old people's faces. Then Victor said that he was going to put a lock on his office door since I apparently didn't understand what was or wasn't acceptable to say while he was on a conference call.

This isn't to say that I'm completely averse to cosmetic surgery or even that I've never had it before. Victor recently found a picture labeled "Jenny, age seven. *After the procedure.*" I was unconscious and I had an enormous cast on my head.

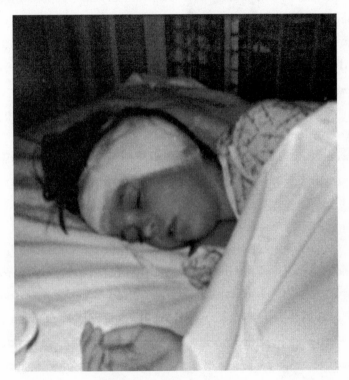

(*Courtesy of Nelda Dusek*)

"*What in the hell happened to you?*" he asked. "And are those *metal bars on the windows?*"

I leaned over to glance at the photo. "I think the bars were on the hospital bed to keep me from falling out. I was always falling out of beds at that age."

He stared at the giant brain cast, and then at me, and then nodded to himself. "This explains *so* much," he whispered.

It looks worse than it really was. The doctor who did my tonsillectomy decided that since I was already under anesthesia they should fix the wonky ear I'd been born with. I suspect it was not his area of expertise and that he was just bored or high and thought, "Hang on, I wanna try something," because I woke up to a misshapen head cast where giant bushels of hair stuck out in awkward clumps. I looked like if a drunken child tried to make a papier-mâché hat on an angry Snuffle-upagus. A week later they removed the cast, some of my hair, and what little dignity I had left. My ear looked *exactly* the same as before, so the doctor told me to sleep with a headband over my ear for the next year because that would work just like a retainer. And it absolutely did if the point of retainers is not to work at all.

Twenty years later I tried elective surgery again when I got tired of wearing glasses and decided to get laser eye surgery. The clinic tried to up-sell me on what they referred to as "superhuman eyesight" but I told them that I wouldn't want to be able to see through clothes because that would really ruin Thanksgiving dinners for me. They explained that it just meant that I'd have better than twenty-twenty vision but it was too expensive and honestly I prefer things a little soft and fuzzy around the edges. The world always looks nicer when it's a little blurry—that's why so many of us have a second glass of wine at dinner.

The eye surgery was fine except that they used an older suction tool that made me go temporarily blind in whatever eye they were working on, which was unsettling.

"THIS IS THE OPPOSITE OF WHAT I WANT," I may have screamed during the procedure.

Apparently it was a rarish reaction so they don't warn people of it beforehand. Also, I was like, "You guys? I smell something burning." And then I realized it was me. The doctor later explained that it was the smell of a chemical reaction, which just happens to smell *exactly* like burning flesh. And this is why I don't trust doctors anymore. That and the ear thing.

Still, the eye surgery mostly worked and I got to stop wearing glasses for several years until my eyes got all shitty again. That happens. You expect that you're fixed forever but your eyesight continues to fade as you get older, which ends up being a nice coincidence because the older you get the less clearly you want to see yourself in the mirror.

A few weeks ago my friend Brooke Shaden came to take my photograph. She was set to do it a few years ago but I was always sure I'd be thinner the next month and so I kept procrastinating and putting it off until Brooke eventually decided to just come to me. She's one of my favorite photographers. Her work is dark and unsettling and beautiful and I imagined the photo shoot would be glamorous and insightful. And it was at least half of those things.

We drove to a swamp where I wore a thrift-store evening gown and a cape made out of a tablecloth. Brooke wanted me to sit on a tree branch that was several feet above my head. Victor and Hailey had come along for the ride so Victor decided to grab my feet and throw me into the tree, which actually worked. But then when it was time to come back down I was totally stuck. Victor suggested that I step into his clasped hands and then fall over onto him, but apparently I wasn't doing it right because Victor kept grunting and yelling, *"Just fall into me, Jenny."* I said, "I *AM* FALLING," and he said, "NO, YOU'RE JUST CROUCHING ON MY HANDS. *FALL ONTO ME*," and I was like, *"I'M FALLING AS HARD AS I CAN, VICTOR,"* and he yelled, "YOU'RE NOT FALLING RIGHT," and I said, "FALLING IS THE *ONLY* THING I CAN DO RIGHT. *I CAN'T FALL ANY BETTER THAN THIS,"* and then Hailey yelled, "YOU GUYS, I FOUND A KITTY," and that was disconcerting because we were in a swamp and most swamp kitties end up being rabid skunks. But it was good timing because it caught me off guard and I fell across Victor's shoulder. Unfortunately, the pressure of Victor's shoulder was like being punched in the stomach and caused me to fart extraordinarily loudly.

And that was me: farting and screaming and flailing upside down and grabbing on to the back of Victor's pants to prop myself up so I could frantically scan the swamp for diseased skunks. I'm not sure I have the words to describe that moment but if there's a word that means the exact opposite of "ladylike," that would be a good start. It was mortifying but Brooke smiled widely and said it was perfect because she thought she'd captured my essence. Victor volunteered that it would have been hard to *avoid* my essence but I'm pretty sure he was making a cheap fart joke.

A week later Brooke finished my portrait, a photograph of me as the oxymoronic Bluebird of Happiness, locked in my cage but still blithely optimistic even as dark clouds swept around me.

It was me, with all my bumps and wrinkles, and even a hint of my wonky ear. And it wasn't pretty. It was *better* than pretty.

It was goddamn *potaterrific*.

(Courtesy of Brooke Shaden)

It's Called "Catouflage"

For the past several months I've been getting these giant goose-egg bumps on my head. I called my sister (who was an EMT for several years) to ask if she thought they were cancer. Lisa sighed and said I needed to stop thinking everything was cancer, as it was more likely that the bumps were silent twins I'd absorbed in the womb who were just now starting to sprout into new heads who, she hoped, would not inherit my habit of calling her at three a.m. to ask if they had cancer. Then she hung up because she has a terrible bedside manner. Or maybe her EMT license had expired and she wasn't allowed to diagnose cancer over the phone anymore. I don't know. I sort of preferred the job she had before she was an EMT, when she was a professional clown, because she always had candy in her pockets and if I was sad she'd make me a balloon poodle.

The bumps would appear almost overnight. They were the size of itchy half-golf balls and eventually turned into smaller bumps, which I assumed were hives from my anxiety disorder. My shrink agreed but suggested I visit the dermatologist next door just to make sure it wasn't something more serious.

A few days later I went in for the exam and the doctor glanced at my scalp and said, rather dismissively, "Oh, that's just a folliculitis staph infection." Then I stared at him and he explained, "Your rheumatoid arthritis is an autoimmune disease, which makes you more likely to get infections like this. Take these pills." I explained that I was concerned because I'd always heard that staph could be super deadly but he said, "You'll be fine. It's like acne, but on your scalp. No one ever died from acne."

I thought he was being awfully nonchalant and he thought I was overreacting. I pointed out that he had just told me I have a staph infection spreading toward my brain, and he was all, *"Where are you getting this from? You have a rash on your head,"* and I clarified that my brain lives in my head, and I was a little concerned that I had to point that out since *he's* the one who's supposed to be the doctor. Then he shook his head in almost the same way Victor does, told me to stay off the Internet, and walked out of the room to call in my prescription. Of course, I immediately pulled out my phone to see what he was so afraid of my looking up because I'm pretty sure "Stay off the Internet" is code for "I fucking *dare* you to Google that shit."

"This is a terribly lazy way to tell me I'm dying," I thought.

When the doctor returned I showed him my phone accusingly and asked him why he was prescribing medication that treated "malaria, anthrax, and cholera." He told me that was *exactly* why he didn't want me on the Internet and pointed out that this specific medication was also used for treating acne. And he's right, but it's still disconcerting. It's like taking a pill for a stubbed toe that also cures the plague and grows back missing arms. I was getting mixed messages. Was this a serious medical affliction that I should be getting pity and bed rest for, or was it nothing? He assured me it was *"mostly* nothing" and told me to take the malaria pills twice a day. Then I showed him a weird bump I've had on my leg for the last eight years and he said, "Yeah, that's just a bump," and then I started to question whether this man was even a real doctor.

Regardless, it is nice to hear "No, it's not cancer" and I suppose it's also nice not to have to worry about picking up malaria, even though it wasn't really a worry I had before this appointment.

The most unsettling part of the visit, however, came when the doctor casually asked if I'd ever considered having any work done, as they were having a special on Botox. Then I stabbed him in the knee with a pen. But just in my mind, because you can never find a pen when you really need one. In reality I just told him that I wasn't a fan of paying money to inject paralyzing poison into my face and that I was actually quite proud of my laugh lines, which I view as a badge that tells people I'm not an asshole. He countered that it was really the frown line between my eyebrows that he'd focus on. I pointed out that I'd gone through a *lot* of living to get that frowny wrinkle and I wasn't about to erase it now.

"MY HUSBAND *MADE* THAT LINE," I said, with a defensiveness that surprised even me. "This line represents every time I have ever argued with him about everything in the damn world. It's a line that says, 'Don't cross me or I will cut you.' It's practically a medal for time served *and I EARNED IT.*"

He nodded (surprisingly easily) and went back to filling out my chart.

"But," I admitted, "I *would* be okay with you taking that weird bump off my leg. I don't have any personal relationship with that bump." He looked at it closer and told me that he could remove it but that it would leave a big hole and a scar. I decided to pass because it seemed wasteful to pay to have a different type of disfigurement when I could just keep the one I accidentally grew for free.

As the doctor walked me out he told me to "stop worrying so much" because it's possible that some of the rash actually *is* hives caused by nerves, and I made a note to tell my shrink the breaking news that the medical world finally found the cure for my severe anxiety disorder and that the prescription is "Just stop worrying so much."

My God, we've come so far with science.

Later I called Lisa to get a second opinion and she reminded me again that she wasn't a doctor, that we lived in very different time zones, and that she was going to start turning off her ringer after midnight, but she perked up when I mentioned my leg bump because she realized that she has the *exact* same bump on her leg. I asked if she'd ever had it looked at and she was like, *"Why would I have it looked at? It's just a bump, dingus."* And that's when I realized that she would have made a great doctor. She told me that it was good I was on malaria pills because with my luck I probably already had malaria anyway, and she had a point. She also said that I should have the surgery to remove my leg bump because then I could use the hole where it had been for people who wanted to do body shots out of it. I was pretty sure no one would want to drink alcohol from my scarred, puckered leg hole and she said, "Come to LA. There's always a market for something." She's probably right, but I suspect that the people who would *want* to get drunk out of my leg hole wouldn't be the people *I'd* want to have getting drunk out of my leg hole. That's just one of those truisms of life. Lisa said that I'd never get a job as a living leg shot-glass with that attitude. I'd like to think that job doesn't exist with any attitude.

Regardless, now I feel old and wrinkly and I probably *would* be considering Botox right this moment if my friend hadn't just had it done and now one of her eyebrows is slightly lower than the other one because it's *too* relaxed. She asked if it was noticeable and I told her no, and that it looked like she was constantly puzzling over something, so if anything it just made her look pensive and intellectual. She seemed fine with my answer, I think. Or she was really mad. That's the bad thing about talking to someone whose face is slightly paralyzed. You never know if they're leaning toward you for a hug or to punch you in the neck.

Lisa groggily took all this in and pointed out that it seemed slightly suspect that my therapist encouraged me to go to a doctor who then made me feel old so that I would be forced to make another appointment with my shrink to discuss the midlife crisis that I didn't even know I was having until he brought it on.

I nodded. "And then when I go back to see my shrink she'll probably rub poison ivy all over my chair so I'll have to keep seeing the dermatologist. And eventually I'd probably start to suspect that I was being played but no one would ever believe that my shrink was poisoning me so Victor would force me to see my shrink *again* to get treated for my '*unfounded* paranoia.'"

"*Bingo,*" Lisa said. "Now you're thinking like a doctor. Or maybe a psychopath."

It was more likely the latter because my shrink is as sweet as pie and has the clear and innocent face of someone utterly unfettered by a guilty conscience. Or, possibly, of someone who has an addiction to Botox that she's financing by sending the dermatologist extra clients.

Either way, I probably need to stop thinking about this. It's giving me wrinkles.

PS: My doctor assured me that staph-infection-of-the-head is easily treated and most likely won't eventually spread to my face, brain, and body, but (just in case) I've been practicing using a cat for camouflage. I call it "**cat**ouflage" because it's more fun to say. Basically I just carry the cat around and put him up to my face to cover any imperfections, blemishes, double chins, etc.

Sadly, I now have to use catouflage to cover up cat scratches as well, so it's a bit of a catch-22. It's nice though because you get to wear fur, but no one from PETA is going to yell at you about it. Unless I staple Ferris Mewler to my neck. Then they'd probably get pissy about cat-stapling. But I would never do that because that would be ridiculous and cruel and would probably lead to even *more* infections, and then Dr. *Yep-that's-a-bump-all-right* would be like, "Yes, I know you *think* these marks are vampire bites but you probably just have an infection from stapling cats to your neck. Stop doing that. Here's a pill for that, and also it cures testicular decay and loss of eyeballs." So that's why I'm thinking that maybe I should just get a baby sling to put Ferris Mewler in, so that I can wear him on my chest without staples.

Someone get me a BabyBjörn with a tail hole cut in it.

And some bed rest.

And some malaria.

Might as well get my money's worth.

We're Better Than Galileo.
Because He's Dead.

I have learned that every person in the world is on the spectrum of mental illness. Many people barely register on the scale, while others have far more than they could be expected to handle. Even specific disorders are incredibly individualized. For example, my depressive disorder comes and goes and when it's gone I have a hard time remembering how I could ever have felt as lost or numb as I get during those times. My anxiety disorder, on the other hand, is always with me and comes with all sorts of niggling "bonus" disorders and phobias, like some sort of terrible boxed set.

I struggle with a host of phobias, like agoraphobia—the fear of being in a situation where escape is impossible if things go shitty. I have acute social anxiety disorder (a.k.a. anthropophobia), which is the fear of people. I *don't* have arachnophobia (irrational fear of spiders) because fear of spiders is perfectly rational so I refuse to recognize it as a "disorder." I also have arachno-anthropophobia, which is the fear of people who are covered in spiders. I made up that last one but it's still a valid concern.

The fear of people is something I think most introverted, socially awkward people understand, but I tend to take it a step further . . . into a place filled with weird shame. The disorder manifests itself in strange ways, but when I'm having a bad spell I can't make myself interact with the outside world. I even find myself hiding in my own home, my panicked heartbeat in my ears when someone comes to the door.

This would be easier to handle if I were in another room but I'm inevitably home alone and sitting in my office near the front door when the doorbell rings. Usually my blinds are closed but they're always raised a few inches so that the cats can look out at the world I'm avoiding.

"Can they see my feet?" I wonder as I freeze and hold my breath, waiting for whoever is at the door to leave. "Maybe they'll think I'm a mannequin," I whisper to myself.

I slowly bring my feet up to my chair seat, my knees at my chin. Quietly and in slow motion to avoid catching their attention. Watching their feet to see if they respond to mine, if they've noticed me.

Then I sit there, perched in a fetal position, and feel ridiculous, physically hiding from the world. The cats look at me strangely. I'm being judged by cats. Mostly because they wonder where my lap has gone since it's their favorite chair.

The worst thing is when the person outside waits and rings again. Someone who rings once is just doing his job, but someone who rings twice is a madman. The real psychopaths will keep waiting and sometimes even call our home phone as I sit there, paralyzed, thinking, "The call is coming from outside the house."

I never answer.

Eventually the person leaves and I'm left to wonder who they were. These are dark times. It could have been a serial killer. Or a member of the local church. Someone to tell me a bill was late. A magician with a wagon of magic. A utility worker to warn me of a gas leak.

Or perhaps it's just a person who wonders who I am. Who was that girl who lifted her feet *almost* out of sight to hide from a perfect stranger for no conceivable reason at all? *Who would do that?*

Honestly, sometimes I wonder myself.

It's hard to explain anxiety disorders to people. The things that scare others don't scare me. I'm fine with snakes, and clowns, and needles. I can sit in morgues or hang out with the dead. I can look down from dizzying heights or hunt for ghosts in abandoned asylums.

Most people are afraid of speaking in public, but I am fine onstage and I can comfortably speak in front of a thousand people. The scary thing is not being onstage . . . the terror and dread is in the millions of potential problems *getting* to that stage. What if I get lost? What if someone recognizes me? What if no one does? Where do I hide until it's time to go on? What if when I'm hiding people see the real me . . . the terrified me who is boring and strange and has frightened, panicked animal eyes until she's onstage and knows she's in the right place and has no other choice but to speak? Then the terror melts away for a few minutes because at least for those moments I don't have to make decisions or wonder what my face is doing. I can relax because for that brief time I have no other choice but to breathe and move forward.

Some people are afraid of flying, and I am too, but not in the way you think. I'm afraid of getting stuck, and lost, and paralyzed every single step of the way from my house to the plane. The only time my fear abates is when I'm actually in my seat and the plane takes off. It's not until that moment that I have no other choices or mistakes to make and so I can relax for a few minutes while the people who are afraid of flying in a normal, understandable way suddenly tense up and clench their armrests in panic. I look at them with pity and wish I could explain to them that their fear is irrational. That we'll be fine and that even if we aren't it'll be over soon and there's nothing we can do about it. I consider telling them that, but then I worry they'll keep talking to me and I can't have that because I need the hour before we land to be quiet so I have time to study and memorize the terminal maps of the airport we'll be landing in, and triple-check that my notes about every step of the travel are right, and worry about the unknown place we'll land and the myriad of spots I could become lost. The normal scared-of-flying people will exit the plane with obvious relief and I can't help but feel envious, both that their irrational fear is one normal people understand, and also that it's one that ends as they leave the plane. My fear is just ratcheting up again and it will last until the moment I'm back in my own home and can melt.

Your body isn't made to deal with that much fear for that long, so when I travel a lot I get sick, physically and mentally. I explain to people that it's my autoimmune disease and people understand but my autoimmune issues are just one part of the puzzle. It's also the terror of leaving my safe space at home where I've built up a smooth veneer of protection, which cracks so quickly. It wears away each minute until I'm finally exposed and raw and can't move from exhaustion.

It's a conflicting bundle of emotions. When I travel on book tours I meet the most amazing people. Some who love the humor. Some who love the dark. Some who stare at me with my own terrified eyes and whisper that this is the first time they've left their house in weeks. Those are my favorite people . . . The ones who, like me, are scared but come out anyway, alone, and find themselves making friends with other people in line who are just like them. It's what happens every week in the comment section of my blog, but it's so much more lovely to see it in real life.

During my first book tour I didn't know how draining and terrifying it would be. A week and a half into one of the tours I sort of lost it. It wasn't a *complete* breakdown. (That would come later when I got home and couldn't move for weeks.) This was simply overstimulation and terror and having no routine to calm me. When things got really bad Victor and Hailey would fly to wherever I was that day and we'd hide in the hotel room and watch TV and snuggle. It was exactly what I needed. Better than the massages I was too afraid to book, or the parties I couldn't make myself go to, or the vacations I turned down.

It's hard to write about this without giving the wrong impression, and I worry about that. I *love* that a special tribe of people understands and enjoys my writing and I am incredibly lucky to have found them. I love walking into a signing and finding out that the bookstore is out of seats and that the book vendors are shocked by the turnout of hundreds of strange and wonderful misfits who are standing and smiling and wearing red ball gowns and holding metal chickens. I love that such a strange little book was a bestseller because of the amazing groundswell of underground readers who supported the book, and who got the attention of others who found the book or blog and found their place in our strange community.

It's hard to understand anyone's being depressed or anxious when they've been given a gift it seems anyone would kill for. At best it seems ungrateful. At worst it seems disgraceful. But still, it happens. Some of the moments that (from a normal person's perspective) seem like they should've been the greatest moments of my life were actually sometimes the worst moments. No one ever tells you that. Probably because it sounds crazy. But that doesn't make it any less true.

I wish someone had told me this simple but confusing truth: Even when *everything's going your way* you can still be sad. Or anxious. Or uncomfortably numb. Because you can't always control your brain or your emotions even when things are perfect.

The really scary thing is that sometimes that makes it worse. You're supposed to be sad when things are shitty, but if you're sad when you have everything you're ever supposed to want? That's utterly terrifying. Why am I curled in a ball in my hotel room bed, too self-conscious to enjoy life? Feeling like a failure and a fraud while a party in my honor rages on? How can I feel so awful and sick and guilty and sweaty with panic when things are so perfect?

If everything is perfect and I'm miserable, then is this as good as it gets?

And the answer is no.

It gets better.

You get better.

You learn to appreciate the fact that what drives *you* is very different from what you're *told* should make you happy. You learn that it's okay to prefer your personal idea of heaven (live-tweeting zombie movies from under a blanket of kittens) rather than someone else's idea that fame/fortune/parties are the pinnacle we should all reach for. And there's something surprisingly freeing about that.

It is an amazing gift to be able to recognize that the things that make you the happiest are so much easier to grasp than you thought. There is such freedom in being able to celebrate and appreciate the unique moments that recharge you and give you peace and joy. Sure, some people want red carpets and paparazzi. Turns out I just want banana Popsicles dipped in Malibu rum. It doesn't mean I'm a failure at appreciating the good things in life. It means I'm successful in recognizing what the good things in life are *for me.* This makes sense because at the end of your life no one ever says shit like, "Thank God I got to ride an elephant." Instead they say, "I wish I'd spent more time with loved ones." So if you spent an hour playing the-floor-is-made-of-lava with your kid then you're better off than the girl who traveled all the way to Sri Lanka. Plus, you didn't get cholera. Probably. Depends, I guess.

This doesn't mean I don't make myself go to conferences and

tours and vacations, because I do. I know that I'd become a hermit if I didn't push myself outside so I try to say yes enough to experience wonderful things and meet amazing people without overwhelming myself. I'm just very picky about what I do because I know I don't have enough spoons to do it all.

Do you know about the spoons? Because you should.

The Spoon Theory was created by a friend of mine, Christine Miserandino, to explain the limits you have when you live with chronic illness. Most healthy people have a seemingly infinite number of spoons at their disposal, each one representing the energy needed to do a task. You get up in the morning. That's a spoon. You take a shower. That's a spoon. You work, and play, and clean, and love, and hate, and that's lots of damn spoons . . . but if you are young and healthy you still have spoons left over as you fall asleep and wait for the new supply of spoons to be delivered in the morning.

But if you are sick or in pain, your exhaustion changes you and the number of spoons you have. Autoimmune disease or chronic pain like I have with my arthritis cuts down on your spoons. Depression or anxiety takes away even more. Maybe you only have six spoons to use that day. Sometimes you have even fewer. And you look at the things you need to do and realize that you don't have enough spoons to do them all. If you clean the house you won't have any spoons left to exercise. You can visit a friend but you won't have enough spoons to drive yourself back home. You can accomplish everything a normal person does for hours but then you hit a wall and fall into bed thinking, "I wish I could stop breathing for an hour because it's exhausting, all this inhaling and exhaling." And then your husband sees you lying on the bed and raises his eyebrow seductively and you say, "No. I can't have sex with you today because there aren't enough spoons," and he looks at you strangely because that sounds kinky, and not in a good way. And you know you should explain the Spoon Theory so he won't get mad but you don't have the energy to explain properly because you used your last spoon of the morning picking up his dry cleaning so instead you just defensively yell: "I SPENT ALL MY SPOONS ON YOUR LAUNDRY," and he says, "What the . . . You can't pay for dry cleaning *with spoons. What is wrong with you?*"

Now you're mad because this is his fault too but you're too tired to fight out loud and so you have the argument in your mind, but it doesn't go well because you're too tired to defend yourself even in your head, and the critical internal voices take over and you're too tired not to believe them. Then you get *more* depressed and the next day you wake up with even *fewer* spoons and so you try to make spoons out of caffeine and willpower but that never really works. The only thing that *does* work is realizing that your lack of spoons is not your fault, and to remind yourself of that fact over and over as you compare your fucked-up life to everyone else's just-as-fucked-up-but-not-as-noticeably-to-outsiders lives.

Really, the only people you should be comparing yourself to would be people who make you feel better by comparison. For instance, people who are in comas, because those people have no spoons at all and you don't see anyone judging *them.* Personally, I always compare myself to Galileo because everyone knows he's fantastic, but he has no spoons at all because he's dead. So technically I'm better than Galileo because all I've done is take a shower and already I've accomplished more than him today. If we were having a competition I'd have beaten him in daily accomplishments every damn day of my life. But I'm not gloating because Galileo can't control his current spoon supply any more than I can, and if Galileo couldn't figure out how to keep his dwindling spoon supply I think it's pretty unfair of me to judge myself for mine.

I've learned to use my spoons wisely. To say no. To push myself, but not too hard. To try to enjoy the amazingness of life while teetering at the edge of terror and fatigue.

This weekend was the perfect example of that. I was asked to speak at a conference and I said yes, but just getting from my house to the hotel in San Francisco was exhausting so I was too tired to go to the conference, or to eat, or to even get a cab. I locked housekeeping out because I needed to feel like my hotel room was a protected place, that no other emotions, which I might have to battle with, were mingling with mine.

That sounds mad, but it's true. I can feel other people's emotions. Their life force, maybe? Something. It's uncomfortable but in a way that's hard to define. Like a sweater you can't appreciate because it's itchy from an allergic reaction you can't explain. I take pills to dull my over-active senses and it makes me able to love the sweaters, and people, and life. But then the pills wear off and I'm terrified again and I want to run away and scream and have someone rescue me, but the only one who can rescue me is me, which is hopeless because I am unreli-able and paralyzed and my stomach lurches and then I know I'm going to be physically ill . . . a physical manifestation of my brain that equates to my body ridding itself of everything it can. I used to think it was fight or flight. On my worst days I think it's my body's way of mutinying . . . of deserting me in any way it possibly can.

The hotel I was booked in was in the bad part of the Tenderloin district, seedy and fascinating and scary and depressing and exciting. It was also filled with homeless people, who seemed to be huddled in groups on every street. I'd managed to successfully avoid seeing any-one but there was no room service so if I wanted to eat I'd have to walk down the street. The problem was that I couldn't get more than a few steps without being blocked by a man or woman who was either severely mentally ill or very high or both. I'd walk a few feet and see a shirtless man sitting in a doorway screaming, "GIMME A DOLLAR" to people as he grabbed at their feet and spat at them. Then I'd turn and go the other way and see a furious woman screaming angrily at someone who wasn't there. It happened on every street and I kept turning back until I had no other street to walk down and so I just walked back to my room to eat the peanut butter crackers I'd brought with me.

It's not that I'm afraid of homeless people any more than non-homeless people. I'm afraid of something much more complicated. I look at them and think, "Is that my future?" Because that's what I'd become if I got stuck and was forced to be around people without a break. Screaming and terrorized and stuck huddled in a doorway each day. Lost. Never moving. No options. It's how I feel now, except that I'm blessed to be stuck in a room with clean sheets and a bottle of pills that I carry with me that I hope will give me the numb courage I'll eventually need to call a cab and go to the airport and do a myriad of things normal people don't think about, but that I obsess about over and over until I've taken that taxi and gotten lost in the airport one hundred times in my mind before I actually have to do it for real.

I panic that I'll get stuck. I stand at the door of my hotel room and look out at the real world and I'm terrified that I'll just stop. That I won't be able to leave. Or to call a cab. Or to get on the plane. That I'll be stuck, forever, like those people in the streets.

I'm lucky because I have options. I have medications and therapeutic tools and breathing techniques. I have friends and family I can call to come rescue me if things get too bad. And I have the Internet. That sounds weird, but Twitter is a lot like having a large, invisible gang of equally messed-up people who will hide with you in bathrooms and make you laugh under the pillow fort you've built in a lonely hotel room. Many of them suffer from the same fears, which keep them similarly isolated, but we've found a way to be alone together.

There's something wonderful about experiencing life with friendly strangers and stranger-friends who all fit in your pocket. They celebrate your successes. They send you videos of hedgehogs in bathtubs when you are down. They tell you that you are not alone. *And suddenly? You aren't.* They turn horrific experiences into ones you can laugh about with your friends, these odd strangers who walk with you, keeping you company late at night during a panic attack. Or when you're awkwardly sitting alone at a table in a public place and accidentally mortify yourself, which is—coincidentally—exactly what happened to me that weekend at the conference.

Since the hotel I was staying in didn't offer room service I'd been surviving on the peanut butter crackers I'd brought with me. But on the final day I decided I needed real food before I had to do my speech, so I decided to brave the world and go to the restaurant attached to my hotel. What followed was a humiliating series of events, which would have left me devastated had I not been able to laugh about them with Twitter. (And that's the awesome thing about introverts. They're often on their phones or computers so it's like you're with friends even when you're alone.)

In a nutshell, I tried to take a subtle selfie of how awkwardly alone I was in the dark restaurant but I forgot my flash was on and then when I tweeted the picture my phone made a loud wolf-whistle. In my rush to leave, I tripped on the edge of their fancy koi pond and stepped on a fish. The fish was fine but my right shoe was a mess so I tried to use the ceiling fan in my room to dry my shoe but it was taking too long and I couldn't go speak with a shoe that was making squelching noises so I stuck my shoe onto the fan blade because I thought inertia would force the water out. It seemed to be working until I turned the fan up too high and my shoe shot off the blade and hit me in the face. It was like I was being kicked in the head with my own stupidity.

But Twitter was there through it all, reminding me that if I did actually get my shit together no one would know who I was anymore.

And that? *That* is why I love the Internet. Because they turned a really horrific moment into a memory I could laugh about later because I was experiencing it with people who could commiserate, or at least appreciate it as a terrible train wreck. And it was good. And terrifying. And I survived even though I had to go onstage with a slightly squelchy shoe and then hide in my room immediately afterward.

I continue to do what I do because that is life, and because one day I'll maybe get used to this. Maybe one day I'll have the same reaction to life that I have when I'm locked in a plane or onstage. Maybe I'll be able to relax and enjoy my life without letting fear keep me from living it. Maybe one day I'll easily acknowledge the frank truth . . . that I have no other choice but to breathe and move forward.

Things My Father Taught Me

- Always pull a tank dog out of a hole by the tail. Also "tank dog" is a fairly awesome name for an armadillo.

- You can't leave a donkey in the car. But you CAN take it into a bar. And then you can never go back to that bar again.

- If you have too much grass, and your neighbor has too many goats, you should just rent some of your neighbor's goats to eat your grass. But make sure you get all female ones because otherwise you'll end up with too many goats too. Too much grass and not enough birth control: that's how goats are made.

- If you want to learn the Native American way to skin buffalo you should let a bunch of them come live in your yard. Native Americans, that is. Not buffalo. Honestly, we barely had room for all those goats.

- The grass is greener on the other side of the fence but only because most people don't have a bunch of rented goats in their backyards. Those fucking goats eat *everything*.

- You can trade three goats for one slightly used kid's motorcycle.

- You can trade one slightly used and now vaguely crashed kid's motorcycle back for those same goats if you just make sure to trade really bad goats the first time around. They should change "You can't handle the truth" to "You can't handle these goats" because it's more realistic. Goats are terrible to handle.

- When life gives you lemons you should freeze them and use them to throw at your enemies using some sort of trebuchet. Also, you should never ask your father what a trebuchet is because he will show you. It's like a catapult but more complicated, and inevitably it breaks or the goats wander into its path and run away dazed.

- On the other side of fear is freedom. And usually fewer fingers than you started with.

- Everyone is born with extra fingers. God expects you to cut a few off during your journey. Otherwise he wouldn't have made power tools so awesome.

- If you toss a freshly killed deer on the kitchen table with its stomach on the tabletop and its front legs on one side and back legs on the other it'll look less like it's flying and more like it's just badly failed at the hurdles. It's a bit funny and horrible all at once. Much like life.

- Always shoot first. Because bears don't shoot. They just eat you. You'll never win if you wait for the bear to get the first shot. This is all basic hunting 101.

- There will be moments when you have to be a grown-up. Those moments are tricks. Do not fall for them.

- Refrigerators are good for keeping homemade moonshine less gross. Freezers are good for keeping rattlesnakes less angry. Garages are good to hide in when your wife finds either.

- If you leave the freezer open, the rattlesnakes will thaw and bite your hand. (I'm not sure if this is an actual fact or just a way for my father to get my sister and me to close the freezer quickly before letting all the cold air out. This is such an electricity saver that I'm considering using the same tactic on my daughter. But without the actual rattlesnakes. Because that would be insane.)

- Don't make the same mistakes that everyone else makes. Make wonderful mistakes. Make the kind of mistakes that make people so shocked that they have no other choice but to be a little impressed.

- Sometimes stunned silence is better than applause.

- You don't have to go to some special private school to be an artist. Just look at the intricate beauty of cobwebs. Spiders make them with their butts.

- Be happy in front of people who hate you. That way they know they haven't gotten to you. Plus, it pisses them off like crazy.

- You can make a hat out of a cat's face but that doesn't make it a good hat. Unless you line it first.

- Don't sabotage yourself. There are plenty of other people willing to do that for free.

- It's okay to keep a broken oven in your yard as long as you call it art.

- If you're going to buy glass eyeballs you should buy them in bulk because you're going to need more. Glass eyeballs are like Pringles. No one can have just one. Mostly because you seldom taxidermy one-eyed animals. Unless maybe you make them wink at each other. Or make them pirates.

- If you stick a couple of giant glass eyeballs made for taxidermied cow heads inside your glasses you will freak a bunch of people out. You'll probably also fall and break your hip. But it'll totally be worth it.

- There's a point when roadkill is much too decomposed to be used in taxidermy. It's several weeks after a normal person would expect.

- You can make a very convincing taxidermied Sasquatch out of a deer's ass. They don't sell well in the taxidermy shop but it's very entertaining when gullible people get an inch away from a deer's butthole to stare at it with wonder and skepticism.

- Most Sasquatch sightings are probably just deer who are walking away from drunken hunters.

- Normal is boring. Weird is better. Goats are awesome, but only in small quantities.

- Hand me those eyeballs.

I'm Going to Die. Eventually.

"So," said my psychiatrist, "what's going on today?"

I took a deep breath. "I'm going to die."

"Oh," she replied, eyes opening in surprise.

"I mean . . . *eventually,*" I added.

Her eyes narrowed. "*Right.* So, everything is normal."

"It's not normal. *I'm dying.* **You're** dying. WE'RE **ALL** DYING."

She crossed her legs. "That's a normal phase of life."

"Dying? *No.* Dying is like *the opposite of life.*" I crossed my arms. "Aren't you a medical doctor? Because I think you should know that."

"No," she replied. "I meant that thinking about your mortality is a normal phase of life."

"I can't trust anything you say right now. You just found out you're dying and you're obviously in shock."

She raised an eyebrow. "I *already* knew I was dying."

"Oh my God, I'm so sorry."

"*No,*" she said. "I'm not dying *now.* I'm just the regular kind of dying. It's called 'aging.' *And that's a good thing.* Each day is another chance to enjoy life."

"It's also another chance to get kidnapped by a serial killer," I countered. "Or to end up at the bottom of a well. **Or both.** That's probably where serial killers dump their victims. Which is probably why we don't use wells anymore."

"Hmm," she replied absently, writing something on her notepad. "What about wishing wells?"

"You know, I always assumed that the dead girls in the wells were the ones giving out the wishes. And that's why my wishes never came true. *Because dead girls don't give wishes.*"

"Huh."

"You know," I said, "I feel a lot of silence coming from you and it's feeling a lot like judgment."

She put down her pen. "Okay. Is this fear of death a real thing that we need to discuss, or . . . ?"

"Not really. Just coming up with small talk. Which is sort of weird because I'm paying you to talk to me and yet **I'm** the one having to come up with topics of conversation."

She paused. "Do you want me to come up with the conversation?"

"I'm just saying, you could try a little harder."

"You seem a little defensive today. What's going on with you?" she asked.

"Okay." I took a deep breath. "The entire time I was driving here I was thinking about what I wanted to talk about today and for once *I'm totally doing okay,* and now I don't know how to entertain you for the next forty minutes."

She glanced at the clock. "*Thirty minutes,* actually."

"Yeah. I've been meaning to ask you . . . why do therapy hours only last fifty minutes? Because that's sort of fucked up. What if I tried to pay you with a five-dollar bill and I told you it was a 'therapy six-dollar bill'? That's not a thing anywhere other than therapy and I think that's probably because you guys know you're dealing with crazy people so you're pretty sure you can get away with it."

She tilted her head to one side. "Is this really what you want to talk about or are you just being defensive again?"

"I'm being defensive." I sighed. "**Damn**, you *are good*."

"Yeah." She nodded. "It's my job. You don't have anything you want to talk about?"

"Okay. Here's one. Every time I walk into a public bathroom I do it cautiously and tentatively because I'm always convinced there will be a dead body in the toilet stall. Every. Single. Time."

"Why do you think that is?"

"No idea. I almost never find dead bodies but I do find a lot of *potential* dead bodies. Those are the black plastic trash sacks abandoned on the side of the road. I always want to open them because I'm convinced there might be a body in there, but then I don't because I'm not responsible enough to take care of a dead body. I mean, like, to call the police and have them take care of it. Not like 'Here's your new goldfish so take care of it.' You don't have to take care of dead bodies. That's one of the few positives about them. If you don't feed a dead body it doesn't look at you accusingly, and it never gets deader. In fact, dead bodies make much better pets than goldfish because someone has already killed them for you so there's not as much potential guilt attached."

My doctor lifted her pencil as if wondering where to start.

I continued, trying to explain myself. "I'm always afraid that once I find the first dead body it'll start a weird streak because I'll never stop opening garbage bags after the first one pays off and eventually the police will finger me as a suspect. That's probably why so many people distrust the police. Because they'd rather assume you were a murderer than think you were just really lucky at finding bodies."

My doctor removed her glasses and rubbed the bridge of her nose. "Well . . . it's an unusual way of looking at it but really, a phobia of dead bodies is very common."

"Oh, I don't have a phobia of dead bodies," I countered. "'Phobia' implies an unreasonable fear and this fear is perfectly reasonable. You are *supposed* to be afraid of dead bodies. It's what keeps you from hanging out with them and getting cholera.

"Of course," I admitted, "'fear of finding dead bodies on toilets and in bags' is maybe a more uncommon variant, but people find dead bodies everywhere.[1] A DJ friend of mine once went to the radio station at midnight because there was dead air and she found her boss dead of a heart attack on the soundboard. She had to DJ over his dead body while waiting for the police to arrive, which her coworkers at the radio station found brave and dedicated, but which I thought was a bit

---

1. It's quite freeing to write about this because I realize the chances of my walking in on a dead body in the toilet are admittedly slim, but it seems like it would be even *more* unlikely for someone who just *wrote* about her fear of walking in on toilet corpses to actually discover a toilet corpse. So effectively, this chapter is lowering my chances of that happening.

And raising the chances of its happening to you.

I'm sorry, but that's how statistics work. It's not like writing this is going to keep people from dying on the toilet. *I'm not Jesus, people.* I can't bring bathroom corpses back from the dead. They're still out there and someone has to find them, and odds are it will most likely be you rather than me since I just wrote this.

Except now that I think about it, what are the odds that you (*who just read about the minute chances of finding bathroom corpses*) would actually find a bathroom corpse now? Getting slimmer by the sentence I'd say. If anything I'm helping you.

You're welcome.

In fact, you should encourage all your friends and family to read this book to lower *their* chances of finding a bathroom corpse too. That's what we do for people we love. We hold their hair when they vomit, and we help them move, and we protect them from toilet corpses. I suggest buying all of your loved ones this book and inscribing it: "I bought you this to keep you safe from bathroom corpses *because I love you.*" That way they'll know you mean business.

bizarre and unsettling. *Just put on a long record and go hide in a less corpsey room, lady.* If anything, *she's* the weird one. Not me."

"Anything else?"

"Whenever I go to wash my hands, if the automatic sink doesn't work I immediately assume that I've died in the bathroom stall and that it's my ghost trying to wash my hands."

"Huh."

"Because the automatic sensors won't work since I'm a ghost," I added.

"Yeah, I got that."

"Also, I'm really, really good at peeing . . . like almost *too* good. It's like a superpower."

She looked at me critically. "Is this an issue?"

"Yes. Because I'm such a fast pee-er that I always have to stand inside the bathroom and count to twenty so that the people outside don't think that I'm skipping washing my hands." I waited for her expression to change to impressed but it seemed like I'd be waiting a long time. "Also, I can't stop pronouncing the 'p' in 'hamster.'"

"There is no 'p' in 'hamster.'"

"Well, obviously you've never squeezed one hard enough. There's *tons* of pee in them."

She stared at me.

"That was a joke," I explained. "Not a very good one," I admitted. "But seriously, it should be spelled 'hampster.' We're all saying it that way anyway."

"So," she asked, "do you think you're finished with therapy?"

"Every time I get a pimple I worry that it's the beginning of a new nipple."

She stared at me in silence.

"And that was *not* the answer to your question. I'm sorry. I jumped ahead."

"To tell me about your nipples?" she asked calmly.

"And then I assume the nipple will turn into a new person and I'll be a late-blooming conjoined twin. This is what it's like in my mind pretty much ALL THE TIME."

"So, I'll pencil you in for next week?"

"Yeah." I nodded. "I'll clear my whole day."

And This Is Why I Prefer to Cut
My Own Hair

ME: I just need a trim and maybe some highlights.

BEAUTICIAN: You know what we should do? We should get you a Brazilian blowout.

ME: Oh **HELL NO.**

BEAUTICIAN: Why not? It'd look great. And we're doing them for $150 this week.

ME: Seriously? *That sounds like torture.* I have *no idea* how you convince someone to sit for that, much less *pay* for it.

BEAUTICIAN: It's not that bad. It just takes some time and you have to be extra careful for the first day or two. You can't, like, put your hair in a ponytail or anything, or it could compromise the treatment.

ME: WHAT THE SHIT? *WHO PUTS THEIR PUBIC HAIR IN A PONYTAIL?*

BEAUTICIAN: Wh . . . what?

ME: I just don't get it. Every year I hear about women doing more and more with their pubic hair and I just don't understand it. Vajazzling, waxing. I don't want anyone helping me style my pubic hair into a ponytail. And frankly it makes me a little weirded out that people have enough that they can put it in a ponytail. I mean, no judgment, but I didn't even know I was supposed to be coveting extra-long pubic hair. I can't even keep up with the stuff that's on my head, much less on my lady garden.

BEAUTICIAN: I am . . . *so* confused right now.

ME: That makes two of us.

BEAUTICIAN: Okay, a Brazilian blowout is a blow-drying treatment for the hair *on your head*. It straightens it and makes it less frizzy.

ME: *Oh.*

BEAUTICIAN: Yeah.

ME: So I can understand why you look so confused.

BEAUTICIAN: Yeah.

ME: But in my defense? If I asked you for a Brazilian you'd take me in the back and style my pubic hair, so I just assumed a Brazilian blowout meant that you'd just blow-dry it first.

BEAUTICIAN: Huh. That'd be . . . messed up.

ME: Frankly it's not that much more messed up than me asking you to take me to the back and rip out all of my pubic hair by the roots. Honestly, it's all a matter of perspective. *Either way?* You're still styling pubic hair.

BEAUTICIAN: No. I'm not. We don't do any sort of waxing here. We only deal with the hair on your head.

ME: *Ah*. So now I understand why this might have been the first time you ever had to have this conversation.

BEAUTICIAN: I'd like to think it was the first time that *anyone* has ever had this conversation.

ME: Touché.

It's All in How You Look at It
(The Book of Nelda)

When I was young we were quite poor, but we never really talked about it. There was no need to. It's the same reason why hippos don't talk about being hippos. Or at least, one of the reasons. I did, though, as a teenager, mention to my mom (Nelda) that we were dirt-poor and she promptly stopped drying the dishes, raised an eyebrow in baffled amusement, and said, "Nonsense. We have plenty of dirt. Too much if anything. We're practically buried in it. In fact, we eventually plan to be buried in it. THAT'S HOW MUCH WE HAVE."

"Semitics," I harrumphed in that sarcastically bored way that only stupid fourteen-year-old girls can properly master.

"I think you mean 'semantics.' 'Semitics' is . . . *I dunno* . . . when you really like Jewish people, I think? Get up off the kitchen floor and go look it up."

"There's an entire word for just liking Jewish people?" I asked. "That seems strange. Is there a word for people who really like Christians?"

"Yes," sighed my atheist mother as she side-eyed the pictures of Jesus my father had hung on the wall. " '*Tolerant.*'

"The point is," she continued, "we are *not* dirt-poor. We are wealthy with dirt. Our whole house is built on it and I suspect it's what's keeping most of the furniture stuck together. That's why you should never dust too much. Because dust is what holds the world together. The whole world is made up of it. Dust from the wind. Dust from dinosaur bones. Stardust. We are wealthy with dirt. I can assure you, we are *far* from dirt-poor. *It's all in how you look at it.*"

My mother's words have echoed through my head for years. Mostly because they're a really good excuse to not dust. (And technically my sister and I never minded if she didn't dust because her dust cloths were usually my father's old pairs of underwear. It's weird knowing that the house was cleanest when it'd been wiped down by your father's underpants.) Plus, it's a really good way to get out of cleaning because whenever I try to explain my mom's dusting theory to Victor his eyes get all squinty and he accuses me of being insane and I just scream, "IT'S A FAMILY TRADITION, VICTOR. YOU WOULDN'T UNDERSTAND IT."

Dust as a metaphor for life, now that I'm thinking about it, is a pretty tired cliché. Even Jesus used it in the Bible during his "Ashes to ashes" speech. Except my mom just read this over my shoulder and reminded me that Jesus didn't actually write anything himself and that most of the Bible chapters were named for the guys who actually did all the work (probably soberly) editing and writing down all the good shit. *My God*, that woman knows a lot about Jesus for an atheist. Also, she pointed out a lot of grammatical errors. If this were the Bible this chapter would be called "The Book of Nelda."

Nonetheless, there's a reason why dust and life go together naturally. Sometimes it comes together in the most perfect way to make the very building blocks of life. Sometimes it sweeps in and makes everything seem hazy and dark. Sometimes it gets in my amaretto and then I have to pour a new glass, but mainly that's cat fur, which is not really the same thing.

I have had a very odd and strange life, filled with more ups and downs than the average woman could shake a stick at. (Which would be weird because it's been my personal experience that average women hardly ever shake sticks at anything. Normally it's strange women like me shaking sticks against windmills, and cougars, and bushes that you thought were cougars because you've had too much amaretto.)

When I look at my life I see high-water marks of happiness and I see the lower places where I had to convince myself that suicide wasn't an answer. And in between I see my life. I see that the sadness and tragedy in my life made the euphoria and delicious ecstasy that much more sweet. I see that stretching out my soul to feel every inch of horrific depression gave me more room to grow and enjoy the beauty of life that others might not ever appreciate. I see that there is dust in the air that will eventually settle onto the floor to be swept out the door as a nuisance, but before that, for *one brilliant moment* I see the dust motes catch sunlight and sparkle and dance like stardust. I see the beginning and the end of all things. I see my life. It is beautifully ugly and tarnished in just the right way. It sparkles with debris. There is wonder and joy in the simplest of things. My mother was right.

It's all in the way you look at it.

Well at Least Your Nipples Are Covered

The Fifth Argument I Had with Victor This Week

ME: Does this outfit look okay?

VICTOR: Yeah. It looks okay.

[*I huff off to change.*]

VICTOR: *Why are you changing?* WE NEED TO GO.

ME: Because you hate my outfit so now I have to change.

VICTOR: I SAID YOU LOOKED FINE.

ME: *No.* You said I looked "*okay*," which is pretty much the same thing as saying, "*Well, at least your nipples are covered.*" If you'd said I looked "*fine*" I'd feel better but I'd probably still change, because "fine" equals

"You might as well just give up." Which I won't, because **I** care about my personal appearance.

VICTOR: That is the craziest fucking thing you have ever said.

ME: Not even remotely. If you *really* thought I looked okay you should have said that I look great.

VICTOR: YOU LOOK GREAT. STOP BEING MENTAL AND GET IN THE DAMN CAR.

ME: *No.* Not until I look okay.

VICTOR: I **TOLD** YOU THAT YOU LOOKED OKAY.

ME: EXACTLY. But *my* "okay" is not *your* "okay." I CAN'T BE-LIEVE I'M EVEN HAVING TO EXPLAIN THIS.

VICTOR: THAT MAKES TWO OF US.

ME: Okay, let me put it in perspective. Imagine we just had sex for the first time. You ask me how it was. I say, "*It was okay.*"

VICTOR: Ah.

ME: *Exactly.*

VICTOR: Fine. *You look amazing.*

ME: Really? So I look okay?

VICTOR: I don't even know what to say here. Is this a trick question?

ME: No. Just nod and say something nice about my shoes or my hair or something.

VICTOR: Fine.

ME: . . . Sooner rather than later would be nice.

VICTOR: I'm thinking.

ME: *Wow.*

VICTOR: I like your skin because it keeps your organs from falling out onto the carpet.

ME: If I had a nickel for every time a man told me that . . .

Winner: Victor. Because now he understands how words work.

Death by Swans Is Not as Glamorous as You'd Expect

We recently moved, continuing our pattern of buying a house, fixing it up, and then putting it up for sale about fifteen minutes before it actually feels like home. When Victor decided we should move again I told him that this house would be the last one because I wasn't moving again unless it was in my coffin. Then he waited until I was out of town and bought an old (but very sweet) house that needed massive repairs, had lots of issues, and could probably kill us. In short, he bought the *"me"* of houses.

Before we moved, Hailey, Victor, and I all decided on the one thing we wanted in "the perfect house."

Victor wanted something safer in a gated community because I had a bit of a stalker problem last year. (Please don't stalk me. I'm very boring in real life, I assure you.) I wanted a smaller place with big trees and a nice yard. Hailey wanted a pool.

The week we moved to our new, gated community a man rammed the front gate and had a full-on shoot-out in his driveway with the local police department. Luckily for him, the police have extremely bad aim and just arrested him. The alleged gunman in question lives in our neighborhood. *We have succeeded in locking the crazies in with us.* Also, we got a flier from the homeowners' association saying that a cougar had come down off the mountain nearby and eaten some lady's dog WHILE SHE WAS WALKING IT. We were told to keep our animals indoors but I was a little concerned that would just make the cougar even hungrier. What if the dog was just the appetizer and the cougar is now hungry for people? This is all true, by the way. (Also, I just assume the sewers are filled with panthers because that's the direction this seems to be taking.)

A few weeks later, I watched as a man ardently sprayed what I thought was ant killer all over our green lawn. Turns out he was ardently spraying *plant poison*. Apparently he had the wrong address and was supposed to be destroying the yard on the next street so they could put in different grass. He did an excellent job doing exactly the opposite of what we'd want. We are now dirt farmers and *the harvest is plentiful.*

The view from our front door. I'm sure our neighbors are
very pleased that we've moved in.

After that debacle I decided to just take a break from all the insanity of busted pipes and roof replacements and angry mountain lions and simply relax in the pool.

Someone bring me a damn piña colada. (*Courtesy of Victor Lawson*)

Also, the house was old and had a lot of issues, which is how we were able to live in a fairly fancy, country-club neighborhood. But it meant a lot of contractors at our home all the time to bring the house up to code, and to pull down all the pieces of the house that apparently wanted to kill us. If you've ever remodeled your house, or added on, or just brought contractors in to see if your marriage can survive it, then you already know the particular hell it is. If you haven't, let me expound . . .

The Subtle Changes Between Your First Thoughts and Your Final Thoughts During the Process of Redoing an Older House

Your child says she saw a kitty frolicking near the house.

A giant possum is under your crawl space.

A giant dead possum is under your crawl space.

A giant dead possum is marking the spot where the gas leak is.

The gas leak is actually spirits escaping from the Indian burial ground that was desecrated when this house was built.

The angry spirits now have your chain saws. Plus, they killed your possum.

The contractors have come to fix the angry spirit/possum problem. They estimate it will cost four dollars and take twelve to sixteen minutes to complete.

The contractors have to leave because it's dark, and it's taking longer than expected because they didn't realize that "purple is a color" or some other ridiculous bullshit that sounds made-up but that you can't question them about because you don't understand enough about possums or angry spirits.

A gust of air the intensity of a newborn kitten sneezing rips down the plastic tarp the contractors affixed to the twenty-foot hole they cut into the side of your house. Also, the plastic tarp was affixed with spit and air and a shitload of hopelessness.

There are now forty-two possums living in the twenty-foot hole on the side of your house. They create a wild, all-night disco after partnering with the angry entities. They play "Call Me Maybe" and "Gangnam Style" on a loop and sell ecstasy to the neighborhood children.

The contractors say they'll be there within the hour to fix the problems, which they've actually made worse. They are referring to an hour that will occur sometime in the year 2032. They send you a bill for eleventy billion dollars for the work they've done so far. The possums eat the bill. The contractors sue you and you lose the house. You end up living in the crawl space with the bitey possums, who are like, the worst roommates ever.

You ask the contractors to please finish the last paragraph of this post since they now own this computer and WE'LL BE BACK TO FIX THIS "TOMORROW." HAHAHAHA. YOU OWE US ELEV-ENTY BILLION DOLLARS.

I am a girl who believes in signs. Not necessarily traffic signs (which I think of more as helpful but unnecessary suggestions from an overly concerned great-aunt) or signs from God (which I only got once, when God sent me a mushroom on my lawn that looked like a severed boob and my very religious grandfather assured me it was less a sign from God and more of a sign that I was watering the lawn too much). No. I'm talking about giant flashing signs from the universe that you are doing awesome, or that you are fucking it up for everyone and need to get your shit together. I received one of those glaring, blinking signs the first week we moved to our new house.

The new house seemed perfect. It was old, but the trees were beautiful, the neighborhood was tranquil, and there was a rumor that Stone Cold Steve Austin lived on the next block. (True story: A famous honky-tonk singer lives four doors down from me. Technically it's three doors, a small mountain, a heavily guarded gate, and then another door, but still . . . it's our claim to fame and we've seized it.)

Our former old country house had been wonderful, but after several years of rattlesnakes and scorpions and chupacabras we were ready for something a little more suburban. This gated community seemed perfect for the kind of people we were pretending to be (normal people who had their shit together). I was fairly certain I'd immediately be found out for an imposter.

The first day we moved in I still felt out of place as I walked down our road toward the picturesque little neighborhood park and tried to look as if I belonged. I sat down on the slope of a man-made stream and that's when I saw my sign. Two beautiful, snowy-white swans turned around the bend of the pond and glided over to me, staring at me curiously. I sat perfectly still, mesmerized, as the noble birds swam together, making accidental heart shapes with their bowed necks as they crossed each other's path. And then I sighed a sigh I didn't even know was there, and I realized that I was going to be okay.

And then a herd of swans tried to eat me.

At this point you're probably rereading that last line and wondering what's wrong with me and the answer to that is that SWANS TRIED TO EAT ME. THAT'S WHAT'S WRONG WITH ME. *Surely*, you're probably saying to yourself, *you exaggerate. Swans don't eat people.* And let me assure you that *oh yes, they fucking well do.*

These swans jumped out of the water, snorting and hissing and running at me like goddamn cheetahs. Cheetahs who were good at football and had been coached on how to surround their victim. I screamed and ran back toward our house, certain I could hear the deadly flip-flopping of webbed feet behind me. When I got near the house I saw Victor out front watering the lawn and I screamed, "ARE THEY BEHIND ME?" He turned and looked at me. I was certain they must still be because he looked fucking terrified, but then I looked back and there was nothing. It turns out he was terrified because his wife was running down the road screaming, "ARE THEY BEHIND

ME?" like it was the beginning of the zombie apocalypse and no one had thought to tell him. I stopped to catch my breath and was about to inform him that I'd just been accosted by an angry mob of swans, but then I considered how that might sound. Also I wasn't sure if two swans could be classified as a mob but then I decided that you should always be honest in marriage. Victor disagrees with me about this, mostly because my honesty often ends with me insisting that I've just been assaulted by swans. And, yes, I know that it's not *technically* assault if they didn't actually touch me or pull out a knife, but I can recognize intent and I'm fairly certain that the swans were not furiously chasing me down in order to scream "HUG ME!!!" Mostly because swans are mute. And maybe that's why they're so angry. Maybe it's because they can't scream their feelings. I don't know the psychology of swans.

Victor insisted I had misunderstood the swans and so I looked swans up on the Internet and it was mostly pictures of their being all graceful and regal but when I looked hard enough there were plenty of websites saying "Oh, those motherfuckers will tear a bitch a down. DO NOT FUCK WITH THOSE ASSHOLES." Seriously, they will break a man's arm with a well-placed kick and last year they drowned a man in England. This is true and not just something I found in the *National Enquirer.* Swans are dangerous but are never held accountable, I suspect because of racial profiling. Also, according to the Internet if you're attacked the best way to escape is to "grab the swan by the neck and heave it as far as you can," which sounds like an Olympic event that PETA would be boycotting. You can also slap it across the face as hard as you can but I'm fairly certain that I'd fail at that because swan heads are notoriously tiny. It would be like playing tetherball, except that the pole would be moving and the rope would be a neck and the ball would be trying to eat you. Deadliest tetherball ever.

"Oh, holy hell . . . this website says I might have been impregnated," I yelled at Victor.

"From a swan *running* at you?" he asked incredulously. "Do you even realize how crazy you sound right now?"

"Well, I'm problemly in shock. And possibly pregnant with water-fowl, *so god knows what my hormones are doing right now*. I just found a medical journal that says you need to seek 'prophylactics' after a swan attack. THAT'S HOW DEVIOUS SWANS ARE."

Then Victor tried to explain that "prophylactics" means "preventa-tive care" and doesn't *automatically* equal birth control but I was too busy to listen because I may have just been forcibly impregnated by a murder of swans. Then Victor pointed out that it's a "murder of crows" and that a group of swans is called a "lamentation" but I'm pretty sure that just proves my point because swans are mute, yet they're named after a word that means "wailing in horrible pain"? If that's not a sign then I don't know what is. Victor says he agrees, but less about the fact that it's a sign and more about the fact that I don't know what a sign is.

Regardless, it was an issue and I couldn't get near the swan pond without fear of being attacked by the swans, whom I had named Whitey and Klaus Bananasnatch. Whitey was the more violent of the two, but neither would ever make a move when any other human wit-nesses were near and at most they'd just walk at me semi-aggressively. Probably to make people doubt me so that they wouldn't be suspects in my certain and untimely future murder.

After that day I'd drive slowly by the swan pond on the way home and the swans would glare at my car. I'd pass by (as they likely plotted ripping off my bumper or disabling my brakes), and I'd roll down the window and scream, "DON'T EVEN START WITH ME, WHITEY!" which, admittedly, is one of the worst things to scream in the middle of a posh Republican-stronghold neighborhood, but I had no real hope for ever fitting in and so I had already given up. (In fact, our new neighbor invited Victor and me to a welcome-to-the-neighborhood party, which sounded terrifying, but then she mentioned that it would also be a

Republican fund-raiser and that was a relief because then I had an excellent excuse not to go. I explained that I was the designated non-Republican in our marriage and she said it would be fine so I handed her a copy of my first book. A week later I got a very nice letter from her explaining that she'd read the book and now understood why I shouldn't come. So basically I was uninvited in writing but in a way that we all felt good about.)

Victor blamed my "imagined" swan persecution on a manifestation of imposter syndrome, a very real problem I struggle with. Basically, it's when you're convinced that any success you have is due to luck and that at any moment everyone will realize that you are a tremendous loser and that you aren't as cool as they thought you were. It's disconcerting because most people think I'm insane at best, so I think that means that I'm convinced that I'm not even successful enough at being crazy, which is sort of the definition of being crazy. Regardless, I'm pretty sure these swans were onto me. They had identified me as an outsider, which should have endeared me to them since all swans start out as ugly ducklings, but no. These swans had obviously forgotten where they came from and they were doing their best to make sure that nobody else remembered either.

No one else ever seemed to have any problems with the swans but I'm still certain they would eat you if given the chance. Victor disagrees but I'm pretty sure that swans have probably eaten a lot of people and they're just really good at it and that's why no one ever suspects them. They're like the Spanish Inquisition of flightless waterfowl. In fact, I have a hunch that most of the missing people of the world were outright eaten by swans. Victor suspects I've had too much to drink. It's possible we're both right.

But this was not the only sign.

Several months after moving in we were finally able to fix the pool. One particular morning I was enjoying the pool alone, as Hailey was at drama camp and Victor was out of town.

The tall red-tips behind the pool blocked out the sun and they rustled in the breeze. But there was no breeze. And still there was rustling. I peered into the dense, ten-foot foliage directly behind the pool and then I realized that someone was in the bushes. The red-tips shook hard and there was a cracking sound of branches breaking. I was trying to back away from the bushes when suddenly I heard something tumbling and saw that an enormous squirrel was desperately clinging to a mostly broken branch. Then I realized that the mostly broken branch was hanging directly over the pool. Then I realized that the squirrel was, in fact, a goddamn wild possum.

My first instinct was to scream, "Possum!" which was unhelpful because he already knew he was a possum and also because it just succeeded in freaking him out more. He desperately tried to scurry back up the limb but it wasn't happening. I fucking *hate* possums but I suddenly found myself rooting for the little guy. Mostly because he was clinging frantically upside down on a branch looking almost identical to the way I did the time I was hanging upside down on the monkey bars in second grade and realized I didn't have enough ab strength to lift myself back up. I'd had to rely on Mrs. Gilly to come and rescue me, but no elementary school teacher would be coming for this frantic possum as it did its furious acrobatics. It was as if the possum was part of Cirque du Soleil, or a frightened BASE jumper, and I was unable to look away.

I reached over for the net I used to skim bugs off the surface so I could use it to help the possum regain its footing but it was too late and in an instant I saw a look on the possum's face that said, "Fuck. I'm comin' in, lady." And then the possum was like "CANNON-BAAAALLL" and it dove in with fairly good form, and I thought, "Shit, now we have to boil it." (The pool, I mean. Not the possum. Possum tastes awful. It's not even great for giblets, and giblets are sort of the end of the line for food.)

I screamed and jumped out of the pool and the possum scurried out behind me toward the bushes but then it flopped over suddenly as if it were there for a tanning session, but I suspected it was just playing possum. I called Victor on the cell and screamed, "There's a possum in the bush!" and he paused and asked, "Is this your idea of phone sex? Because, I gotta tell ya, it's not really working for me."

I wasn't sure if I was more scared that the possum was still alive or that it was dead. Victor suggested that I nudge it with my foot but I was afraid it might maul me so instead I poked it gently with a pool noodle while saying, "Hey, possum. Are you dead? *Hello?*" But it just lay there and I thought it was either *really, really* talented or *really, really* dead, and it's weird that those things are either/or. Honestly, it could only have been better at playing possum if it'd had some intestines in its pockets and spread those around, because that's how you know you've got a possum who is really committed to the role. I went inside to look for a shovel and when I came back the possum was gone. It's possible that it was resurrected like Jesus. Or that it was playing dead and wandered off when I left. Or that it was taken by a mountain lion. Or eaten by a swan. Anyone's guess really.

Regardless, I sat there for a minute and realized that the fancy neighborhood I'd felt so alien in had just dropped a possum on me and it's fairly hard to respect the snootiness of any neighborhood that drops possums[1] and that's when I started to think that maybe we'd fit in anyway. Or that we'd just play dead until the country club members left. It seems to work for possums.

---

1. I know it seems like there are a lot of possums in here but this is a memoir and you don't get to pick what you get attacked by. If I did I'd pick a baby penguin because they're slow and fucking adorable. But then no one would ever believe that one had attacked me because they're so cute, and that's profiling. Much like the swans that people think are graceful and not out to eat you. Full circle, y'all.

The Big Quiz

Today I wrote a post on my blog. It wasn't particularly well written but I was struggling and I needed help, so I asked for it.

The post:

Okay. This isn't a funny post so feel free to skip it. I just need to know something and I need you to tell me the truth rather than just make me feel better, so please be honest.

I realize that I've accomplished a lot in life and deep down I know that, but it doesn't change the fact that I only have a few days a month where I actually feel like I was good at life. I know I'm a good person (as in "not evil or intentionally arsonistic"), but I'm not very good at **being** a person. I don't know if that makes sense and it's not me fishing for compliments. Please don't tell me the things I'm good at because that's not what this is about. It's just that at the end of each day I usually lie in bed and think, "Shit. I'm fucking shit up. I accomplished **nothing** today except the basics of existing." I feel like I'm treading water and that I'm always another half day behind in life. Even the great things are overshadowed by shame and anxiety, and yes, I realize a lot of this might have to do with the fact that I have mental illness, but I still feel like a failure more often than I feel like I'm doing well.

My pride that Hailey is the best speller in her class is overshadowed by the embarrassment that I don't have the energy to be a PTA mom. I'm happy my first book was so successful, but I suffer with writer's block so much that I'm always sure I'll never write again and that I'll never finish my second book. I feel like from the outside looking in I seem successful and happy, but I can't help but think that if people looked closer they'd see the cracks and the dirt and shame of a million projects that never get done.

Part of this is me. I have depression and anxiety and a number of disorders that make it hard for me to see myself correctly. Part of it is that I judge myself by the shiny, pretty people I see at parent-teacher meetings, or on Facebook, or Pinterest, who seem to totally have their shit together and never have unwashed hair. They never wait until Thursday night to help their kid with the entire week's homework. They don't have piles of dusty boxes in corners waiting to be opened from the move before last. They have pretty, pastel lives, and they are happy, and they own picnic baskets and napkins and know how to recycle, and they never run out of toilet paper or get their electricity turned off. And it's not even that I want to be one of those people. I fucking hate picnics. If God wanted us to eat on the ground He wouldn't have invented couches. I just don't want to feel like a failure because my biggest accomplishment of the day was going to the bank.

I just need an honest assessment to see if this is just me (and if I need to just find a way to change, or to increase my meds) or if this is just normal and people just don't talk about it.

Please tell me the truth (anonymous answers are fine). How many days in a month do you actually feel like you kicked ass, or were just generally a successful person? What makes you feel the worst? What do you do to make yourself feel more successful?

Please be honest. Because I'm about to be.

I feel successful 3–4 days a month. The other days I feel like I'm barely accomplishing the minimum or that I'm a loser. I have imposter syndrome so even when I get compliments they are difficult to take and I just feel like I'm a bigger fraud than before. I feel the worst when I get so paralyzed by fear that I end up huddled in bed and fall further and further behind. To make myself feel more successful I spend real time with my daughter every day, even if it's just huddling under a blanket and watching *Doctor Who* reruns on TV. I also try to remind myself that people like Dorothy Parker and Hunter S. Thompson struggled as well, and that this struggle might make me stronger, if it doesn't first destroy me.

I'm hoping that by writing and posting this it will make me face this head-on and make some changes, either in forcing myself to change the way I see success, or in forcing myself to get shit done and stop feeling such dread and anxiety every day. I'm hoping that I'll get hints from you guys about what you do to feel like a good, successful person or what you avoid that I can try to avoid as well. I'm hoping to stop the voices in my head. At least the ones who don't like me very much.

Your turn.

PS: For those of you who are new here, I'm already doing cognitive therapy and I'm already on a lot of drugs for anxiety, depression, and ADD, but I'm really fine. Honestly. I just want to be better. I'm just struggling with being human and I could use some pointers. My guess is that a lot of us could.

PPS: The Oxford dictionary says the word "arsonistic" doesn't exist, but it totally does. It's the same thing as being artistic, but instead of being sensitive to or good at art, you're just really good at arson. Then again, this is the same dictionary that just added "twerk." I question everything now.

PPPS: Sorry. This post is all over the place. My ADD drugs haven't kicked in yet. I'm failing at writing a post about how I'm failing. I think I've just set a record. A bad one.

And then I sat back and waited for people to say, "Oh, you're not bad. Cheer up, little ninja!" But they didn't. Instead, thousands of people responded with "Me too. These are the things I whisper at night to my husband, or to my girlfriend, or to my cat. These are the scary things that I know are true. These thoughts are the monsters in our closets. You might be a failure. But we're right there with you. Failing." And it was amazing. And a little depressing. But mostly amazing.

A few people commented that this seemed to be an American problem, because the places where they lived (mainly Europe) judged success less by things and accomplishments and more by feelings.

Happiness came from spending time with people, and more non-Americans seemed to think that spending a few hours watching TV with the kids on the couch was something to celebrate and enjoy, rather than feel guilty about.

Then more comments came in; some were platitudes to help to remind people that they aren't alone. They were helpful, but I come from a place of deep and abiding sarcasm so I internally tacked on my responses.

"Comparison is the death of joy."

I liked this one so much that I looked it up and found out it was Mark Twain who penned it and then I felt like shit again because all the best quotes are from Mark Twain and he's used them all up so now I feel bad in comparison to Mark Twain regarding his quote about how comparison makes you feel bad, so I'm basically just proving Mark Twain more right for making me feel like an asshole. I'm caught in a Mark Twain shame-spiral.

"Don't compare your insides to someone else's outsides."

This makes sense because I've seen my insides and they are disgusting. It's mainly fat and gristle and blood and a liver that would probably cut its way free of my body if it had a sharp knife. People almost never look as bad on the outside as I do on the inside, but that's sort of nice because it reminds me that even when I'm having a bad hair day my ponytail is still more aesthetically pleasing than Gwyneth Paltrow's bile duct. In fact, I think the whole quote should be rewritten to say, "Even the ugliest person's cellulite is more attractive than the most beautiful supermodel's lower intestine." I'd put that on a T-shirt but probably Mark Twain already said it.

> "Don't compare your behind-the-scenes look to
> everyone else's highlight reel."

This one makes sense because the DVD commentary is never as good as the actual movie, but my first response was, *"EVERYONE ELSE HAS A HIGHLIGHT REEL? I don't even have a goddamn blooper reel."* Conclusion: I ruin everything.

> "The only person you need to be better than is
> the person you were yesterday."

This is nice because the bar is set super low since all I did yesterday was eat a lot of Funyuns. Like, a crazy amount of Funyuns. It was almost sort of impressive. But basically the thing I got from that is that if I have a really good day I'm setting myself up for failure because then I have to be better tomorrow and so maybe I should just continue to be an unsuccessful shut-in who is only proud of her Funyun consumption. Or maybe just murder a village and then the next day murder one less person and keep getting better until your idea of being successful is just kicking three blind people in the face. This is probably how serial killers and tyrants start.

But I noticed something in common with each of those quotes. One was my ability to fuck all of them up. The second was that they were all better quotes than anything I'd ever write. And the third, and most important, was that perhaps I was judging myself by the wrong sets of standards.

I started to think about the way that I viewed success and realized that I didn't really want to lower the bar (because the bar was already so low that I kept tripping on it) but that I wanted to take the bar and throw it like an Olympic spear into the leg of Mark Twain and all of the other shiny, successful, imaginary people I was judging myself against. And then I realized that this would be illegal and would also require me to go outside and have better aim and get a lawyer and so instead I said "fuck it" and decided to stop even looking at the shiny people (who were possibly only shiny because they were hiding very dark secrets that I would pay good money to hear) and instead just change the way I define success. And you can do it too.

Are you successful? Let's see. I'm a big fan of self-tests. The ones where you end up a dog, or a tree, or a *Game of Thrones* character. Let's do one now:

The Very Important Quiz

Are you reading this or listening to this on tape? That means that you care about being a better person, or that you want advice on how to spear people in the leg. Either way, you're attempting to better yourself. Give yourself 10 points.

Now add 10 points for every time you accomplished the following:

- Didn't kill a spider. (Double the points if you helped it outside by shooing it and talking to it. Triple point score if the spider got on you and you didn't automatically smoosh it.)

- Didn't punch an asshole in the neck even though you really wanted to.

- Fell and didn't immediately yell at whoever was closest to you.

- Didn't use the word "supposably," "liberry," or "flustrated."

- Took care of an animal. (This amount doubles each time you walked a dog in the rain, rescued a stray animal who was in the middle of the road, or emptied a litter box. Emptying a litter box is basically like serving as a cat's toilet. It's the best way to humble yourself ever. Add 10 more points for being an awesome toilet.)

- Showed compassion. (Double points if it was for yourself.)

- Didn't die. (This seems small but people die all the time. Cemeteries are full of them. Even Jesus died. Some might point out that Jesus was resurrected and you haven't been, but to your credit, you haven't actually died yet, so who knows. Unless you *did* die and were resurrected. Then give yourself another 10 points. Or maybe you're a vampire. Give yourself 50 points if you're a vampire. Subtract 40 points if you're a sparkly vampire.)

Now add up your results:

If you scored between zero and 8,000: You are you. You're more you than yesterday but not as much as tomorrow. Keep going. You're on the right track. Also, your hair looks great today.

In other words, stop judging yourself against shiny people. Avoid the shiny people. The shiny people are a lie. Or get to know them enough to realize they aren't so shiny after all. Shiny people aren't the enemy. Sometimes *we're* the enemy when we listen to our malfunctioning brains that try to tell us that we're alone in our self-doubt, or that it's obvious to everyone that we don't know what the shit we're doing.

Hell, there are probably people out there right now who consider us to be shiny people (*bless their stupid, stupid hearts*) and that's pretty much proof that none of our brains can be trusted to accurately measure the value of anyone, much less ourselves.

How can we be expected to properly judge ourselves? We know all of our worst secrets. We are biased, and overly critical, and occasionally filled with shame. So you'll have to just trust me when I say that you are worthy, important, and necessary. And smart.

You may ask how I know and I'll tell you how. It's because right now? YOU'RE READING. That's what the sexy people do. Other, less awesome people might currently be in their front yards chasing down and punching squirrels, but not you. You're quietly curled up with a book designed to make you a better, happier, more introspective person.

You win.[1] You are amazing.

---

1. Unless you're reading this while you're punching squirrels. Then you might need to see a therapist, although I do applaud your ability to multitask. I can't even text and talk at the same time. Frankly, I'm a little jealous. And concerned. Put down the squirrel.

Cat Lamination

The Sixth Argument I Had with Victor This Week

VICTOR: There's cat fur all over the back of your dress. Like, it looks like you just shit out a cat and then did a bad job of wiping.

ME: It's because Ferris Mewler sits on my office chair all night. I bought a new pet-fur roller but it totally doesn't work. I say we just nip it in the bud and laminate the cats.

VICTOR: That's . . . probably not a good idea.

ME: But we'd leave their heads and paws and buttholes free, obviously.

VICTOR: *Obviously.*

ME: And a patch of skin so they don't go all *Goldfinger* on us.

VICTOR: So they don't *what*?

ME: You know . . . that lady that they painted gold in that James Bond movie and she suffocated because her skin couldn't breathe?

VICTOR: Yeah, that's an urban myth.

ME: Well, even better, because that means we can laminate the whole cat and not have to leave a small shaved patch of cat hanging in the breeze. Because that shit would look weird.

VICTOR: I don't even know where to start disagreeing with you on this one.

ME: Does Kinko's do laminating? Do you think they would laminate a cat?

VICTOR: No. Plus, I'm not sure Kinko's even exists anymore.

ME: Probably because they refused to do cat lamination. *You have to move with the times, Kinko's.* Change is coming. And by "change" I mean "my cat." My cat is coming to get laminated. Open back up, Kinko's. I'm about to save your business.

VICTOR: No.

ME: Then how about Saran wrap? DIY.

VICTOR: Are you trying to punish me for something?

ME: TINFOIL! Because they'll be cool, and they'll look like they're wearing armor or like they're tiny robots that run after laser beams.

Plus, if we make them tinfoil hats the government can't read their cat thoughts. EVERYONE WINS.

VICTOR: Huh.

ME: I mean, except the government. They'll probably be concerned when three cats suddenly disappear off the grid. It's gonna be like *The Matrix*. But for cats.

VICTOR: Right. I'm going to sell you to a carnival.

ME: Someone bring me some tinfoil and duct tape.

Winner: The government, I guess, because the cats stubbornly refuse to keep the tinfoil hats on. It's like they want *the government to read their minds. Which they actually might, now that I'm thinking about it, because they might be sending messages to the government asking to be removed from this house before they get laminated. I can see their point.*

That Baby Was *Delicious*

I don't even remember the first time I did meth in front of my child.

This is mostly because I've never actually done meth. But it's a good way to start out a chapter about how you fear you're failing as a parent because it sets the bar of child-rearing very, very low and everything you do that *isn't* meth in front of your children seems incredibly impressive by comparison.

My daughter, Hailey, is now nine and so far she shows none of the anxiety and crippling shyness that I'd already begun perfecting at her age. When people who know me spend time with her they are always shocked at how well adjusted and happy she is. This is an incredibly insulting compliment, but one I have a hard time arguing with, so I usually just say, "Thank you?"

Frankly, I think parents have very little input in creating the positive aspects of their children's personalities. My sister and I were raised in the exact same way and we could not be more different. This is not to say that you can't fuck up a kid by being an asshole, because children are small sponges and will mimic all of your worst behaviors at the least opportune time. But I believe that usually your kids' positive qualities come less from your making them awesome and more from just not intentionally squashing the random things they're inherently born with that *make* them awesome.

Some people think this is a cop-out that people like me use in order to justify the fact that I don't have my child enrolled in 287 different extracurricular activities and lessons, and those people are right. I'm sorry. You were probably expecting something defensive and brave right there but the truth is that I'm terrible at being one of those moms who can sit in the bleachers or dance studios and make forced small talk with parents who all seem to know (and secretly hate) each other and who never seem to show up in pajamas or mismatched shoes. I'm continually saying something awkward and inappropriate, like "I thought this was just for fun" or "No, actually I don't think that toddler is too fat for ballet."

I believe it was Sartre who said, "Hell is other people," and I suspect he wrote that after spending an hour with overinvolved parents who won't stop yelling at coaches, instructors, or crying four-year-olds who really just want a snow cone.

Even if you do enroll your kid in one or two lessons or clubs you're always hearing about some other, better, and more exclusive club where they learn to twirl batons while reciting Mandarin poetry. You immediately worry that if you don't enroll your child there they will end up homeless or legless or be turned into carpet or something. Whatever it is, it must be awful, because almost all of the parents I know seem to be competing to see how much shit they can pack into their child's life.

I'm not judging those people though, because it's not like I haven't tried that route myself. Hailey's done gymnastics, piano, jazz, hip-hop, ballet, tumbling, choir, but none of them held her attention for more than a year. She rather enjoyed dance classes but seemed to be setting a record for how many times she could fall. Honestly, she is smart and beautiful and kind but she could manage to fall while duct-taped flat on her back on the floor.

When she was five she took ballet lessons at one of those classes where the parents aren't allowed inside the studio (because some parents are yelly assholes and most studios recognize this) but the lesson played on a closed-circuit television in the lobby so we could all watch an hour of kindergartners not following instructions in French. Victor and I watched while the small children leaped across the floor until it was Hailey's turn and she did really well except that she was so busy watching herself in the mirror that she ran right into the wall and then bounced off the wall and fell headfirst into a large, rubber trash can. Her tiny, flailing legs were the only things we could see and we were panicked, but Hailey thought it was hilarious (after she was pulled out of the trash can). The people who did not find it hilarious were the other parents in the lobby, who were not happy about the distraction. I tried to lighten the mood by saying, "Wow. I love that kid, but she can-*not* hold her alcohol, am I right?" No one laughed.

Soon afterward we moved to the one thing she really excelled at, drama classes. She's a natural on the stage and loves performing in front of hundreds of strangers. I suspect she was switched at birth.

When I was a kid in rural Texas none of this stuff seemed to exist. I didn't know anyone who took dance classes. No one knew martial arts. You could take band classes in school, but only if you could afford to buy or rent an instrument, and my family couldn't, so instead when the other kids went to band I stayed with the poorer kids and we had a class called Music Memory. It was basically a room filled with old records and a teacher who was usually asleep, and we'd listen to scratchy Mozart pieces while showing each other how switchblades worked and learning how to pick locks. This sounds like comedic exaggeration, but it's not. I felt a little sorry for myself at the time because all the cool kids had their shiny boxes of spit valves and flutes, but I learned a lot in Music Memory and I've had more occasions to pick a lock than I've ever had to play a bassoon, so I suppose it all worked out in the end.

Still, you feel shitty as a parent if your kids aren't doing what all the other kids are doing. My mom could not have been a more perfect mother, but she never took me to lessons or dedicated entire days to forced quality time with me. So, I guess sometimes the example you set is the lesson, and the lesson I took was learning that the world didn't center on me and that I was responsible for making the most of my time. But my mom read. Lots. To me, and (more importantly) in front of me. And that made all the difference. So I guess I also learned that my mom's time was important too, and that's a lesson I'm still trying to learn now when the guilt about Hailey's not having a perfectly scheduled life creeps in.

Occasionally Hailey complains of being bored, but boredom is good. It makes up most of your life and if you don't figure out how to conquer it when you're a kid then you're sort of fucked as an adult. Learning to combat boredom is a lesson in and of itself and it's one you don't have to drive your kid anywhere for them to learn. The downside though is that your kid is probably just like you, in that boredom sometimes drives them to do *incredibly* stupid things. Necessity is the mother of invention but boredom is the mother of doing bafflingly stupid shit. Setting things on fire, taking apart the TV, riding goats, accidentally eating foot powder, letting twenty-five tadpoles hatch into frogs in my bedroom because I forgot I hid them under my bed, exploring abandoned buildings, burning my eyebrows off with a lighter . . . these were all things that happened to me during periods of boredom and they were also all things to which I honestly answered "*I don't know*" when my baffled mother would see the evidence of wrongdoing and ask me what in the hell I was thinking. Frankly, I *still* don't know what I'm doing or why I'm doing it most of the time, but at least I learned early on that this is a normal state of mind (and also that I shouldn't be trusted with fire).

Boredom makes you rely on your own imagination, or makes you realize how little you have. My sister, Lisa, and I spent a great deal of our childhood digging holes on our surrounding land for no reason at all. Perhaps when we started we were making caves or looking for bodies, but in the end it just became a matter of digging holes deep enough that we could easily drop into them and disappear completely because it freaked out people driving by to see a child waving furiously in an empty field and then suddenly vanishing completely as if being sucked into some sort of parallel dimension. Or at least, that's what we imagined it looked like. It probably just looked like little girls jumping into holes, which is just as baffling to watch. Later, Lisa pointed out that the place where we were often aggressively digging was directly on top of the rusty propane tank buried in the yard, which was probably not the safest thing ever.

Luckily the god of How-Did-Children-Survive-in-the-Seventies was looking out for us and we never ended up in a giant fireball, although we once lost a series of holes in the tall grass and forgot about them completely until several months later when we looked up just in time to see our mother drive the riding lawn mower into what looked like a sinkhole. And then she was like, "WHY ARE THERE SO MANY HOLES?" We considered claiming it was the mole people who'd created some sort of Scooby-Doo trap but we didn't have time to go over all the details so instead we just calmly explained that there were holes because we'd dug them and then she asked why and we honestly stared at each other and said, "*I don't know*," and that was the truth. We were baffled by it ourselves. And maybe that's why people overschedule their kids now. Maybe it's to avoid driving your lawn mower over a small cliff made by gopherlike children.

But still, it seems like it's overkill to schedule away any chance of boredom. It's like when your cat brings you dead mice and you want to yell at her but you can't because she's just doing it because she thinks you're a really shitty cat who won't survive on your own. We're sort of like that with our children, bringing them private lessons and participation medals and beauty pageant tiaras as if we suspect they don't have the ability to succeed at stuff without our forcing them into repetitive drills and buying expensive costumes and spending long weekends at competitions and pageants. Plus, now we've set up our kids to expect to win at everything and they feel shitty if they don't because they can see how unaccountably emotionally invested we are in their ability to beat other children.

When I was a kid I never won anything and when I mentioned it to my mom she looked up from her book and pointed out that I had once been *the youngest person in the entire world*. Sure, it was only for a millisecond, but it was a record I'd set without even trying. Then I went back to my own book and forgot all about competitions until my own child was born. Then *she* took the title. Excellence runs in our family, I guess.

No one ever warns you about the complicated and political decisions regarding lessons and classes and sports you'll have to make when you become a parent. When I was in eighth grade everyone in Home Economics had to care for flour-sack babies for two weeks to teach us about parenting and no one ever mentioned enrolling your flour baby in sports. Basically, everyone got a sealed paper sack of flour that puffed out flour dust whenever you moved it. You were forced to carry it around everywhere because I guess it was supposed to teach you that babies are fragile and also that they leave stains on all of your shirts. At the end of the two weeks your baby was weighed and if it lost too much weight that meant you were too haphazard with it and were not ready to be a parent. It was a fairly unrealistic child-rearing lesson. Basically all we learned about babies in that class was that you could use superglue to seal your baby's head after you dropped it. And that eighth-grade boys will play keep-away with your baby if they see it so it's really safer in the trunk of your car. And that you should just wrap your baby up in plastic cling wrap so that its insides don't explode when it's rolling around in the trunk on your way home. And also that if you don't properly store your baby in the freezer your baby will get weevils and then you have to throw your baby in the garbage instead of later making it into a cake that you'll be graded on. (The next two weeks of class focused on cooking and I used my flour baby to make a pineapple upside-down cake. My baby was *delicious*. These are the things you never realize are weird until you start writing them down.)

Recently Hailey decided she wanted to be in Girl Scouts. I told her I thought it was a cookie pyramid scheme, but she loves it. I go to her troop meetings and hide in the back and try not to look like I'm uncomfortable around the other parents.

Last week I sat in my usual corner and as another mom sat down next to me and struck up a light conversation I silently congratulated myself on being a normal person. A few seconds later Hailey looked up from across the room with the other Girl Scouts and, smiling widely, exclaimed, "MOMMY! You made a friend! *Good for you!*" And then I fell through the floor because being embarrassed by your child when you're an adult is much like being embarrassed by your parents when you're a teenager, but worse, because you can't roll your eyes at them and pretend that they just don't understand you. Kids *totally* understand you. *So* much more than you want them to.

And maybe *that's* why they're sent off to so many lessons and camps. Maybe it's so their parents can stay home during that time and secretly watch bad TV and cry and eat a bucket of mashed potatoes and put clothes on the cats without getting harshly but accurately judged by their own children.

Now it all makes a little more sense.

These Cookies Know Nothing of My Work

"BUT I DON'T *WANT* TO BE A GROWN-UP," I screamed from a vaguely fetal position in the corner of the office. *"I'M JUST NOT READY FOR THIS YET."*

It was a major psychological breakthrough and one I felt certain my shrink would have been very proud of, had she actually been there. Instead, my husband and our CPA stared at me as if this were the first time something like this had ever happened during an initial financial-planning meeting.

"I'm not really with her," Victor mumbled.

He said it out of habit but it seemed a bit of a weak argument considering that he was holding a giant folder of papers proving that we'd bought a lot of shit together in the last seventeen years. Or perhaps it was the folder of evidence he was compiling to have me committed. If it was the latter, I was fairly sure that this incident was going to end up in there.

"Whoa there. No judgments here," said our CPA (Maury) as he held up his hands with caution, like you might to someone about to jump off the edge of a building, or to a rabid dog that you hoped under-stood English. Then he said something about how he was "just here to help people get their finances in order" but what I heard was, "We're here to discuss how terrible you are at being a responsible, normal per-son. There are hidden cameras everywhere and this is all going on YouTube. I'm going to be super rich."

Honestly, I consider myself to be fairly good at finances if you don't compare me to normal people. I make more money than I deserve and then I give away a lot because it makes me nervous to have it around. I pay bills when the paper they're printed on turns pink or gets threatening, and if my debit card is still accepted then I feel like I'm winning. At the end of the year I go to the tax office and throw a box of receipts marked "EVIDENCE" at the tax lady (there's a proper word for her job but I've never learned it) and then run away before she can tell me that I'm fired from being her client. She'll usually scream something like "QUICKBOOKS!" and then I scream back: "*I'm totally going to do that starting today, pinkie promise!*" and then I duck into the bushes before she can realize that most of the receipts are actually just napkins with scribbles on them, like "I needed to buy a kangaroo outfit for work but the flea market doesn't give out receipts. It was $15 but it was worth like $100. I can't confirm this but the blond guy at the flea market who doesn't use deodorant said he can be a witness if we need him."

This seems like it's a terrible way of keeping records, but I can as-sure you that it's much better than the year I meticulously attempted to keep all of my receipts in a box under my desk until the cat mistook it for a litter box, or the year I kept a bunch of receipts in a clear plastic envelope and then when I went to pull them all out half of them were just blank pieces of paper. Turns out that if you expose receipts to sun-light they eventually just fade away, much like my intentions to keep receipts. Instead I just wrote what I thought should be on the now-blank pieces of paper. Things like "I bought a dead weasel for $40 but then I dressed her up and made her into Christmas cards for clients," or "I think this was a receipt for a haunted Kewpie doll that I wrote about and then sold on eBay. But then eBay cancelled the auction because I mentioned that the doll possibly contained the souls of eaten children, and eBay said it was against the rules to sell souls. This is all on my blog if you need proof."

In my defense, I suspect that my tax accountant probably enjoys doing my returns. I'd enjoy them too if math weren't involved, because looking through them is a glimpse into a life well lived. Or a life that needs massive sorting out.

A few of my business expenses:

- Taxidermied wolf I wore to watch *Twilight* at the local theater. His name is Wolf Blitzer and he died of natural causes. (GO TEAM JACOB.)
- Full-body kangaroo costume worn to impress and infiltrate a band of wild kangaroos while on writing assignment in Australia. (See "Koalas Are Full of Chlamydia.")
- Tetanus shot needed immediately after trip to Australia.
- Postage to ship home a brain that someone gave me while I was on a book tour.
- A taxidermied Pegasus for the cats to ride on.
- A box of cobra.
- A rented live sloth.
- Stylish outfits for cats.
- Two super-ecstatic taxidermied raccoon corpses for late-night cat rodeos.

Then the tax lady would call and say, "But what about your server costs and your office supplies and your real operating expenses?" And

I would explain that I don't really know them because I only keep up with interesting receipts. Then she'd call Victor to get his help and he would scream at me: "You're paying too much in taxes because you're not being responsible with deductions!" And I'd scream back, "Well, maybe the government needs the money more than I do!" Then Victor would question why he'd ever married anyone who wasn't Republican and I'd question why anyone would ever trust me to do taxes to begin with.

And this was probably why I was feeling a little defensive at the CPA's office. It was our first meeting and was filled with questions that made me immediately uncomfortable and sort of defensively stabby.

Maury asked if I had life insurance and I assured him that I didn't because I didn't want Victor to be arrested. There was a pause in the conversation.

"She thinks life insurance is only taken out on people about to be murdered," Victor explained stoically.

"It's true, though," I continued. "Whenever someone ends up in the meat grinder the authorities are always quick to arrest whoever the beneficiary is on the insurance policy."

Victor rolled his eyes.

"*I'M TRYING TO HELP YOU WITH YOUR MURDER DEFENSE*," I yelled politely. Then Victor huffed a bit but probably because I'd accidentally said "meat grinder" instead of "chipper-shredder." Victor would *never* murder me with our meat grinder. He's such a germophobe that he can't even handle it if I leave a used Kleenex on my desk, so there's no way he's going to be able to make his summer sausage after he knows I've been through our grinder. I mean, who knows where I've been?

Eventually Victor and Maury got back to discussing investment strategies and mathy stuff and I blanked out a bit until I noticed that they were both staring at me. Maury repeated himself. "Do you have any questions so far, or anything you'd like to add?"

I didn't but I wanted to contribute to the conversation so I asked, "Why is there a gold standard?"

Victor and Maury looked at me because the question apparently had nothing to do with what they'd been discussing but I thought it was still a good question, so I continued:

"I just don't get the gold standard. If America found a planet made of gold would that make us super rich, or would it make all gold worthless? And if it did make us super rich, what's keeping all the other countries from being like, 'We don't like gold anymore because this isn't fair. We like spiders now. Pay us in spiders.' Would that make our economy collapse? Could you buy spiders with gold? What would the exchange rate be? Would it be in metric or imperial? I already can't remember how to convert to metric and it's going to get worse if I have to convert to metric spiders. And that's why I don't think we should go around mining on other planets and looking for trouble. *Because I don't want to carry a purse around filled with hordes of spiders. That's why.*"

"You're blocking out all of our conversations because you're too focused on how you'd pay for things with spiders?" Victor asked with disbelief.

"I guess so," I said. "Having a purse full of spiders is actually less scary than having to think about finances. *Wow.* That's sort of a breakthrough." I let out a deep breath and looked at Maury. "I should totally come see you instead of my normal shrink."

"Huh," Maury replied.

"Would it be tax deductible if I came to see you for mental problems?" I asked. "Also, are you licensed to prescribe drugs? Because that's sort of a deal breaker."

Victor shook his head. "It's like you're allergic to making sense." He seemed a bit snappish, but probably because of the spider thing. I'd be pissed too if I'd spent years trying to save money and suddenly realized it could all be replaced by spiders and I'd be fucked.

I placed a soothing hand on Victor's sleeve and whispered, *"I hear and acknowledge your pain."*

"This is not therapy," he barked. *"This is financial planning."* He looked slightly frazzled and I considered slipping some of my Xanax into his coffee, but then I thought that maybe my possible new therapist would see me as being a little *too* free with drugs and so instead I just said, "Well, it's sort of both, isn't it?"

Maury changed the subject to funeral planning and wills and I blanked out a little. Personally, I've always been a little bit icked out by wills. Mostly because of the math involved. I'm fine with funeral planning and dead bodies and all that stuff. In fact, I recently saw a coffin in a magazine that I wanted that had "Hi coffin. You look nice" written on the side and I thought that was very clever and would put everyone at ease while they were grieving me, and so I told Victor that he could buy me that one, or if it was too expensive he could just buy me a cheap casket and stencil that shit on the side himself, but then Victor got all yelly about my talking about funerals again, probably because he's bad at arts and crafts. Or maybe because he knows that after going through the chipper-shredder I won't need anything more than a small cocktail shaker to hold what's left of me. In a way that would be nice though, because I'd finally get to go to an event where I was the thinnest person there.

Then I realized that Victor and Maury were staring at me and that they'd asked me a question about the will but I couldn't remember what it was so I just said, "When I die I'd like all my stuff to be left to my cat." Then Victor just rubbed his temples and I explained, "Not really though, because there's *no* way Ferris Mewler is outliving me and Hunter S. Thomcat is way too irresponsible to take on that sort of money, but this way you can just tell everyone that I'm obviously insane if I'm leaving shit to a cat and then you can just handle all the will stuff yourself and I don't have to do any of this paperwork. *WE ALL*

WIN. Except Hunter S. Thomcat, I guess. He'd better find himself a sugar mama or something."

Victor sighed, but frankly I'm not really sure what he'd expected. It was my job to accidentally make money and his job to make sure that I didn't lose it when I was doing wobbly cartwheels in the parking lot after the bars closed. Our roles had been clearly defined.

Maury cleared his throat. "We can come back to wills later. How about retirement plans?"

Victor spent the next several minutes speaking in a combination of words and letters that I'm pretty sure meant "I have a retirement plan and it's quite good."

Maury looked at me expectantly.

"I have a drawer I put change into."

Victor put his head in his hands.

"Not quarters though. I use those for gum."

Then Victor and Maury talked about dividends and stipends and split ends and then Victor woke me up an hour later to sign things that looked far too important for me to sign. I agreed to sign them if he'd take me somewhere for lunch where I could have some booze and Maury recommended a place in the same building, which was convenient because I was so overwhelmed I didn't think I could make it very far. In fact, when we got downstairs to the café the waiter asked what I'd like to drink and I said, "I would like booze, but I don't have it in me to make any more decisions today so you just pick something for me, will you?" He did and it was very strong and I suspect that Maury sends all of his easily overwhelmed clients there and that's probably "the Maury Special." I laid my head down on the table and Victor wondered aloud how I would ever manage to live if he wasn't there.

"Well, my life would be much simpler," I explained with perfect honesty. "I don't know how the eight remotes for the TV work so I'd never use it again, and when the lights burned out I'd just sort of leave them if I couldn't reach them with a chair, and when the computers broke I'd just throw them in a ditch, and when my car stopped working I'd probably just buy a donkey to ride into town to buy provisions from the gas station. I suspect I'd become accidentally Amish within a year. In fact, I bet the Amish are just a whole tribe of people who didn't have someone around to turn the TV on for them for several generations and finally said, 'Fuck it. We're just going to live life this way.'"

"I'm pretty sure that's not even *remotely* accurate," Victor replied.

"Well, I'd look it up online but I tried to update iTunes this morning and now my phone is frozen so I think I'm going to use it as a paperweight from now on."

Victor stared at me.

"That was a joke," I explained. "But, actually, I *did* manage to somehow delete half of my icons, so if you could help me out there I'd appreciate it. No rush though. I know you've had a tough morning."

"You have no idea," he said.

"Actually, I do. I mean, I realize that I'm ridiculously inept when it comes to . . . you know . . . *things.* Stuff like money and planning and complicated television sets. But what you *don't* think about is that I'm fantastic with people. Except when I'm hiding from them, obviously. And I'm there to make things lovely and good and to make sure that everyone is happy. Everyone except for maybe Maury, I mean. He seemed a bit flustered."

"Yeah, there's a lot of that going around," Victor replied. But he said it in a way that made me think that he agreed, or that he just didn't have a way to respond properly. "Just please do your best to be a little more financially responsible and we'll be fine."

I nodded, kissed him on the cheek, and then excused myself to powder my nose, but then when I was walking down the hall to go to the bathroom I saw it. The giant Zoltar fortune-telling machine from the movie *Big.*

The same one that turned Tom Hanks into a successful grown-up. And so I immediately decided that I needed to have my fortune told and I ran back to Victor and told him I needed some quarters to see what our fortune was.

"You want take our money and throw it away on a fortune-telling machine? *Have you learned nothing today?*"

"Well, I learned you're pretty stingy with quarters. You know perfectly well I've spent all mine on gum. Plus, it's only fifty cents for advisement on our fortune. Or for getting a fortune. Something like that. And that's what this whole day has been about, right?"

Then he sighed and fished out a bunch of quarters.

The first fortune was for me and it was so perfect I ran back to the table to share it:

So basically Zoltar told me that I'm fiscally sound and that I'd wasted the whole day setting up retirement plans when I just needed to spend as much as I could out of my never-ending chest of money. Victor did not agree.

So I went to get his fortune so that I could prove how remarkably accurate it was. This was his fortune:

"See!" I said. "According to Zoltar, you've got tons of happiness in your future and it's all caused by your perseverance and clever ways of handling your domestic problems."

"I think *you* might be my domestic problems."

"Well, either way, everything's coming up roses, right?"

And then Victor laughed, in spite of himself. And that's how you know that you've got a real fortune. Because money can't buy the happiness of a good and understanding spouse. But it can buy a new phone when you accidentally drop it in the toilet after having too many Maury Specials.

PS: After dinner the waiter brought us fortune cookies and I was like, "FOUR FORTUNES IN ONE DAY! WHAT A BOON!" Victor said cookies weren't really the same thing as actual fortune, but I think Victor's underestimating the importance of cookies. But then we opened them and decided to just stick with Zoltar because mine said, "No snowflake in an avalanche ever feels responsible," and I'm pretty sure that's supposed to be insulting, although it also implies that I'm somehow "responsible" and I think that proves I'd gotten the wrong cookie. But then Victor opened his and said, "Mine says, 'Never argue with a fool.'"

"What?" I said. *"THAT'S WHAT OUR WHOLE MARRIAGE IS BASED ON."*

Victor shrugged. "This cookie is telling me not to talk to you."

I crossed my arms. "Well, *this* cookie is making me feel guilty and I don't even know what I've done."

Victor nodded. "Well, the cookie has a point."

"YOU CAN'T TELL US WHAT TO DO, COOKIES. YOU DON'T EVEN KNOW US," I might have yelled.

And that's when we decided not to take advice from cookies anymore and Victor also tried to make me not take advice from fortune-telling robots near bathrooms but I said that's just throwing the baby out with the bathwater and that's bad financial advice for everyone. Unless your baby is really spendy. But still, I think it's a good idea to keep them even if they do end up costing you time and money because they're worth all the fuss because of the joy they bring into your life.

And Victor smiled and held my hand and agreed.

I don't think we were talking about the same thing, but it was nice to see him smile so I smiled back and we walked out of the restaurant to face the future together . . .

. . . unknown, uncertain, dangerously entertaining, and *furiously happy.*

It Might Be Easier.
But It Wouldn't Be Better.

I'm at the final part of a severe rheumatoid arthritis flare-up. I only get a few a year, but when they hit it's simply a matter of surviving from day to day. That sounds ridiculous and overblown, since I at least know that eventually the pain will fade and I'll be able to get out of bed and not bite back screams. The first few days seem like they should be the worst since they're the most painful and always end with a trip to the emergency room. The next few days it hurts less, but you're so brittle from a lack of sleep and unending pain that you still feel just as miserable. Your family members and friends understand and care, but after half a week of seeing you hobbling around the house and crying in the bathroom, even they can get worn-out by it all. Then comes two days of fatigue so intense that you feel drugged. You want to get up and work and clean and smile, but you find yourself falling asleep at your daughter's first play, and you have to leave to get back to bed while everyone else celebrates.

Life passes. Then comes the depression. That feeling that you'll never be right again. The fear that these outbreaks will become more familiar, or worse, never go away. You're so tired from fighting that you start to listen to all the little lies your brain tells you. The ones that say that you're a drain on your family. The ones that say that it's all in your head. The ones that say that if you were stronger or better this wouldn't be happening to you. The ones that say that there's a reason why your body is trying to kill you, and that you should just stop all the injections and steroids and drugs and therapies.

Last month, as Victor drove me home so I could rest, I told him that sometimes I felt like his life would be easier without me. He paused a moment in thought and then said, "It might be easier. But it wouldn't be *better*."

I remind myself of that sentence on days when the darkness seems like it'll never end. But I know it will pass. I know that tomorrow things will seem a little brighter. I know that next week I'll look back on this sentence and think, "I should stop listening to my brain when it's trying to kill me. *Why did I even write this?*" And that's precisely *why* I'm writing this now. Because it's so easy to forget that I've been here before and come out the other side, and perhaps if I have this to read I'll remember it again next time and it will help me to keep on breathing until the medications take hold and I'm out of the hole again.

I used to feel a lot of guilt about having depression but then I realized that's a lot like feeling guilty for having brown hair. Still, even though it's unrealistic, it's normal. I felt the same when Smokey the Bear was all, "ONLY YOU CAN PREVENT FOREST FIRES," and I was like, "Shit. *Only me?* Because that really seems like it should be more of a team effort." And also I don't think I should take orders about forests from bears, because some bears use forests to hide in so that they can eat you. So basically I have some demanding bear shaming me into creating a less fiery dining room for him to devour me. And also, that doesn't even make any sense because aren't some forest fires caused by lightning? Because I can't stop lightning, bears. I'm not God. I can't stop lightning, or swamp gas, or spontaneous combustion, or depression. These are all things that just happen and shouldn't be blamed on me.

Stop blaming the victim, bears.

In the years since I first came out about struggling with mental illness I've been asked if I regret it . . . if the stigma is too much to handle.

It's not.

There are terrible sides to illness (mental and physical) but it's strangely freeing that my personal struggle is obvious and has to be acknowledged. In a way I'm lucky. My depressions and periods of anxiety and paranoia were so extreme that I couldn't keep them much of a secret. I felt like not writing about them was creating a false history, and honestly, when I first wrote about them I expected I'd lose readers. I expected that I'd scare people. I expected that some people would feel betrayed that someone they turned to for light and funny fluff was pulling them into serious and difficult dreck. I expected silence.

I did not expect what I was given.

What I got back in return for being honest about my struggle was an enormous wave of voices saying, "You aren't alone," and "We suspected you were crazy anyway. We're still here." "I'm proud of you." And louder than all of that were the whispers that became stronger every day from thousands and thousands of people creeping to the edge and quietly admitting, "*Me too. I thought it was just me.*" And the whispers became a roar. And the roar became an anthem that carried me through some of my darkest moments. I did not ride that wave alone.

I have a folder that's labeled "The Folder of 24." Inside it are letters from twenty-four people who were actively in the process of planning their suicide, but who stopped and got help—not because of what I wrote on my blog, but because of the amazing response from the community of people who read it and said, "Me too." They were saved by the people who wrote about losing their mother or father or child to suicide and how they'd do anything to go back and convince them not to believe the lies mental illness tells you. They were saved by the people who offered up encouragement and songs and lyrics and poems and talismans and mantras that worked for them and that might work for a stranger in need. There are twenty-four people alive today who are still here because people were brave enough to talk about their struggles, or compassionate enough to convince others of their worth, or who simply said, "I don't understand your illness, but I know that the world is better with you in it."

In the days when I was doing my book tour for *Let's Pretend This Never Happened* I was often asked whether I regretted going public with my struggles and my answer is still the same . . . those twenty-four letters are the best payment I ever got for writing, and I never would have gotten any of them without the amazing community that helped save those lives. I'm incredibly lucky and grateful to be a part of a movement that made such a difference.

And it doesn't stop.

When I first started talking about my "Folder of 24" I was shocked at how many people would whisper in my ear at book signings that they were number twenty-five. One girl was fifteen and her parents were with her. One woman had two small children. One man who decided to get therapy instead of commit suicide brought his whole family with him. Each time I wondered at how *any* of them could ever consider that life would be better without them, and then I remembered that it's the same thing I struggle with when my brain tries to kill me. And so they've saved me too. That's why I continue to talk about mental illness, even at the cost of scaring people off or having people judge me. I try to be honest about the shame I feel because with honesty comes empowerment. And also, understanding. I know that if I go out on a stage and have a panic attack, I can duck behind the podium and hide for a minute and no one is going to judge me. They already know I'm crazy. And they still love me in spite of it. In fact, some love me because of it. Because there is something wonderful in accepting someone else's flaws, especially when it gives you the chance to accept your own and see that those flaws are the things that make us human.

I do worry that one day other kids will taunt my daughter when they're old enough to read and know my story. Sometimes I wonder if the best thing to do is just to be quiet and stop waving the banner of "fucked up and proud of it," but I don't think I'll put down this banner until someone takes it away from me.

Because quitting might be easier, but it wouldn't be *better*.

Epilogue:
Deep in the Trenches

To all who walk the dark path, and to those who walk in the sunshine but hold out a hand in the darkness to travel beside us:

Brighter days are coming.

Clearer sight will arrive.

And you will arrive too.

No, it might not be forever. The bright moments might be for a few days at a time, but hold on for those days. Those days are worth the dark.

In the dark you find yourself, all bones and exhaustion and helplessness. In the dark you find your basest self. In the dark you find the bottom of watery trenches the rest of the world only sees the surface of. You will see things that no normal person will ever see. Terrible things. Mysterious things. Things that try to burrow into your mind like a bad seed. Things that whisper dark and horrid secrets that you want to forget. Things that scream lies. Things that want you dead. Things that will stop at nothing to pull you down further and kill you in the most terrible way of all . . . by your own trembling hand. These things are fearsome monsters . . . the kind you always knew would sink in their needle-sharp teeth and pull you under the bed if you left a dangling limb out. You know they aren't real, but when you're in that black, watery hole with them they are the realest thing there is. And they want us dead.

And sometimes they succeed.

But not always. And not with you. You are alive. You have fought and battled them. You are scarred and worn and sometimes exhausted and were perhaps even close to giving up, but you did not.

You have won many battles. There are no medals given out for these fights, but you wear your armor and your scars like an invisible skin, and each time you learn a little more. You learn how to fight. You learn which weapons work. You learn who your allies are. You learn that those monsters are exquisite liars who will stop at nothing to get you to surrender. Sometimes you fight valiantly with fists and words and fury. Sometimes you fight by pulling yourself into a tiny ball, blotting out the monsters along with the rest of the world. Sometimes you fight by giving up and turning it over to someone else who can fight for you.

Sometimes you just fall deeper.

And in the deepest, night-blind fathoms you're certain that you're alone. You aren't. I'm there with you. And I'm not alone. Some of the best people are here too . . . feeling blindly. Waiting. Crying. Surviving. Painfully stretching their souls so that they can learn to breathe underwater . . . so that they can do what the monsters say is impossible. So that they can live. And so that they can find their way back to the surface with the knowledge of things that go bump in the night. So that they can dry themselves in the warm light that shines so brightly and easily for those above the surface. So that they can walk with others in the sunlight but with different eyes . . . eyes that still see the people underwater, allowing them to reach out into the darkness to pull up fellow fighters, or to simply hold their cold hands and sit beside the water to wait patiently for them to come up for air.

Ground zero is where the normal people live their lives, but not us. We live in the negatives so often that we begin to understand that life when the sun shines should be lived full throttle, soaring. The invisible tether that binds the normal people on their steady course doesn't hold us in the same way. Sometimes we walk in sunlight with everyone else. Sometimes we live underwater and fight and grow.

And sometimes . . .

. . . sometimes we fly.

Acknowledgments

I owe an immense debt to my parents and sister for giving me these stories, and also the ability to truly appreciate how bizarre and wonderful they are. Thank you to my husband for being the straight man in this book and the funny man in my life. You are my home. Thank you to my daughter for being amazing and for letting me write about her even though she did refuse to let me write that one really funny thing about Ada Lovelace. Hailey, I assume you're not letting me write about it because you're keeping it for your own future memoir and I salute you for your foresight.

Thank you to my dead grandparents for not haunting me. Thank you to my live grandparents for supporting me even when normal people would distance themselves. I love you all.

Thank you to Neeti Madan, the greatest agent ever, who understands my weirdness and calls me after every professional conference phone call because she knows I'll need someone to tell me I'm not an idiot. Thank you to the brilliant Amy Einhorn, who continues to believe in me even though I refuse to use proper punctuation and randomly make up words. Thank you to the editors and proofreaders who are probably all angry alcoholics after working on this book.

Thank you to Jeremy Johnson for making Rory I and Rory II, and to my father for spending an entire day wiring and sculpting prosthetic limbs for my dead raccoon amputee.

Thank you to the wonderful group of people who read my stuff before it's even close to being polished and who listen to my insane chapters over and over at ridiculous hours. Laura Mayes, Maile Wilson, Karen Walrond, Brené Brown, Lisa Bir, and Stephen Parolini. *These books would not exist without you.*

Thank you to the lovely and talented Andrew Kantor, who took that picture of a vicious possum so I didn't have to. You are one of God's bravest creatures, Andrew.

Thank you to Mary Phiroz, who keeps me out of jail and makes me seem like a grown-up. Thank you to Brooke Shaden, the immortal Nancy W. Kappes (paralegal), Jason Wilson, Doctor Q, Allie Brosh, Neil Gaiman, Wil and Anne Wheaton, Bonnie Burton, Deni Kendig, Kim Bauer (oneclassymotha), Kregg, Amanda, Felicia, Christine Miserandino from butyoudontlooksick.com and everyone else who has helped so generously.

Thank you to my dedicated readers who bought my first book even though there was a dead mouse on it, and to the booksellers, librarians, book buyers and the people who work in bookshops who write nice things about me. Thank you to the people who sneak into bookshops, find my books, and put them up front in illegal displays. Thank you to everyone who ever came to a book tour or was brave enough to suggest one of my books for their book club. A giant (and vaguely passive-aggressive) thank-you to my fellow writers and bloggers who just keep getting better and make me have to work harder. Thank you to everyone who helped me dispose of a body. Thank you to my first-grade teacher, who celebrated my weirdness. Thank you to my eighth-grade teacher, who said I wouldn't amount to anything, because it spurred me to prove you wrong, and also to glue your desk shut. Thank you to the people who voted in the poll about whether I could write "He was later drug to his death by catfish" instead of "He was later dragged to his death by catfish."[1] And thank you to everyone who realized that "foxen" and "problemly" were intentional mistakes.

Thank you to the person I forgot to list here for being so incredibly understanding and forgiving. Everyone said you'd be bitter and butt-hurt but I knew better.

And finally, thank you to you. For being you. You are better than enchiladas or cupcakes. Or enchilada cupcakes. Which should totally exist.

---

1. *Poll results, in case you're interested:*

31%—"Sweet baby Jesus. I will punch you in the neck if you use the word 'drug' incorrectly."

23%—"You can use 'drug' as dialect but only if you are prepared to get yelled at."

18%—"Can't you just say 'yanked'?"

14%—"As long as you don't use the phrase 'fixin' to' you're fine by me."

14%—"I never use words improperly. I cannot believe you drug me into this mess."